Monument Culture

Monument Culture

*International Perspectives
on the Future of Monuments in a
Changing World*

EDITED BY LAURA A. MACALUSO

ROWMAN & LITTLEFIELD
Lanham • Boulder • New York • London

Published by Rowman & Littlefield
A wholly owned subsidary of The Rowman & Littlefield Publishing Group, Inc.
4501 Forbes Boulevard, Suite 200, Lanham, Maryland 20706
www.rowman.com

6 Tinworth Street, London SE11 5AL

British Library Cataloguing in Publication Information Available

Library of Congress Cataloging-in-Publication Data

Names: Macaluso, Laura A., editor.
Title: Monument culture : international perspectives on the future of monuments in a changing world /
edited by Laura A. Macaluso.
Description: Lanham, Maryland : Rowman & Littlefield, 2019. | Series: American Association for
State and Local History | "Section 1: Monument Culture: Leading Essay Chapter 1 Homage to
Charlottesville: A Familiar Essay Alex Vernon Section 2: Monument Culture: Land, People, and Place
Chapter 2 Implications of Erasure in Polynesia Carmen S. Tomfohrde Chapter 3 Monuments in
Antarctica: Commemoration of Historic Events or Claims for Sovereignty. Ingo Heidbrink Chapter 4
Phnom Penh's Independence Monument and Vientiane's Patuxai: Complex Symbols of Postcolonial
Nationhood in Cold War Era Southeast Asia Roger Nelson Chapter 5 Enshrining Racial Hierarchy
through Settler Commemoration in the American West Cynthia C. Prescott Section 3: Monument
Culture: Trauma/Violence and Reconciliation/Reparations Chapter 6 In Defense of Historical Stains:
How Clean Approaches to the Past Can Keep Us Dirty Dan Haumschild Chapter 7 Repairing and
Reconciling with the Past: El Ojo que Llora and Peru's Public Monuments ; Ñusta Carranza Ko Chapter
8 Ruptures and Continuities in the Post-Apartheid Political and Cultural Landscape: A Reading of
South African Monument Culture Runette Kruger Chapter 9 Beyond Ruins: Borgoño's Barracks and
the Struggle over Memory in Today's Chile Basil Farraj Section 4: Monument Culture: Migration and
Identity Chapter 10 Iconoclasm and Imperial Symbols: The Gough and Victoria Monuments in Ireland
and the British World, 1880–1990 Derek N. Boetcher Chapter 11 Monuments of Refugee Identity:
Pain, Unity, and Belonging in Three Monuments of Cappadocian Greeks Zeliha Nilüfer Nahya and
Saim Örnek Chapter 12 Kindertransports in National and International Memory Amy Williams
Chapter 13 A Cubist Portrait of Christopher Columbus: Studying Monuments as Transcultural
Works Chiara Grilli Section 5: Monument Culture: Ambiguities and Alternatives Chapter 14 Visible
Differently: Roni Horn's Vatnasafn/Library of Water as Memorial Elliot Krasnopoler Chapter 15
Monuments and Other Things That Change: Several Attempts at Titling a Photograph Masha Vlasova
Chapter 16 Illegal Monuments: Memorials between Crime and State Endorsement Nauskiaä El-Mecky
Chapter 17 Transnational Social Media Monuments, Counter Monuments, and the Future of the
Nation-State Johnny Alam Section 6: Monument Culture: Strategies and Actions Chapter 18 Citizens
as Walking Memorials: Rethinking the Monument Genre in the Twenty-First Century Tanja Schult
Chapter 19 Exhibiting Spectacle and Recasting Memory: Commemorating the First World War in New
Zealand Kingsley Baird Chapter 20 Dealing with a Dictatorial Past: Fascist Monuments and Conflicting
Memory in Contemporary Italy Flaminia Bartolini Chapter 21 Avoiding Iconoclasm: How the Counter
Monument Could Settle a Monumental Debate Scott McDonald Section 7: Monument Culture:
Closing Essay Chapter 22 On Creating a Useable Future: An Introduction to Future Monuments
Evander Price." |
Includes bibliographical references and index.
| Identifiers: LCCN 2019000968 (print) | LCCN 2019002471 (ebook) | ISBN 9781538114162
(electronic) | ISBN 9781538114148 (cloth : alk. paper) | ISBN 9781538114155 (pbk. : alk. paper)
Subjects: LCSH: Monuments—Political aspects. | Monuments—Social aspects. | Memorialization—
Political aspects. | Memorialization—Social aspects. | Collective memory.
Classification: LCC NA9345 (ebook) | LCC NA9345 .M65 2019 (print) | DDC 725/.94—dc23
LC record available at https://lccn.loc.gov/2019000968

Printed in the United States of America

Contents

SECTION 6: MONUMENT CULTURE: STRATEGIES AND ACTIONS

SECTION 7: MONUMENT CULTURE: CLOSING ESSAY

List of Figures

Preface

CENTRAL VIRGINIA, SOMETIMES ALSO CALLED "JEFFERSON COUNTRY," IS A beguiling place: despite subdivisions, much of the landscape remains rural, and the green rolling hills of the Piedmont sustain old family farms and support a huge array of vineyards, orchards, and other agricultural and cultural tourism enterprises. Life here is generally quiet, the seasons rolling on from one to the next; there is—there *was*—little agitation. Thomas Jefferson himself might be said to have created this Virginian identity. Jefferson's self-defined sensibility for restraint in his public persona was codified in his architectural designs (for example, Monticello, Poplar Forest, and the University of Virginia), which have spread across the state and beyond over the past two hundred years. Many houses, from large 1920s Georgian Revival mansions to small 1950s Capes, are red brick with creamy white trim and Chinese Chippendale details on the door frames. In the nineteenth and twentieth centuries, Virginians wanted to emulate Jeffersonian style and taste.

This emulation, of course, came at a huge price, and it's a price we continue to pay in the twenty-first century. Social justice activism and the turn to "history from below" have helped us to identify the deeply embedded social inequities normalized for generations and reinforced in public culture, which include objects such as school textbooks, the marking of holidays, the creation of historic sites and museums (such as Monticello and Poplar Forest), and the subject of this study, monuments and memorials. I've been researching and writing about monument culture for a long time, but after the events in Charlottesville, it was important to turn my gaze outward and embrace others working with similar materials and perhaps with a similar purpose. The Unite the Right rally on August 11, 2017, around Thomas Jefferson's bronze monument near the Rotunda of the University of Virginia was hideous. The events of the next day, worse still. Monument culture, by then, was already in the news as Confederates and Columbus came under close scrutiny across the country, but this weekend shook the tranquility out of Jefferson Country. I did not want to let the moment go—monument culture had been sidelined for a long time—but now it was center stage (or as center stage as art, history, and material culture could be in the United States).

After placing an open call for proposals, by December 2017, I had received 110, which came from everywhere it seemed, including former Soviet countries and island nations and across the Commonwealth of Virginia as well as from members of the current Commonwealth of Nations, such as Canada, Australia, and New Zealand. I could easily have chosen three times as many essays as were allowed in the book contract. Artists, English professors, sociologists, anthropologists, historians, archaeologists, art historians, and even an economist submitted proposals. I realized too late that the English language requirement was clearly a barrier for many, as was political separation between East and West. Not surprisingly, due to their repressive governments, I received no proposals from anyone in China or Russia and places such as North Africa. Many of the essayists in this collection writing about places far from the United States are attached to this country through immigration or academic affiliation, or else they live in other places but are Americans or Westerners in culture, if not location. In the end, the essays I chose, based on the one-page proposals, were selected for their potential contribution to a global story. The book was set on an abbreviated time frame and needed to move through each stage of the publication process quickly to contribute to contemporary monument culture.

I am grateful to everyone who submitted a proposal and especially to the people who became this book: Johnny Alam, Kingsley Baird, Flaminia Bartolini, Derek Boetcher, Nausikaä El-Mecky, Basil Farraj, Chiara Grilli, Daniel Haumschild, Ingo Heidbrink, Ñusta Carranza Ko, Elliot Krasnopoler, Runette Kruger, Scott McDonald, Nilüfer Nahya, Roger Nelson, Saim Őrnek, Cynthia Prescott, Evander Price, Tanja Schult, Carmen Tomfohrde, Alex Vernon, Masha Vlasova, and Amy Williams. These writers—as it turns out, all academics of one sort or another, from doctoral students and fellows to full-time professors and independent scholars—were eager to prepare their work and did so in a timely way that made my first foray in editing an essay collection a pleasure. I am grateful as well to the peer reviewers, who spent time with all twenty-two essays and provided valuable criticism, and to John Marks, the American Association for State and Local History's senior manager of strategic initiatives, who also serves as the managing editor of the book series. Importantly, he, as well as Bob Beatty, now of the Lyndhurst Group, supported my vision for an attempt at integration from differing disciplinary and literary perspectives. Many thanks are due to Charles Harmon, Michael Tan, and Della Vache of Rowman & Littlefield for their work.

The essays were grouped into five themes: Land, People, and Place; Trauma/Violence and Reconciliation/Reparations; Migration and Identity; Ambiguities and Alternatives; and Strategies and Actions. This grouping could be reshaped many times over due to the fact that monuments are objects with multiple forms and meanings—with points of connection that can fit together in different ways. It is instructive to know that the origin of the Latin verb *monere* is a "calling to mind," which denotes little about form/style/place/meaning. Most essays can be reassigned into alternate or multiple categories because monument culture encompasses multiple disciplines within the object and place. Readers may find their own connective tissue between essays—I certainly hope so. From these writers, then, we are able to learn something about monument culture in Ireland as well as in Iceland, Antarctica, Peru, Chile, England, Italy, Greece, Polynesia, Spain, Rwanda, Austria, Germany, South Africa, Kyrgyz Republic, Cambodia, Laos, Australia, New Zealand, and the United States. But it is the twenty-first century, and now we must also recognize monument culture is part and parcel of the digital world too.

My hope is that *Monument Culture* makes a constructive collective statement and reaches across time and place to connect people and ideas. Monument culture gives us a past but also attempts to shape a future. That we keep falling short of control over both boils down to the limitations of humanity.

Introduction

MONUMENT CULTURE: INTERNATIONAL PERSPECTIVES ON THE FUTURE OF MONUMENTS IN A CHANGING WORLD compiles new scholarship about monuments from around the world, providing an international dimension to contemporary discussions regarding the meaning and use of monuments and memorials. The essays pack a lot of information—geographies, methodologies, content, and literary style—into one book, which is intended to provide brief introductions for interested readers and others to the wide-ranging world of scholarship around monument culture. For some, this effort might be disorienting, but I believe the essays open a pathway to international perspectives on monument culture, serving as a departure point for more detailed investigations for anyone who has such interest. Certainly, all of the authors here are open to public conversations and would welcome inquiries into their work.

In these essays, readers will find discussions of traditional monuments as shaping national narratives and erasing particular pasts; the problems of incorporating and appropriating culture; race and public commemoration; questions about what defines a monument; and the uses of monument culture and more traditional art historical techniques of iconography, rhetoric, and architectural forms. This collection also goes beyond physical monuments to "social media monuments" and "citizens as walking memorials," reminding readers that monuments are no longer limited to groupings of bronze figures or the ancient forms of arches, obelisks, sarcophagi, monoliths, and colonnades. Today, monumentalizing and its relation, memorializing, come in as many shapes and forms as culture can create, and that shape has radically changed in the twenty-first century. The directions in which to study monument culture are as varied as the parts of its being: questions about participation in monument-making processes are part of monument culture, as is the creation of exhibits (both temporary and "permanent") and the installation or removal of physical objects to append new ideas to old objects as well as the integration of the analog and digital worlds, a practice enveloping more and more of our attention.

Monument Culture opens with an essay by Alex Vernon, who provides a lyrical leading work, bringing readers with him as he moves backward and forward in time, connecting the events in Charlottesville to the intertwined sociopolitical histories of the United States and Europe and the slippery slope that we find ourselves on when speaking to the meaning of monument culture—something once thought of as permanent and unyielding to change. Vernon, a professor of English and an author, comes to monument culture from a place different than the others in this volume. Not bound by the disciplinary strictures of academic writing, Vernon's "familiar essay" is a view into the immediate personal set against the uses of history. For those of us who spend a lot of time in the analytical thinking and writing mode of specific disciplines, Vernon's essay is a reminder that everyone has a place in this conversation—a conversation usually dominated by historians—which brings insight into why monuments serve as connections across discipline, place, and time. After inviting readers to place their thoughts again in the unfolding events in 2017, which Vernon ably captures in "Homage to Charlottesville," *Monument Culture* offers five sections of four essays each, grouped thematically.

Section 2 is created out of studies concerned with deploying monuments to shape identity, community, and history via the physical landscape and place. Carmen Tomfohrde's essay "Implications of Erasure in Polynesia" uses historical and contemporary examples of monuments from the central and southern Pacific Ocean islands and their relationship to a changed culture with mass conversion to Christianity in the first half of the nineteenth century, which changed shape yet again by the end of the twentieth century. Tomfohdre asks how monuments are used in this "continual negotiation of history," in which the secular coexists with the religious over the concept of "deep time," but also if these monuments have meaning today and tomorrow. Ingo Heidbrink's essay, "Monuments in Antarctica: Commemoration of Historic Events or Claims for Sovereignty?" similarly looks at monument culture from the perspective of the future. Heidbrink argues that various countries have erected monuments not only to commemorate historic events but, in all actuality, to substantiate future territorial claims on a continent where there is no traditional sovereignty. Beyond reminding readers that there is no place on planet Earth without monument culture, Heidbrink's essay demonstrates that monuments can and do serve a function without a visiting public.

Roger Nelson's contribution, "Phnom Penh's Independence Monument and Vientiane's Patuxai: Complex Symbols of Postcolonial Nationhood in Cold War–Era Southeast Asia," uses the theme of "redeployment," that is, the use and reuse of colonial and local architectural forms for the creation of postcolonial nationhood in Cambodia and Laos. His essay points to the use of the same monuments by successive political regimes as symbols of differing ideologies. Using a comparative approach to tease out the application of meaning ascribed to the monumental forms, Nelson's work considers the capital cities and nations in which these monuments are sited and the renewed interest shown in them due to new urban features. The last contribution to this section, focused on the function of monuments in the construction of land, people, and place, is Cynthia Prescott's "Enshrining Racial Hierarchy through Settler Commemoration in the American West." Prescott studied 185 pioneer monuments located in the American West and beyond to find that the western movement of Jeffersonian agrarian ideals translated on the ground to indigenous dispossession and that the monuments marking these white settlers' placement on the landscape encoded racial hierarchies in subtle and sometimes not-so-subtle ways. The theme of land, people, and place in monument culture appears in varying degrees in the essays to follow as well because it is a foundational construct of human identity making in use since the first *Homo sapiens* (and now even earlier hominids) began painting on cave walls in prehistory.

Section 3 is a group of essays concerned with the twinning of trauma and violence to reconciliation and reparation in monument culture. Dan Haumschild's essay, "In Defense of Historical Stains: How Clean Approaches to the Past Can Keep Us Dirty," employs examples of monument culture situated in traumatic environments—specifically, Berlin, Germany, and Kigali, Rwanda— to ask how the concept of "futurity," that is, to learn from the trauma of the past so as to never repeat it, is better served through a "clean" versus a "dirty" representation of trauma. The point, for Haumschild, is to move toward futurity and therefore far from the origin of the trauma, which he sees occurring when monument visitors "inherit the past." Ñusta Carranza Ko's essay, "Repairing and Reconciling with the Past: *El Ojo que Llora* and Peru's Public Monuments," instead, presents a view into the workings of monument culture in Peru, which centralized itself on reparations processes using a newly created public space— not the scene of trauma—which binds the narratives of violence of the past to the present through allegorical/performative portrayals of political victims.

Like Peru's memorializing site *El Ojo que Llora*, South Africa's National Heritage Monument is viewed as a tool to build new collective memory and foster social cohesion. In "Ruptures and Continuities in the Post-Apartheid Political and Cultural Landscape: A Reading of South African Monument Culture," Runette Kruger discusses the site of the National Heritage Monument in the Groenkloof Nature Reserve on the outskirts of Tshwane/Pretoria, the country's capitol city, and the true-to-life bronze statues of "ordinary" South Africans, dehumanized under the Apartheid regime but humanized and celebrated here, liberating a "ruthlessly one-sided history." Basil Farraj comes to his subject, the memorializing of the Cuartel Borgoño in Chile, through ethnographic fieldwork. In his essay, "Beyond Ruins: Borgoño's Barracks and the Struggle over Memory in Today's Chile," Farraj traces the research done to "recuperate" (from the Spanish *recuperar*), meaning to restore and bring to life that which has been lost and silenced. His essay uncovers the individual response to the building's violent past use and attempts by these political prisoners to fight against official erasure as the country attempts to come to terms with its dictatorial past.

Section 4 is built around the theme of migration and identity and the ways in which content codified in monument culture travels across networks, changing shape with each geographic site. Derek N. Boetcher's essay, "Iconoclasm and Imperial Symbols: The Gough and Victoria Monuments in Ireland and the British World, 1880–1990," tracks the forced migration of imperial monuments before, during, and after colonialism. These monuments, once erected in colonial communities, were casualties of iconoclasm, which put the works into a migratory network, re-erected in other places that assign new meanings. Boetcher sees this as a useful and expanded definition and application of iconoclasm, in that destruction may be thought to "stimulate the production of new objects." The next chapter, "Monuments of Refugee Identity: Pain, Unity, and Belonging in Three Monuments of Cappadocian Greeks" by Zeliha Nilüfer Nahya and Saim Örnek, explores the way in which refugees "build their own monuments expressing and transmitting their past to new generations." Nahya and Örnek visited these monument sites and documented religious affiliation, the reshaping of identity through emigration and immigration, and the use of monuments as centers of social activity for refugees.

While the essays by Boetcher and Nahya and Örnek offer positive readings on the theme of migratory monuments and their usefulness, Amy Williams, in her essay, "Kindertransports in National and International Memory," problematizes a form of monument making that lost its sheen due to the changing perceptions of history and contemporary challenges to refugees in Britain and western Europe. As Williams notes, monuments to Kindertransports have recently come under scrutiny due to the noted parallels between the World War II–era forced migrations of Jewish children to the current refugee crisis, raising questions about "separation, loss, and estrangement" and lack of government action to address humanistic concerns. Kindertransport monuments are networked across Europe and Britain, so too are monuments to Columbus, which are found across an ocean and beyond. In her essay, "A Cubist Portrait of Christopher Columbus: Studying Monuments as Transcultural Works," Chiara Grilli suggests that the current (but already old) controversy about the place of Columbus in monument culture needs to be reframed as a Cubist work of art; that is, each monument—including Columbus—requires a comprehensive analysis of all of its facets. For monuments to Columbus, Grilli suggests that critics have yet to understand the importance of "Italian-

American myths of migration and identity, folk heroes, and collective emotion." Taken together, these essays remind readers that migration—whether of object, idea, or people—is a platform for the reshaping of identities and that monument culture plays a role in that work, for both the migrant and the memory-making work around the migration.

Section 5 of *Monument Culture* embraces differing forms of monument culture, away from the common focus on objects built of granite and bronze and erected for formal, often sanctioned entities. Elliot Krasnopoler sees an installation in the library of a small Icelandic town as a memorialization to the current and future loss of glaciers due to climate change but also a reading of the local, human-scaled experience of the landscape. His essay, "Visible Differently: Roni Horn's *Vatnasafn/Library of Water* as Memorial," argues that Horn's work becomes a nonmonumental memorial through this pendulum swing between the local and the global. Masha Vlasova's contribution also uses the idea of movement, but hers is the idea of "monument rotations," where one pedestal in the city of Bishkek in the Kyrgyz Republic hosted changing figures, following changes in political leadership. In "Monuments and Other Things That Change: Several Attempts at Titling a Photograph," Vlasova presents varied readings of an image of the pedestal with Vladimir Lenin installed, revealing a fluid relationship to a monumental past, unique to that city's landscape. Similarly, Nauskiaä El-Mecky asks readers to consider another form of monument making in transition—objects she calls "illegal protest monuments," objects that may be ephemeral (or not) that challenge the long process of monument making, serving to critique/attack regimes in power or draw attention to neglected people and events. In her essay, "Illegal Monuments: Memorials between Crime and State Endorsement," El-Mecky says that though these illegal monuments are often created out of materials that disappear, they live on in the digital world and can become permanent, changing monument culture by forcing the question, "What is a monument today?" Johnny Alam's paper, "Transnational Social Media Monuments, Counter Monuments, and the Future of the Nation-State," offers case studies to examine this question from the perspective of the transnational practice of memorializing via social media, as when Facebook users applied the French flag to their profiles after the terrorist attacks of November 2015 in Paris. Alam delves into questions about this contemporary form of monument culture, asking how this transnational practice contributes to or controls the work of memory and what this means to the future of nation-states.

Section 6, the last grouping of essays, continues to consider the differing ways monument culture is shaped and applied in contemporary contexts around the world, especially those dealing with controversial, difficult, or "dark" history. Tanja Schult offers walking as a different strategy in "doing" monument culture. In her essay, "Citizens as Walking Memorials: Rethinking the Monument Genre in the Twenty-First Century," Schult ably describes Christoph Mayer's memorializing project, *The Invisible Camp—Audio Walk Gusen*, located in Austria at the site of a forgotten Nazi concentration camp for Jews. Schult analyzes Mayer's audio walk through the landscape and finds a unique experience different from traditional audio walks (such as in a museum) that successfully conveys the history of the site through a "collage-based" structure, but which asks much from the listener/walker to make the experience work. Kingsley Baird, in his chapter, "Exhibiting Spectacle and Recasting Memory: Commemorating the First World War in New Zealand," notes that the publicly popular memorial exhibit on Gallipoli, created of colossal figures by the Weta workshop, does not offer an opportunity to critique war as one of the foundational myths of New Zealand identity. An alternative action to the colossi are the artist's small-scale bronze sculptures, which he believes can serve to encompass "recognition of sacrifice and duty while critiquing the use of the past in the present." The role of monument culture in working with a troubled past is also the focus of Flaminia Bartolini's essay, "Dealing with a Dictatorial Past: Fascist Monuments and Conflicting Memory in Contemporary Italy." Here, Bartolini highlights two ways in which Italy presents its fascist past via monument culture: the first, the town of Affile, which celebrates its connection to Rodolfo Graziani, and the second, the town of Bolzano, which critiqued its own fascist monument by the installation of artwork by philosopher Hannah Arendt via digital technology. The last chapter in this section, Scott McDonald's "Avoiding Iconoclasm: How the Counter Monument Could Settle a Monumental Debate," believes that the American-centric discussion around Confederate monuments falls short of considering the alternative: as with Bartolini's description of the changes to Bolzano's Town Hall, McDonald believes controversial monuments should be "manipulated and challenged by artists with input from the local community." His reasoning is based on work done in Northern Ireland, which has a more than thirty-year history of creating new social connective tissue out of a desperate social divide.

Monument Culture's closing essay is Evander Price's "On Creating a Useable Future: An Introduction to Future Monuments," which considers a little-talked-about subject: the future monument. Price notes that future monuments are intended to "explicitly reify and manifest an imagination of the future." There is something very twentieth-century about this—Price discusses examples from the 1939 World's Fair and Carl Sagan's "Golden Record," which is currently in space—a celebratory idea, but one also full of social anxiety about control over the future. Scholars and students of monument culture spend much time trying to link past to present, but as Price points out, the risks inherent in creating a "useable past" also extend to usable future monuments.

CHAPTER 1

Homage to Charlottesville

A Familiar Essay

Alex Vernon

We are all drowning in filth. When I talk to anyone or read the writings of anyone who has any axe to grind, I feel that intellectual honesty and balanced judgement have simply disappeared from the face of the earth. Everyone's thought is forensic, everyone is simply putting a "case" with deliberate suppression of his opponent's point of view, and, what is more, with complete insensitiveness to any sufferings except those of himself and his friends. . . . One notices this in the case of people one disagrees with, such as Fascists or pacifists but in fact everyone is the same, at least everyone is utterly heartless towards people who are outside the immediate range of his own interests. What is most striking of all is the way sympathy can be turned on and off like a tap according to political expediency.

—George Orwell's diary, April 27, 1942[1]

Friday evening, August 11, 2017, the first of the weekend's incoming news updates from Charlottesville hit my smartphone: White Nationalists March on University of Virginia. Over a dozen such organizations were descending upon the newly renamed Emancipation Park to protest the potential removal of a statue of the Confederate General Robert E. Lee. They were to be met on Saturday by a diversity of counter-protestors. Luckily, we had canceled our cable subscription, freeing me from that medium's irresistible news hypnosis. I needed to absorb the events and images on my own emotional terms and schedule. From the radio, I learned about the car ramming into the crowd of counter-protestors. I didn't need an assault by video footage to know more; I could read about it, read about the entire depressing mess, online.

Web browser opened, cable news channel website found, and there it was, the first frame of the video. Looking past the car's rear end, its spoiler and GVF 111 license plate, my eyes follow what from the image's perspective is the car's axis of advance to its most prominent visual end point. *What the . . . ?* Am I seeing what I think I'm seeing, waving there in the background, above and slightly to the left of the car, above what must be the last cluster of anti-racist counter-protestors? A few minutes studying other images online confirm it. It's the red-yellow-purple triband flag of the Second Spanish Republic, 1931–1939.

What the . . . ?

Eighty years earlier and 170 miles from Charlottesville, President Franklin D. Roosevelt spoke at the anniversary of the Battle of Antietam. Seventy-five years earlier, the Union Army had turned back General Lee's first incursion into the north, outside Sharpsburg, Maryland. It remains the bloodiest single day in US military history.

Roosevelt's September 1937 speech acknowledged the painful years of Reconstruction, especially for Southerners. He regretted the "sectionalism" of the postwar years and, for the South, the "economic destruction and the denial to its population of the normal rights of free Americans."[2] That he meant *white* Southerners, that he spoke to white America, became clear in the pretense that the nation's house had finally been restored to order:

> It is too soon to define the history of the present generation; but I venture the belief that it was not until the World War of twenty years ago that we acted once more as a nation of restored unity. I believe also, that the past four years mark the first occasion, certainly since the War between the States, and perhaps during the whole 150 years of our government, that we are not only acting but also thinking in national terms.[3]

In 1862, five days after the battle's symbolic victory, Abraham Lincoln issued his preliminary Emancipation Proclamation. Roosevelt's anniversary remarks overlooked the very people for whose freedom the war was waged.[4] The anniversary included concerts, a small reenactment, and a pageant with Miss Antietam. I have not yet discovered photographic evidence of African Americans among the celebrants. If they were there, I can only somewhat imagine their reactions.

And what of the conflict setting Spain aflame that very moment? It was the most pressing international issue of the day; it could not have been far from Roosevelt's mind. Would he have thought to connect the two civil wars that day, the two republics imperiled by rebellions of those clinging to their exploitative agrarian economic legacy? Roosevelt mentioned the 1898 Spanish-American War as an example of what "young people" consider history, as whatever predated themselves into inconsequence. But was he, was anyone, assembled outside Sharpsburg that day thinking of Spain's pain? Of the Americans who traveled illegally to fight for the Spanish Republic, to fight for their vision of democracy and freedom, having taken as their name the Abraham Lincoln Brigade?[5]

In 1931, an election of democratic Republicans, generally moderate Progressives and Socialists, brought about the end of Spain's monarchy and the birth of the Second Spanish Republic. The next five years saw fierce political fighting among the Republicans, radical Leftists, and various conservative forces for control of the government. The electoral and legislative battles were joined by strikes and suppression, other forms of mob violence, imprisonment, harassment, arson, and murder. A failed military coup in July 1936 by the conservative army and on behalf of conservative Spain devolved into three years of civil war. Those forces—monarchists, landowners, industrialists, the army, fascists, the Catholic Church—fought and won under the banner of Nationalism and the leadership of Francisco Franco, who would rule as fascist dictator until his death in 1975. On the other side, the government collected every center and left-of-center group it could: moderates, socialists, unionists, nonrevolutionary communists, revolutionary communists, syndicalists, anarchists, and regional separatists. To call this coalition *motley* would give it too much cohesion. They shared a common enemy but had competing agendas and worldviews.

Franco's Nationalists openly embraced fascism and received significant financial and military support from Mussolini and Hitler in violation of a nonintervention pact. With the European democracies declining to violate the pact, the Republican government survived as long as it did largely through the interventions of the Communist International, the Soviet Union, and postrevolutionary Mexico. The full extent of Soviet and Communist influence remains a subject of debate. Regardless, many people outside Spain identified oppositionally—in other words, they supported the Republicans as anti-fascist or the Nationalists as anti-communist.[6]

Today, eighty years after the war and more than forty after Franco's death, fresh symbols of the old war repopulate Spain. There—and if you know to look, there is practically everywhere: at University City, the campus on the northwest corner of Madrid where Franco's rebellious Nationalist forces were halted and through which ran the trench lines, stalemated, for the rest of the war, its academic buildings pocky with bullet and shrapnel scores. And there, at old Belchite, a town destroyed during the war whose ruins Franco ordered to remain as a lasting testament to the destruction of the fatherland by his enemy, the legitimate Republican government of Spain. And there, in caves and on medieval forts in the New Castilian countryside south of Madrid. And there and there and there and there, on dumpsters and stanchions and benches and signage—in such places graffiti revives the war's panoply of symbols: yokes and arrows, hammers and sickles, clenched fists, swastikas, circle-A brands, and the acronyms of yesteryears: FAI, CNT, UHP, PCE, POUM.[7]

It's not just graffiti. It's a fascist Falange Española banner in a small town's *plaza mayor*. It's Spaniards whipping out Republican flags to protest pretty much anything, sometimes communist flags too. Those who want to preserve the history and legend of the defenders of the Second Republic hold commemorative marches at major battle sites. Don't imagine a US National Park Service treatment, with shiny canons and welcome centers, a Shiloh or an Antietam—in Spain, a former battlefield is just a piece of land. People carry aloft and wrap themselves in the Republican tricolors and, sometimes, the red drapery of communism. People break out singing "The Internationale." At my first march, at Jarama, a fellow outfitted himself in full Republican military garb. The walk back to our cars during my second such march, this one at Brunete, took us by an equestrian club. With the presumed aristocratic (Nationalist-leaning) riders as the backdrop, fellow marchers posed for cheerful pics clutching open a Republican flag accessorized with a large Atlético Madrid emblem. The people's football club, in opposition to Real Madrid, the club of the royals.

Less than a month before the "Unite the Right" weekend, at the World Gay Pride week in Madrid, rainbow flags with the anarchist circle-A joined regular rainbow flags and Republican flags (and a squad of trotting men wearing nothing but leather straps and pig masks). It is all in good fun, youthful progressive cheeky esprit. It is all quite serious.

I read almost nothing posted online the Saturday of the rally in Charlottesville. Instead, I examine the images. *19 hours ago. 11 hours ago. 2 hours ago. 22 minutes ago.* The swastikas, Confederate battle flags, Nationalist Front banners, and clownish Ku Klux Klan (KKK) regalia don't interest me. They don't surprise. No one needs a photo to picture that scene. But the flag of the Second Spanish Republic, 1931–1939? The usual protest props of Spain have migrated to the Virginia Piedmont?

Apparently so. Look: red flags with the gold hammer and sickle in the corner. Look again: posters with clenched fists, some emblazoned with the word SOLIDARITY. While these fists potentially signify black pride, to face off with the white bigotry of the rally, their red color plus the presence of Republican and Communist flags confuses the message. *Where am I looking at? When am I looking at?* I see among the counter-protesters and their allies in other cities the black flags and the circle-A brand of anarchists, I see black and red flags, I see images of the serpent of fascism, I see anti-fascist language. It's straight from the propaganda art playbook of the Republic's coalition.

At least one person in Charlottesville that August day in 2017—maybe only one person—had the Spanish Civil War in mind, the woman bearing the tricolors. At least one person near Sharpsburg that September day in 1937 had Europe in mind. A rabbinical student, Pinchos J. Chazin, traveled from New York City to speak at the Synagogue of Congregation B'Nai Abraham in Hagerstown. The speech's references point directly to Nazi Germany, never Spain. But the young seminarian addressed Antietam's lessons of liberty and democracy to all dictatorships: "Today, Antietam out of bitter and costly experience steps forth and speaks to dictatorships." To them Antietam says, among other things, "Mankind must not be impaled in the pillories and stocks of medieval reaction for hundreds of years."[8]

In its war to restore power to the traditional ruling class, which included monarchists and the Catholic Church with its inquisition legacy, Franco's Nationalist rhetoric appealed to a fantasy of a true and pure Spain, uncorrupted by the foreign—by Jews, Bolsheviks, and democratic modernity (while aggressively recruiting Moroccan Muslims to fight for Catholic Spain). Roughly a quarter of those who traveled to Spain to fight for the Republic in the International Brigades were Jewish.[9] To fight fascism was in a sense to fight cultural monolithism. The two battalions of volunteers from the United States were the first totally integrated combat units in American military history, and Oliver Law became the first African American to command white and black Americans. He died in July 1937 from wounds suffered in combat at Brunete.

Indeed, African American volunteers and their supporters felt deeply the connection between European fascism, North American racism and segregation, and the plight of Europe's colonies. As Canute Frankson wrote home from Spain in July 1937:

> Since this is a war between whites who for centuries have held us in slavery, and have heaped every kind of insult and abuse upon us, segregated and jim-crowed us; why I, a Negro, who have fought through these years for the rights of my people, am here in Spain?
>
> Because we are no longer an isolated group fighting hopelessly against an immense giant. . . . Because if we crush Fascism here, we'll save our people in America, and in other parts of the world, from the vicious persecution, wholesale imprisonment, and slaughter which the Jewish people suffered and are suffering under Hitler's Fascist heels.
>
> All we have to do is to think of the lynching of our people. We can but look back at the pages of American history stained with the blood of Negroes; stink with the burning bodies of our people hanging from trees; bitter with the groans of our tortured loved ones from whose living bodies, ears, fingers, toes have been cut for souvenirs—living bodies into which red-hot pokers have been thrust. All because of a hate created in the minds of men and women by their masters who

keep us all under their heels while they suck our blood, while they live in their bed of ease by exploiting us. . . .

We will crush them. We will build us a new society—a society of peace and plenty. There will be no color line, no jim-crow trains, no lynching. That is why, my dear, I'm here in Spain.[10]

Black American commentators on the war, such as the poet Langston Hughes, saw in Spain's Moorish history and Europe's dismissal of Spain as more African than European a source of blood and spiritual kinship.[11] Franco was imagined, in cartoons and prose, as belonging to the KKK.

Yet are those bearing Communist, anarchist, and anti-fascist icons in Charlottesville actually happy bedfellows who share a unity of purpose with one another and most especially with those counter-protestors who simply abhor racism? Can one trust that different, potentially conflicting agendas aren't being pursued? "What's eroding," writes Peter Beinart in *The Atlantic*, "is the quality Max Weber considered essential to a functioning state: a monopoly on legitimate violence. As members of a largely anarchist movement, anti-fascists don't want the government to stop white supremacists from gathering. They want to do so themselves, rendering the government impotent."[12] One should not forget the Spanish Republic's bloody internecine war within Spain's bloody internecine war, the May Days of 1937, with anarchists, rival communists, and the government fighting among themselves in the streets of Barcelona and to which George Orwell bore witness in *Homage to Catalonia*. Walking alongside the hammer and sickle as a sympathetic observer during a commemorative event, sure. But severe disquietude hits when I imagine marching beside the hammer and sickle of Stalin's liquidation regime as an activist, even if simply to protest white supremacy. Is a perfect protest, one without complication, reasonable to expect? Is insisting on a single message, well, undemocratic?

A nuanced historic understanding and unity of purpose, whereby the Charlottesville counter-protesters focused upon the anti-racist overlap in the Venn diagram of their gathered symbolism, feels unlikely. Even more unlikely—ridiculously unlikely—would be the expectation that everyone watching them, ideological foes included, would appreciate the nuance. During the Spanish Civil War, all supporters of the Republic, to its foes, were *rojos*. Reds. Everyone in the International Brigades was a *Russo*, a Russian, regardless of country of origin. It is difficult to process mid-twentieth-century rhetoric and symbols resurrected in patchwork and stumbling through the twenty-first century countryside like Frankenstein's monster. Political ideologies, entities, and identities evolve. When should one recall and apply the historical legacy? When should one let it go? Rhetoric and iconography are appropriated, recycled, repurposed. Visual symbols don't easily disambiguate.

The summer before Charlottesville, a controversial photograph from West Point of African American female cadets from the graduating class of 2016 raising clenched fists became national news. The nation had watched Beyoncé's surprise Superbowl performance of "Formation" and was living through the height of the Black Lives Matter response to the killing of black men by police and the exoneration of the officers, their departments, the state.

Did the young women intend to invoke the Black Panthers? Did they even understand fully what that would have meant? Could they recognize the fist's complicated history, stretching at least back to the 1930s' relationship between black America and communism? Was it more about Beyoncé and their love of pop culture than a revolutionary shout-out to the Panthers and a fuck you to the nation-state whose uniform the cadets wore? Was it simply an expression of collective accomplishment that harmlessly if pertly acknowledged their shared identity as black women? The image most closely resembled an assembly of Republican soldiers in Spain circa 1937. And it *could* have simply expressed their accomplishment. After all, President Donald Trump raised his clenched fist moments after taking the oath of office. Surely it wasn't solidarity with the Black Lives Matter movement; given how his 2016 campaign resonated with various white pride groups, could it have been the Aryan Fist, stolen from the Black Panthers? Or a sly salute to Russian President Vladimir Putin, about whom Trump spoke admiringly during the campaign?

The English writer Ralph Bates published a wonderfully strange essay in October 1936 about the burning of Catholic iconography and churches by anarchists in Catalonia, "Compañero Sagasta Burns a Church." Bates writes the scene as witness-participant:

It was a grand bonfire. A little technical commission (to which I was elected) stood at one side of the door, passing judgment on the saints as they were carried out. Compañero Sagasta relies on my judgment.
"This one, compañero?"
"Revolting, burn him."
"Very good, compañero."
Poum! The bearers run to the fire and St. Peter throws up a billow of sparks.
"This one, compañero?"
"Absolutely nauseating, pitch her on the fire." (Why do female saints appear to suffer from permanent disorders of the kind proper to their sex?)
"This one?"
"H'm, looks rather old, the carving's direct; probably deserves a second thought."
"Very good." The saint is dumped on his back among the silver plate candelabra, the books with parchment backs, which may make binding for school-

books, the electric bulbs, the linen, good for bandages, and, in short, anything that possibly has artistic or secular value.

This not-gaudy candelabra, for instance: when it came out I yelled, "Eh, bring that here."

"It's only iron."

"Only iron! Christ Jesus, it's pure Catalan work of the fifteenth century; look, no rivets, no clips, everything is welded and drawn under the hammer."

The iconoclasts reverently placed the candelabra to one side, reverently I say, for a compañero has said this is art, and feeling out of it, they rush into the church for another trophy.[13]

Bates assures his readers that the anarchists took great care in their work, preserving artifacts and architecture of genuine value and declining to burn a Barcelona church whose position gave the enemy no military advantage. They knocked on doors of homes to issue polite warning when they were about to torch a neighborhood church.

I think of Bates's "technical commission" when I read about today's monuments targeted by various groups as needing removal. That 1933 Chicago monument to the creator of Mussolini's air power that would soon be used against Republican Spain, Italo Balbo? Maybe. Maybe not. I—we—require more research, more reflection. Christopher Columbus? In Barcelona in early July, walking past the sixty-meter-high Columbus monument overlooking the port, I hoped to elicit a smile from my teenage daughter by embracing my role as uber-goober dad and so thanked Columbus aloud. Probably with a wave or a half-assed salute. I also think of how, a century ago, the white-robed brethren of the white Christian supremacists of Charlottesville's "Unite the Right" gathering were arguably more anti-Catholic than anti-black, at least in their speeches and publications.[14] That in a previous incarnation they themselves might have cheered on the anti-fascist Compañero Sagasta as well as the anti-Catholic revolutionaries in Mexico. Instead, in Wisconsin in September, in the wake of Charlottesville, vandals defaced a monument to the state's contribution to the International Brigades located across the street from the Gates of Heaven Synagogue. Swastikas, "ANTIFA SUCKS," and "TRUMP RULES," spray-painted in red, appeared hours before Rosh Hashanah commenced.[15]

There is a vast difference, of course, between a self-appointed committee's willy-nilly destruction of icons and the proper, democratic decision-making processes carried out by elected officials over potential statue removal, such as the legislation by three Maryland congressmen to remove the Lee statue at Antietam, introduced two days before the 155th anniversary. When for over twenty years the state of Arkansas celebrated Robert E. Lee Day over the national Martin Luther King, Jr. Day, many Americans can hardly imagine any public testament to Lee as anything but a racial affront. Yet for many defenders of controversial statues, the removal movement can be character-ized by a mobocracy overtaken by self-righteous political correctness mixed up with absurd notions of anti-fascism and anarchist iconoclasm. Will West Point rename Lee Barracks rather than have cadets live in a building named after a fellow graduate, a former academy superintendent, and a leader whose battlefield genius contributes to the school's boast that "the history we teach was made by those we taught"?

I think of the old monument to Spain's colonial army, destroyed during the civil war. It was eventually replaced by a monument to Simón Bolívar, erected by the former colonies to the embodiment of their liberation, a stone's throw from Franco's triumphant arch leading into Madrid. Scores upon scores of commuters pass them every day.

George Orwell's experiences in a Marxist pro-Republican militia defending Catalonia during the war contributed to his rejection of midcentury commu-nism. He remained, however, a committed Progressive Democratic Socialist. In life as well as in language, he bothered—passionately—to discriminate.

In March 1944, two years before his celebrated "Politics and the English Language," Orwell published an essay in his "As I Please" column, which asks, "What is Fascism?" At the height of the world war against fascism, Or-well observes the term's application by pretty much everyone to pretty much everyone else: conservatives, socialists, Communists, Trotskyists, Catholics, war resisters, war supporters, and every stripe of nationalist. "In conversation, of course, it is used even more wildly than in print. I have heard it applied to farmers, shopkeepers, Social Credit, corporal punishment, fox-hunting, bull-fighting, the 1922 Committee, the 1941 Committee, Kipling, Gandhi, Chiang Kai-Shek, homosexuality, Priestley's broadcasts, Youth Hostels, astrology, women, dogs and I do not know what else." He concludes that the word *fascist* has become all but "meaningless" except as a synonym for *bully*. "All one can do for the moment is to use the word with a certain amount of circumspection and not, as is usually done, degrade it to the level of a swearword."[16]

The word *fascism* is hardly alone in its weaponized promiscuity of late, Mr. Orwell. We haven't been listening, sir.

NOTES

1. George Orwell. *My Country Right or Left 1940–1943: The Collected Essays, Jour-nalism, and Letters of George Orwell*, vol. 2, ed. Sonia Orwell and Ian Angus (Har-court, Brace & World, 1968), 423.
2. "Roosevelt Speech at Antietam," *Boston Herald*, September 19, 1937, West-ern Maryland's Historical Library, http://www.whilbr.org/itemdetail.aspx?idEntry=2400&dtPointer=4.
3. Ibid.

4. This brief discussion of a single rhetorical move does not intend to be anything else; one should not infer a general charge of racism in Roosevelt's policies or person.

5. The term Abraham Lincoln Brigade is something of a misnomer because there was no such military unit. There was an Abraham Lincoln Battalion and a shorter-lived George Washington Battalion. The term Abraham Lincoln Brigade refers to all volunteers from the United States regardless of their military assignment.

6. For too many Spaniards, the choices were not easy. One's allegiances, needs, and desires did not readily resolve. There were influences and pressures of family, region or village or neighborhood, and the need to secure work. Often, the decision lay out of the individual's hands. People switched sides. People hid. People pretended. People sought to survive.

7. Federación Anarquista Ibérica; Confederación Nacional del Trabajo; Unión de Hermanos Proletarios; Partido Comunista de España; Partido Obrero de Unificación Marxista. Although "acronyms of yesteryears" is not entirely accurate, as some of the organizations from the 1930s remain active.

8. Germany is not actually named either. "Antietam Address, radio broadcast, undated," Box 12, Folder 14, Pinchos J. Chazin Papers, Temple University Libraries. Though undated in the archives, the document's language exactly matches that quoted by the local newspaper "Rabbi Scores Dictatorship. Visiting Jewish Clergyman Gives Stirring Address Here." *The Daily Mail*, Monday, September 13, 1937, 7F. See also the announcement of the upcoming talk, which mentions that the speech would be broadcast over station WJEJ: "Rabbi Chazin Will Speak at Service Here. 'Antietam Speaks to Dictatorships' Will Be Sunday Topic." *Hagerstown Herald-Mail*, September 10, 1937, www.whilbr.org/itemdetail.aspx?idEntry=2393&dtPointer=7.

9. Helen Graham, *The Spanish Civil War: A Very Short Introduction* (Oxford University Press, 2005), 44. Graham's figure is for all international volunteers, not just those from the United States.

10. "Letter from Canute Frankson, Albacete, Spain, July 6, 1937," in *Madrid 1937: Letters of the Abraham Lincoln Brigade from the Spanish Civil War*, ed. Cary Nelson and Jefferson Hendricks (Routledge, 1996), 33–34. For additional examples, see the writings by Salaria Key and James Bernard (Bunny) Rucker in *The Good Fight Continues: World War II Letters from the Abraham Lincoln Brigade*, ed. Peter N. Carroll, Michael Nash, and Melvin Small (New York University Press, 2006), 27–28, 137–38.

11. See Gayle Rogers, "Negro and Negro: Translating American Blackness in the Shadows of the Spanish Empire," in *Incomparable Empires: Modernism and the Translation of Spanish and American Literature* (Columbia University Press, 2016).

12. Peter Beinart, "The Rise of the Violent Left," *The Atlantic* (September 2017). Although this issue of the magazine appeared after the weekend in Charlottesville, the article does not mention the event—a fact that suggests it was written and sent to press prior to that violence.

13. Ralph Bates, "Compañero Sagasta Burns a Church," *The Left Review* 2, no. 13 (October 1936): 681–87.

14. "While the Klan's list of adversaries was long, some historians have suggested that [in the 1920s] anti-Catholicism was the strongest and most nationally consistent rallying point." Kenneth C. Barnes, *Anti-Catholicism in Arkansas: How Politicians, the Press, the Klan, and Religious Leaders Imagined an Enemy, 1910–1960* (University of Arkansas Press, 2016), 98.
15. The fall of 2017 also saw the terrorist attack in Barcelona that left thirteen dead and the Catalonian independence crisis.
16. George Orwell. *As I Please, 1943–1945: The Collected Essays, Journalism, and Letters of George Orwell*, vol. 3, ed. Sonia Orwell and Ian Angus (Harcourt, Brace & World, 1968), 111–14.

CHAPTER 2

Implications of Erasure in Polynesia

Carmen S. Tomfohrde

LOST AND FOUND

Sheltered among the trees in the public park at Point Venus, a peninsula that forms Matavai Bay, monuments commemorate the historic site where Tahiti experienced its first entanglements with the West. Captain James Cook first anchored in Matavai Bay in April 1769, shortly after fellow British navigator Samuel Wallis's June 1767 "discovery" of Tahiti at the same location. One monument at Matavai Bay remembers Captain Cook; another recalls the ill-fated HMS *Bounty*, lost to mutineers after leaving Tahiti in April 1789. A third monument commemorates an Enlightenment-era ship of a different kind: the missionary ship *Duff*, which arrived at Matavai Bay in March 1797. Approximately two centuries after widespread conversions to Christianity took place in Polynesia, this complex monument encapsulates present-tense recollections of past erasures of religious cultural heritage.

The missionaries' concept of "discovery" was to seek and save people lost in sin and needing salvation, "enlightening" them with the Gospel of Christ. These foreigners were unlike previous visitors: on April 13, 1797, one missionary declared Tahitians "profess hardly to know what we are, and suspect that we are not Englishmen, or like any of the others they have seen who have ever visited their island."[1] The *Duff* missionaries were not the first to attempt to evangelize Tahiti; two Franciscan friars from Peru arrived in 1774 but lasted less than a year. While their evangelical effort was failing miserably, readers in England were enthralled by news of Captain Cook's first (1768–1771) circumnavigation of the globe. Compassion piqued, the London-based Rev. Thomas Haweis spoke with Captain Bligh, secured a rudimentary vocabulary from a *Bounty* passenger, and nearly succeeded in a scheme to send two missionaries with Bligh on his 1791 return voyage to Tahiti for breadfruit. It was not until 1796 that the newly formed Missionary Society purchased the ship *Duff* and dispatched thirty men, six women, and three children to Tahiti, Tonga, and the Marquesas as its inaugural venture. Only four of the *Duff* missionaries were ordained; the others included carpenters, a bricklayer, and a harness maker, each intending to contribute specialized labor not only to survive in this remote island but also to impress Polynesian hosts with their usefulness and develop friendships that should generate opportunities for evangelism.[2]

Within three years, hopes for the *Duff* mission deflated. The lone missionary in the Marquesas returned to England in 1799 having survived a severe famine that included violent skirmishes and cannibalism. Three of the nine Tonga missionaries died in a 1799 civil war, and an excommunicated missionary was left behind when the remaining five missionaries evacuated in 1800. As battles continued to rage, famine drove the missionary who "went native" into desperate circumstances. A visiting ship took him to England in 1801, where he repented of his apostasy in a published memoir.[3] In Tahiti, one year into the *Duff* missionaries' residence, four missionaries were stripped of their clothes and beaten, and armed islanders assembled after missionaries intercepted the sale of guns and gunpowder from a dilapidated visiting ship. When this ship unexpectedly revisited soon after departing, all but eight missionaries and one missionary wife evacuated on it. Although the ship *Royal Admiral* brought a replenishment of missionaries to Tahiti in 1801, almost all of them withdrew seven years later. Tahiti was embroiled in war, and prospects looked bleak for the mission; by 1809, one lone *Duff* missionary, Henry Nott, remained in Polynesia.

When missionaries returned from Australia in 1812 and set up residence on the island of Moʻorea, adjacent to Tahiti, they found the exiled and politically weak "king" Pōmare II a changed man: he wanted a Christian baptism. Doubting Pōmare's sincerity, missionaries delayed his baptism until 1819, but to the missionaries' surprise, their school and worship services became popular. Although hundreds of Society Islanders converted before the 1815 Battle of Fei Pi, that event was pivotal for Christianity in the Society Islands: missionaries reported that after "heathens" waged war on Christians who peacefully assembled for a worship service, Pōmare's merciful treatment of the defeated attackers motivated thousands to convert. A mass movement in favor of Christianity began: by 1816, missionaries stopped registering the names of converts because Christianity had "become national" in both Tahiti and Moʻorea and was quickly spreading through all of the Society Islands.[4] Widespread islander-instigated iconoclasm ensued. New Christian churches were established on the foundations of destroyed *marae* (stone ritual structures used in the religion Christianity supplanted), such as the still-extant octagonal church at Papetoaʻi, Moʻorea, and the missionaries' first printing house repurposed *marae* stones to pave its floor.[5] Rather than describing the widespread demolition of indigenous cultural forms as a cause for grief and bereavement, missionary documents describe a jubilant liberation.

GENEALOGY AND THE *DUFF* MONUMENT

While the distinction between a monument and a historical marker may require clarification in the case of the Matavai Bay monument to the *Bounty*, the monument to the *Duff* is celebratory. Invoking nautical geometry in its abstracted angular form, the monument has a pyramidal stela with a sloped base that bears the *Duff* missionaries' names. Painted red and sharply contrasting with the green foliage surrounding it, the stela bears a surface pattern of bolts and seams, calling to mind the copper sheathing that was attached to the hulls of ships in the late eighteenth century. The monument faces north, the direction from which incoming ships arrive, providing a site-specific spatial orientation that navigationally positions the viewer (figure 2.1).

A low retaining wall surrounds the monument, painted white and embedded with black volcanic stones captioned to identify the years of initial evangelization of other Polynesian islands (figure 2.2). This encircling rim of historical markers gives a specific ancestry to the spread of Christianity and correctly asserts a genealogy of missions that positions Tahiti and neighboring Moʻorea as a central node from which Christianity fanned out across Polynesia. The rapid transformation of Polynesian islands in favor of Christianity began with the London Missionary Society in 1815 but also involved Society Islander missionaries who traveled to the Cook Islands, Tuamotus, and Austral Islands

Figure 2.1. Monument commémoratif de l'arrivée des premiers missionnaires à Tahiti (Commemorative Monument to the Arrival of the First Missionaries in Tahiti, also called the *Duff* monument). Erected at Point Venus, Tahiti, French Polynesia, in 1970. Architect: Rodolphe Weinmann with René Déssirier and Jean Perey.
Photograph by the author.

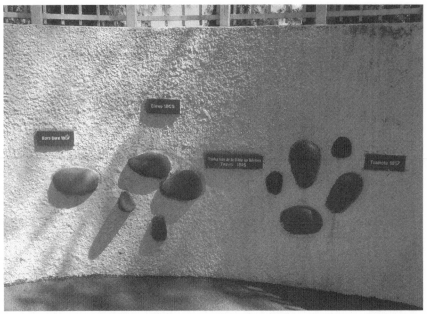

Figure 2.2. Detail, Monument commémoratif de l'arrivée des premiers missionnaires
à Tahiti
Photograph by the author.

as well as Tonga on their way to Fiji; Wesleyan Methodist missionaries from
England in Tonga; and American Congregationalist missionaries in Hawai'i.
Both the London Missionary Society and Wesleyan Methodist Missionary
Society evangelized Samoa after a Tongan convert reached out to Samoans in
1828. The Marquesas largely resisted Protestant missionary attempts before
adopting Roman Catholicism through French missionaries in the 1840s. Foreign missionary presence was often intended as a segue toward indigenization
of Christianity and independence for native churches: the American Board
of Commissioners for Foreign Missions (ABCFM) withdrew from Hawai'i in
1863, and in the Society Islands, missionaries' ill health and the overwhelming
demand for Christian education forced missionaries to rely heavily on indigenous evangelists when widespread conversions began in earnest. Christianity
remains the dominant religion in Polynesia. If Hawai'i and New Zealand are set
aside because of their large immigrant populations, it appears that most Poly-
nesians are Christian today: 84 percent of Cook Island and French Polynesian
residents self-identify as Christian; Samoa and American Samoa claim over 92
and 98 percent, respectively; and Tonga is over 96 percent Christian.[6]

Continuing a present-tense implication of the islands' historical erasure of
pre-Christian religion, the intended dominant narrative deployed by the *Duff*

monument is one of celebration rather than trauma and unification rather than destruction because it collects and integrates stones from elsewhere in Polynesia while retaining echoes of the previous religious system. These black stones reference the ancient Society Islands *marae*. In these open-air gathering places, the gods were invoked through their representations; sacrifices were presented; and ancestors were remembered in a union of politics, culture, and religion. The imposition of *marae* onto Society Islands landscapes allowed chiefs to manage, sanctify, and control their environments, and ancestrally inherited divinity supported claims for use of these structures. Every high-ranking political elite in the Society Islands had a seat at a *marae*, where familial descent lines were marked through wood carvings, called *ti'i* and *unu*, staked into the ground, which anchored living people to this sacred place.[7]

Newly initiated Society Islands *marae* sometimes incorporated a stone removed from the "parent" *marae* from which the new structure descended.[8] Echoing this genealogical index but enacting a reversal of the physical pattern of dispersal, the *Duff* monument at Point Venus assembles stones from elsewhere in Polynesia for chronological incorporation into a unifying symbolic structure. The spread of the new religion is depicted as a historicized unification of geographically dispersed islanders under the umbrella of Christianity, with implied present-tense continuity linking currently living islanders with their converted ancestors as well as their fellow Christians elsewhere in the region. The assembly of Christians in Polynesia took human form at the inauguration of the monument when members of churches in Tahiti and elsewhere in the region assembled for a folk festival in indigenous cultural form.[9] In contrast with a monument's intended persistence through changing generations, this festival was ephemeral, transient, and collectively shared in the presence of others.

ANCIENT AND EPHEMERAL

Approximately two centuries after mass conversions effected intense transformations of Polynesian landscapes, forces of entropy and decay are at work as sites important to long-ago discarded religions lie fallow to the encroaching jungle. In Tonga, unruly vegetation covers the stone slabs of ancient royal tombs (*langi*), which often take the form of stepped pyramids. In small thatched shrines that formerly stood near them, ancestral deities were invoked and summoned. At these locations, burial feasts for the most revered chiefs included days-long processions with extensive self-mutilations that appalled the *Duff* missionaries.[10] Contemporary Christian tombs in Tonga are more cheerful and interactive, often elaborately decorated with white sand, floral arrangements, and colorful quilts. Before the 2018 cyclone Gita inflicted its wrath, a visitor to Tonga would have observed many towering Christian churches, kept pristine and regularly packed with worshippers whose harmonious congregational singing reverberates from the walls; a placard outside the Centenary Church in Nuku'alofa reports a seating capacity of four thousand. A cyclone may have damaged structures in Tonga, but Christianity is a religion of the heart. While Polynesian languages were oral before missionaries developed orthographies for them, both printed texts and oral means are used to keep missionary history alive in Polynesia today through sermons, religious education, and other means of dissemination. Reversing the implications of iconoclasm at Tonga's nineteenth-century pivot toward Christianity, unexpected natural damage to the physical structures of Christianity may actually intensify the beliefs that mobilized their construction by redirecting worshippers to the textual and immaterial basis of the religion.

While the presence and maintenance of towering churches offers visual evidence of the continuing impact of Christianity in Tonga, a diminutive yet conceptually significant monument to an early arrival of missionaries stands in Hihifo, Tongatapu. A *langi* in miniature, the terraced base of the monument is comprised of modern poured concrete, and the monument itself is a vertical granite slab bearing a silhouette of the pages of an open book inscribed with a commemoration of the 1826 arrival of Methodist missionaries at this location. While a visitor must swing open a gate and step across marshy grass on private land to observe the monument, the historical impact of Methodist missionaries on Tonga is incontestable. This monument is celebratory: "So honoured & joyful we are in founding this monument as a token for Almighty God, Father & Son & Holy Spirit having sanctified, placed as free consecrated here the landing of Christian Religion," the monument reads, in a 2008 passage by 'Ilaisa Futa 'i Ha'angana Helu describing the monument's establishment with financial support from Siosifa Filini Sikuea and his family.

Other monuments to missionaries in Polynesia include one to the London Missionary Society's John Williams in Sapapali'i, Savai'i, Samoa, and another honoring him in American Samoa, outside the Siona Chapel in Leone. Not all of them remember foreigners: in the Cook Islands, a group initially evangelized by islander missionaries, a bronze plaque next to a stone in an upraised flower bed in Avarua, Rarotonga, identifies this site as the location where the missionary Papeiha preached his first sermon in 1823. The Hawai'ian 'Ōpūkahai'a, who converted to Christianity in the United States and desperately wished to evangelize Hawai'ians before his 1818 death from typhus, escalated incipient plans for the first mission to Hawai'i. 'Ōpūkahai'a's initial gravesite in Cornwall, Connecticut, memorializes his legacy, as does a small memorial chapel near his birthplace at Punalu'u, Ka'u, Hawai'i, and a cluster of markers at the Kona, Hawai'i site of his 1993 reinterment.

In 2018, ʻŌpūkahaiʻa's legacy became the first in a series of events Hawaiian Mission Houses Historic Site and Archives in Honolulu is presenting in commemoration of the 2020 bicentennial of missionary presence. As ongoing dimensions of its public programming, Mission Houses offers public tours of its site, which include an 1821 frame house erected by missionaries; the presentation of Hawaiʻian *hula*, chant (*mele*), and music; and the staging of living history in the form of "Cemetery Pupu Theater," in which actors in period costume dramatize lives of the deceased buried at the cemetery of the adjacent Kawaiahaʻo Church. Four successive thatched huts preceded this 1842 church, which was constructed of some fourteen thousand coral blocks, each weighing around one thousand pounds, which Hawaiians chiseled from the submerged reef.[11] Other Hawaiʻian sites of missionary heritage are also open to the public: the Baldwin Home and Museum in Lahaina, Maui; the Waiʻoli Mission District at Hanalei Bay, Kauaʻi; and the Lyman Museum and Mission House in Hilo on the Big Island. Similarly, New Zealand preserves historic sites established by the Church Missionary Society (Te Waimate Mission and the Kerikeri Mission Station), the Wesleyan Methodist Missionary Society (Māngungu Mission), and the French Marist Brothers (the Pompallier Mission and Printery).

Expanding the consideration of missionary heritage to churches, chapels, cathedrals, convents, monasteries, and basilicas would generate hundreds of additional sites for discussion, and if monuments to missionaries were removed from Polynesia, monuments *about* them would still exist, including potential sites for pilgrimage. Outside the State Capitol building in Honolulu, a figurative statue remembers Father Damien, who died of leprosy in 1889 while serving the leper colony on the island of Molokaʻi, Hawaiʻi, and was canonized as a saint in 2009 by the Roman Catholic Church. A relic (a bone from his right foot) is located in Honolulu, and another relic, Damien's right hand, is buried in Molokaʻi. His initial tomb on Molokaʻi is a site of remembrance, as is his current resting place in St. Anthony's Chapel in Leuven, Belgium, where his remains were repositioned in 1936. Another monument to Father Damien stands in his Belgian hometown.

IMPLICATIONS OF ERASURE

Since James E. Young coined the term "counter-monument" in 1992, scholars have analyzed a diversity of examples. Counter-monuments may commemorate trauma and victimization rather than heroism, warn of evils of the past, or provoke rather than console viewers. Tactics may include inverting the repertoire of representational codes of traditional monuments, such as imposing scale, solidity, and elevation; embodying ephemerality or transience, including viewer participation and elements that are added or vanish over time; or staging performative actions.[12] Some counter-monuments are established by marginalized groups contesting a master narrative through a competing discourse that corrects, reclaims, or decolonizes history. Counter-monuments sponsored by a nation-state may incorporate ambiguity and abstraction while negotiating complex pasts and including victims of injustice, but such ambivalence and refusal to endorse a singular viewpoint may delegitimize victims' trauma, stoking tension rather than reconciliation, or may simply go unnoticed by oblivious passers-by.[13]

"How does one remember an absence?" Young asked in 1992. "Under what memorial aegis, whose rules, does a nation remember its own barbarity?"[14] In commemorating a past erasure, the *Duff* monument is not conflicted or ambivalent; two centuries ago, Christianity provided the motive and still offers a framework and road map by which past violence is rejected. The *Duff* monument is not an indigenous response to a singular "traditional" monument in the Western iteration of a public sculptural glorification of past achievements, but it does repudiate an entire previous system, which was expressed in still-visible monumental architecture (*marae*), desecrated more than 150 years before the monument emerged.

As the ancient *marae* incorporated stones from preexisting structures, coding their ancestry into sites, the *Duff* monument incorporates indigenous concepts of space and time. The *Duff* monument maintains visible remnants of a past that has been conquered but also simultaneously unifies Polynesian islands in the assertion of a new genealogy, one that gathers stones from geographically dispersed islands to assemble them through a shared Christian heritage. The temptation to conceptualize the *Duff* monument in an oppositional binary between white proto-colonizers and passive Polynesian victims of foreign intrusion dissolves in the collaborative dimensions of this monument's design and continued maintenance. The monument was created in consultation with the government of French Polynesia, which owns the land and financed the construction, and the Evangelical Church of French Polynesia. Parishioners provided free labor at the monument's 1970 construction, and the Mahina district, which is responsible for maintaining the construction, refurbished the monument in 2015.[15] Although the *Duff* departed from England, were this monument solely a state conception erected on public land, the monument could be interpreted as a French colonial apology and attempt at reconciliation; conversely, were it an entirely church-sponsored edifice positioned on or near a Christian site, the secular impact of Christianity in Tahiti could go unrecognized.

Protestant Christianity in Tahiti actively contests a legacy of colonial victimization while preserving the repudiation of its own pre-Christian religious system. The Church does not simply exist to continuously defy ancient Tahitian religion in an oppositional process now more than two centuries in duration, but instead is actively engaged in countering a variety of forms of evil manifested in the contemporary lives of church members. The Protestant church, now renamed the Maʻohi Protestant Church in recognition of its indigenous roots, is currently active in protesting nuclear injustice. Unrelated to the *Duff* monument, Papeʻete, Tahiti, hosts a Memorial Site for Nuclear Testings, erected in 2006 in solemn recognition of the 193 atomic bombs France detonated in French Polynesia from 1966 to 1996. Three thin, vertical, wooden carvings protrude from a small courtyard of stones, reminiscent of the *unu* figures that formerly adorned ancient *marae*. Unlike the *Duff* monument, these representations do not seem to defy the corpus of traditional material heritage from which they are drawn.

The *Duff* monument at Point Venus is actively integrated into festivals and celebrations that continually revitalize this counterpoint to the *marae*, and in counter-monumental function, it warns and educates[16] through its endorsement of Christianity. Each year, French Polynesia celebrates the public holiday "Arrivée de l'Evangile" (Arrival of the Gospel) on March 5, the date of the *Duff*'s arrival. The monument's design also includes interactive features: the retaining wall surrounding the monument is two hundred centimeters high—one centimeter for each year of the mission at its 1997 bicentennial—but the additions of flat stones stacked atop the wall indicate the ongoing progress of evangelization.[17] In their public nature, these "alternative commemorative practices" could be viewed as oppositional to the secretive religious rites held in the ancient *marae*, where prerogatives to manage both sacred and secular power were ancestral.

It would be disingenuous to suggest that Christianity entirely and permanently erased every vestige of precontact Polynesian religion. In recent decades, strides have been made to preserve as well as revive ancient Polynesian traditions, and some ancient Polynesian worship spaces have been renovated and restored. The ancient *marae* Taputapuātea at Opoa in Raʻiātea, Society Islands, achieved status as a UNESCO World Heritage Site in 2017. Missionary William Ellis would not have been impressed; he cited this *marae* as the first site of human sacrifices in the Society Islands, from whence they spread to Tahiti, "where they were offered with great frequency, and in appalling numbers."[18] Although the refurbishment of ancient *marae* could be seen as archaeologically neutral, that would ignore the proud revivals of Polynesian culture, which might be seen either to resuscitate the sites to which the *Duff* monument is a counter-monument or might in fact assert an entirely new history for *marae* structures—one which revitalizes them without endorsing their history of human sacrifices.

This tension emerges from a continual negotiation of history. Whether in monuments, churches, or *marae*, the construction and maintenance of these structures exports into the visible realm indications of a collective effort mobilized for shared communal use, but this activity correlates with a more important operation internal to users of the site. One religion has not simply conquered another in Polynesia; the Christian conversions of two centuries ago were not a singular event, now finished and complete. Each generation must do its own work of remembering histories it never lived through, deciding which elements to retain and in what manner. The *Duff* monument performs this through present-tense assemblies that remember past erasures.

NOTES

1. Wilson 1799, 157.
2. The best-known sources for the history of the *Duff* are Davies 1961; Ellis 1833; LMS *Transactions,* 1804, Vol. I; Lovett 1899; Vason 1840; and Williams 1837. The Missionary Society was renamed the London Missionary Society in 1818.
3. Vason 1840.
4. Davies 1961, 197.
5. Ellis 1833, Vol. 2, 165.
6. Central Intelligence Agency 2017.
7. Wilson 1799, 207–14 for *Duff* descriptions.
8. Williamson 1924, 73–75.
9. Rodolphe Weinmann, personal communication, January 21, 2018.
10. Wilson 1799, 239–44.
11. Kawaiahaʻo Church.
12. Stevens et al. 2010.
13. Strakosch 2010.
14. Young 1992, 290, 270.
15. Rodolphe Weinmann, personal communication, January 21, 2018.
16. Stevens et al. 2012, 955.
17. Tahiti Heritage.
18. Ellis 1833, Vol. 1, 93.

REFERENCES

Central Intelligence Agency. 2017. *The World Factbook.* Washington, DC: Central Intelligence Agency. https://www.cia.gov/library/publications/the-world-factbook/.

Davies, John. *The History of the Tahitian Mission, 1799–1830.* Edited by C. W. Newbury. Cambridge, England: Cambridge University Press (Hakluyt Society), 1961.

Ellis, William. *Polynesian Researches, during a Residence of Nearly Eight Years in the Society and Sandwich Islands.* Vols. 1 and 2. From the latest London edition. New York: J. and J. Harper, 1833.

Kawaiahaʻo Church. "About Us." Accessed January 2018. https://www.kawaiahao.org/about-us/.

[London] Missionary Society. *Transactions of the Missionary Society from Its Institution in the Year 1795, to the End of the Year 1802.* Vol. I. Second Edition. London: T. Williams, 1804. Cited as LMS *Transactions.*

Lovett, Richard. *The History of the London Missionary Society, 1795–1895.* Vol. 1. London: Henry Frowde, 1899.

Stevens, Quentin, Karen A. Franck, and Ruth Fazakerley. "Counter-Monuments: The Anti-Monumental and the Dialogic." *The Journal of Architecture* 17, no. 6 (2012): 951–72. DOI: 10.1080/13602365.2012.746035.

Strakosch, Elizabeth. "Counter-Monuments and Nation-Building in Australia." *Peace Review: A Journal of Social Justice* 22, no. 3 (2010): 268–75. DOI: 10.1080/10402659.2010.502065.

Tahiti Heritage. Arrivée des missionnaires protestants à Tahiti, le 5 mars 1797. https://www.tahitiheritage.pf/arrivee-missionnaires-tahiti/.

Vason, George. *Narrative of the Late George Vason of Nottingham: One of the First Missionaries Sent Out by the London Missionary Society in the Ship* Duff, *Captain Wilson, 1796* [. . .]. Edited by Rev. James Orange. London: Henry Mozley and Sons, 1840.

Williams, John. *A Narrative of Missionary Enterprises in the South Sea Islands, with Remarks Upon the Natural History of the Islands, Origin, Languages, Traditions, and Usages of the Inhabitants.* London: J. Snow, 1837.

Williamson, Robert W. *The Social and Political Systems of Central Polynesia.* Vol. 2. Cambridge, England: Cambridge University Press, 1924.

[Wilson, William]. *A Missionary Voyage to the Southern Pacific Ocean, Performed in the Years 1796, 1797, 1798, in the Ship* Duff, *Commanded by Captain James Wilson. Compiled from Journals of the Officers and Missionaries* [. . .]. London: T. Chapman, 1799.

Young, James E. "The Counter-Monument: Memory Against Itself in Germany Today." *Critical Inquiry* 18, no. 2 (1992): 267–96. http://www.jstor.org.eproxy2.lib.hku.hk/stable/1343784.

CHAPTER 3

Monuments in Antarctica

Commemoration of Historic Events or Claims for National Sovereignty?

Ingo Heidbrink

Horst Wandehn, the president of the German UNESCO World-Heritage Association, stated in 2013, "Ein Denkmal ohne Besucher ist kein Denkmal" [A monument without visitors is no monument], thus raising probably the most important question in the context of any monument in Antarctica.[1] Of course, it's not really true that there are no visitors to monuments in Antarctica, but compared to the millions of visitors to major national monuments around the globe, the hundreds of thousands who visit well-known monuments in more remote areas, or even the hundreds of people who daily pass a monument in a small town, the number of visitors to most Antarctic monuments is negligible. Consequently, the question needs to be asked if the few monuments in the frozen continent are real monuments.

Of course, Wandehn's statement was to a certain degree provocative and part of the discussion as to whether extremely large numbers of tourists visiting a monument should be considered as a threat to the monument or a positive development. In the end, he also raised, at least indirectly, the central question: What is the function of a monument beyond the visitation by whatever number of people and communicating its story or history to the visitors?

Building a monument, regardless of whether it is a small statue or a massive construction, requires a substantial effort, especially if the monument is located in an extremely remote area like Antarctica, where even the apparently simplest transportation requires highly complex logistics and massive funding. Consequently, the question needs to be asked about the motives for the construction of any monument in Antarctica and, more importantly, if there might be hidden motives or goals beyond the obvious and easily recognizable. While certain motives—such as the commemoration of particular historic events in Antarctic history, recognition and celebration of Antarctic explorers, scientific and/or technological breakthroughs, or dramatic and tragic failures—are easily recognizable for a visitor to a monument in Antarctica, the hidden agenda for a monument often requires a deeper look and a good deal

25

of understanding of the complex circumstances of Antarctic politics where the real aims and goals of actors sometimes are as deeply buried as if under the Antarctic ice.

EXAMPLES OF MONUMENTS IN ANTARCTICA[2]

Compared to other continents, the number of monuments in Antarctica is small, but given the effort required to construct these monuments, it can safely be assumed that behind every one of these monuments is a strong motive why the monument was erected. Looking into the motives for some selected monuments is probably the best way to understand the specifics of monuments on the frozen continent.

Bust of Luis Antonio Pardo Villalón at Point Wild on Elephant Island

Besides Scott's and Amundsen's race to the South Pole, Ernest Shackleton's failed Imperial Trans-Antarctic Expedition (1914–1917) is probably one of the best and most widely known stories in Antarctic history.[3] The attempt to cross the continent from the Weddell Sea to the Ross Sea failed completely and most dramatically, with the main expedition ship lost and one group of the expedition crew barely surviving on Elephant Island while the other group faced similar hardships at Cape Evans; the dramatic trip of the *James Caird*, a small open boat, from Elephant Island to South Georgia; and ultimately, the crossing of South Georgia by Shackleton, Worsley, and Crean. With only three casualties in both groups of the expedition, in the end, the expedition needs to be considered lucky despite its complete failure and the fact that none of its objectives were achieved. The financing of the expedition was mainly British with some American contributions; members of the expedition were British subjects, either from the United Kingdom or the Commonwealth.

Consequently, one would expect a monument commemorating the Imperial Trans-Antarctic Expedition to be initiated from the United Kingdom and either commemorating the whole story or representing the main actors, such as Shackleton or his second-in-command, Frank Wild, who led the men while enduring the hopeless time on Elephant Island at a small rocky outcrop now called Point Wild. Actually, the best-known monument in this context tells a completely different story. At Point Wild, there is a bust commemorating the rescue of the members of the Imperial Trans-Antarctic Expedition at Point Wild. The bust, however, represents Luis Antonio Pardo Villalón, a Chilean Navy captain. Pardo was the commanding officer of the Chilean naval tug *Jelcho*, the ship that ultimately brought the men on Elephant Island to safety after their ordeal at Point Wild.

While neglecting Pardo's contribution to the story of the Imperial Trans-Antarctic Expedition would be a misrepresentation of this part of Antarctic history, putting him on the pedestal gives him more importance than his actual contribution. Thus, why is the monument to Pardo and not to Shackleton or Wild?

The simple answer is Antarctic politics at the time when the monument was erected. Like Argentina and the United Kingdom, Chile claims sovereignty over certain parts of Antarctica, and while these claims are currently suspended due to the Antarctic Treaty System (ATS), none of these nations is abandoning its competing and overlapping claims. If it ever comes to the point where the sovereignty issue over certain parts of Antarctica needs to be solved beyond the shared multinational sovereignty of the ATS, contributions to the exploration of the area will most certainly be used as a deciding factor.[4] Using a monument to help claim the Imperial Trans-Antarctic Expedition for Chile is nothing less than bolstering potential future claims for sovereignty in Antarctica. While there may not be many visitors actually seeing the bust of Pardo, its mere existence is enough to claim this part of Antarctic history for Chile.

There is a second copy of the bust at the Chilean station Base Presidente Eduardo Frei Montalva on King Edward Island, which further supports the Chilean claim for this part of Antarctic history, but which is also located at a place that provides a more appropriate context and less of a hidden agenda.

Monuments for *Overwinterers at Argentine Research Stations*

At all major Argentine research stations in Antarctica, there are monuments for those expedition members who have overwintered at the respective station. Normally these monuments consist of a set of bronze plaques simply listing the names of the overwintering crews for all seasons the stations were inhabited. At some of the Argentine stations, these plaques are accompanied by small museums, at least indirectly communicating the relevance of Argentina for the history of Antarctic exploration; the hidden agenda is mainly tied to the commemorative plaques.[5] While this type of monument might look fairly innocent on first glimpse, the actual story behind these monuments is similar to the Pardo bust on Elephant Island. If it comes to a decision on national sovereignty in Antarctica in a potential post–ATS period, active contributions to research and permanent presence in a certain area will certainly be among the factors considered for a decision on attribution of these areas. Again, Argentina, Chile, and the United Kingdom are positioning themselves for a potential decision on sovereignty, and consequently, the purpose behind all the plaques is documenting a permanent presence of one of these countries.

The actual number of visitors seeing these monuments might be even smaller than for the Pardo bust, but again, it's not the number of visitors that counts for the relevance of the monument; rather, it is a hidden claim for potential future sovereignty that is substantiated by the monuments.

Port Lockroy

In the case of the United Kingdom, the third nation among the main competitors for overlapping sovereignty claims in Antarctica, the situation is somewhat different because it is not using a traditional monument as the vehicle to communicate its claim for potential future sovereignty over the contested areas of Antarctica, but a museum. The former British Base A of the British World War II Antarctic activities with the codename Operation Tabarin[6] is today a museum operated by the Antarctic Heritage Trust[7] and includes, besides the museum itself, a post office issuing stamps labeled for British Antarctic Territory, a country that according to the regulations of the ATS, does not exist at all because sovereignty claims in Antarctica are suspended. Nevertheless, the museum is making a powerful claim for British sovereignty over this part of the Antarctic Peninsula region. Tens of thousands of visitors per season return to their cruise ships convinced that the United Kingdom has a clear claim for this region due to its history of ongoing research in the area. Again, a hidden agenda successfully communicated through monument culture.

As the three examples of Antarctic monuments have demonstrated, the main purpose of a monument in Antarctica is not necessarily to tell a specific story to visitors of the monument or to commemorate a specific event in Antarctic history but to relay a message or claim communicated by a monument that does not require visitors to the location of the monument at all. The sheer existence of the monument is enough to claim a certain part of Antarctic history. It does not matter if the monument is dedicated or directly related to the most relevant historic events or actors in the corresponding context, but the existence of the monument alone makes the respective nations' contributions to Antarctic history relevant in retrospect and consequently supports a contemporary political goal, such as the claim for sovereignty in a potential post–ATS period.

MONUMENTS AT THE SOUTH POLE

Because the geographic South Pole is covered by a massive ice sheet, moving approximately ten meters per year, its surface location is not stable. Consequently, any permanent monument at the South Pole after a couple of years would no longer be the Pole, but rather, a good distance away. Nevertheless, the geographic South Pole is prime real estate when it comes to monuments and their purposes in Antarctica. A nation claiming a monument at the South Pole marks its claim for the whole continent. When the Norwegian Roald Amundsen reached the pole on December 14, 1911, he left a tent and a Norwegian flag to mark his achievement but also to mark the Norwegian claim. Despite the temporary nature of such a monument, the tent needs to be understood as the first monument at the pole. It is still officially recognized as a historic monument according to the ATS's list of historic monuments and sites, although it is covered by meters of ice and no one knows its location due to the drift of the ice.[8] In the end, it is a powerful example of an Antarctic monument because it needs few or no visitors and no longer exists. Just the knowledge that it exists somewhere deep in the ice is enough to substantiate a claim or idea with a monument.

The First Argentine Overland Polar Expedition erected another flagpole at the Pole in 1965. While it could be argued whether a flagpole is really a monument or just a continuation of the tradition of taking unknown lands into possession, the flagpole clearly communicates yet another national claim for sovereignty or at least the relevance of a certain nation for Antarctica.

Finally, there is the ceremonial South Pole, a metallic sphere on a pole surrounded by the flags of the original ATS nations. In contrast to the monuments discussed earlier, the ceremonial South Pole does not communicate a hidden story of a claim for national sovereignty but precisely the opposite. The pole itself surrounded by the flags of the original ATS signatory nations affirms that there is no national sovereignty in Antarctica but an international treaty, making Antarctica one of the few regions of the Earth outside the concept of traditional nation-state–based sovereignty.

MONUMENTS AT MCMURDO

The US research station at McMurdo is one of the largest research stations on the continent; thus, it is no surprise that there are two monuments at McMurdo. While the bust of Admiral Richard E. Byrd is a conventional monument commemorating the achievements of Admiral Byrd at the beginning of American Antarctic activities, the second monument is a plaque commemorating the use of nuclear power at McMurdo. From 1962 to 1972, McMurdo station was partially powered by a nuclear power plant.[9] The text on the plaque that was put up by the Naval Nuclear Power Plant Group in 2010 is a bone-dry listing of the technical specifications and the operational dates of the plant. The hidden agenda of this monument is to avoid a broad discussion on the subject commemorated as the concept of using all kinds of nuclear technology in Antarctica does not work well with the idea of a pristine frozen continent peacefully used by many nations for scientific purposes as promoted by the ATS. This begs the question, why have the monument at all if its main purpose is to remain unnoticed?

CROSSES

There are a number of crosses throughout Antarctica, most of them commemorating members of scientific expeditions who lost their lives during the expeditions, such as the well-known cross on Petermann Island. This cross commemorates three members of the British Antarctic Survey who died in 1982 during an attempt to cross the sea ice. Like this cross, these monuments offer neither names nor nationalities of the commemorated and thus should be considered in a personal rather than a political context. Perhaps, they should not even be considered as monuments in the context of this essay and, perhaps, as evidence that not all monuments in Antarctica carry a hidden political agenda.

VISITORS

At the beginning of the chapter, I introduced the somewhat provocative idea that a monument without visitors is no monument at all, while the main argument that followed might be summarized that many Antarctic monuments have a hidden agenda for which the mere existence of the monument is actually more important than visitation. To a certain degree, these two ideas might look like a contradiction in themselves, and thus, it might be useful to have a more detailed look on the visitors to monuments in Antarctica. First and foremost, Antarctica is a continent without any permanent residents, meaning there is no local population that could provide a pool of regular visitors participating in a potential debate on the monuments.

The largest and basically only relevant group of visitors to the majority of Antarctic monuments are the passengers of the expedition cruise ships visiting during the short austral summer. Due to the high costs of these trips, most of the passengers aboard the ships are well-off citizens of Western nations, with the United States and several European countries regularly providing the largest contingents. With a total number of less than fifty thousand tourists going to Antarctica per season and few of them visiting the monuments, the actual number of visitors to each monument is extremely small compared to nearly all other monuments on the globe.[10] Given the demographics of the average passenger on these ships, their influence on public and political debates is above average. While the majority of these passengers are highly educated, only few have in-depth knowledge about Antarctica and, in particular, the issue of sovereignty claims.

Consequently, the situation is just the opposite of many other monuments where there might be large numbers of visitors with at least some knowledge of the respective historic event commemorated by a specific monument and a vested interest in one or another side of the related discussion. Of course, typical passengers onboard the expedition cruise ships do have knowledge about Antarctica, in particular, because many of them save and prepare for such a trip for several years, but based on firsthand experience as a historic lecturer on a variety of expedition cruises to Antarctica, most passengers come with decent knowledge about Antarctic nature but little to no knowledge about

Antarctic history or politics beyond the Amundsen–Scott race to the South Pole in 1911. Thus, the hidden agenda of many Antarctic monuments works extremely well with these passengers because many of them consider an Antarctic cruise to be a learning experience and take the stories conveyed by the monument for face value without having the opportunity or, perhaps, the desire to investigate the broader context. Typically, since none of the passengers have detailed knowledge about the debate behind the hidden agendas and, in particular, overlapping sovereignty claims or the complex issue of sovereignty over Antarctica, normally there will be no controversial discussion about the monuments, and the stories communicated will be accepted as complete. The monuments themselves are enough to make the visitors accept that the nation that erected the monument played a certain role in the history of the respective region of Antarctica and at least indirectly to accept the claim for sovereignty.

NORTH–SOUTH MONUMENTS

It might also be useful to have a look at a monument partly inside Antarctica and partly in other places of the globe. A typical example of such a monument is the Antarctic Monument by the British Antarctic Monument Trust, with its northern monument in Cambridge (United Kingdom) and the corresponding southern monument in Stanley (Falkland Islands/Islas Malvinas). The two abstract monuments were erected to "promote good citizenship by honoring those explorers and scientists who have carried out hazardous duties in the pursuit of scientific knowledge in the British Antarctic Territory,"[11] but also serve to increase the awareness of the British peoples, and others, of "Britain's contributions to the exploration and understanding of this remote area and the significance their discoveries have on us today and our future lives."[12] In this case, the hidden agenda is not hidden at all but central to the monument. Contrary to the monuments in Antarctica, the northern monument in Cambridge will be seen by many visitors, therefore making an extremely strong and successful statement supporting the British claim on Antarctica and its history, a peculiar claim, considering the monument is not in the place it claims.

SOME FINAL THOUGHTS

The few examples of monuments in Antarctica discussed clearly show that many monuments on the frozen continent not only have a hidden agenda; they are directly related to the issue of overlapping sovereignty claims even with all these claims currently suspended by the ATS. While the ATS is a successful example of international governance over a whole continent, the issue of sovereignty is complex. Officially, the ATS entering in force ended the debate on traditional national sovereignty over Antarctica, but a good number of nations continue to position for a potential reopening of the discussion and monuments in Antarctica as they set the contribution of a certain nation to the history of the respective area of Antarctica in stone, sometimes literally.

With the number of visitors to the actual monuments being marginal, these monuments also show that, sometimes, it is not necessary for monuments to be visited by large numbers of people but that the mere existence of such monuments is enough to make or support a political claim, in particular if the related political issue is not really known to the broad public but only to a small group of specialists more or less directly involved in the debate. The increasing number of tourists in Antarctica may bring at least some new monuments in Antarctica, in particular, those in the Antarctic Peninsula region, thereby increasing visitor numbers in the future. But compared to most other monuments on the globe, the absolute numbers will remain small, and for the foreseeable future, the number of visitors will not rise to a level that will change the current meaning of the monument.

In the end, these monuments in Antarctica directly showcase the power of monuments for all kinds of political debate. Once a monument is erected, its story becomes to a certain degree not only more visible but also more important than stories not commemorated by a monument even if these other stories might be more important to professional historians. It is by no means intended by this article to imply that the stories commemorated and told by monuments in Antarctica are incorrect or fake. It may need to be understood that monuments are a powerful tool for communicating hidden agendas and relating a story that did happen but was not the most appropriate for center stage. After all, monuments are an easy way to emphasize one perspective on a multifaceted history regardless of whether they are in Antarctica or elsewhere in the world.

Visitors will accept the story told by a monument to be true unless there is a reason for them to doubt this perspective and their lack of knowledge about the complex history of Antarctica will not make them suspicious. Social scientists, politicians, and historians dealing with Antarctic issues will easily recognize the hidden agendas behind the various monuments in Antarctica, whereas the average visitor will most likely take them for face value. As a result, a monument in Antarctica does not only mean to commemorate a certain part of history but often to claim this history and maybe at least indirectly to claim the frozen continent.

Erecting a monument that will be seen by no or few visitors might seem like a useless endeavor, a folly, but if this monument supports a potential future claim for sovereignty, it is not useless nor a folly but actually a calculated political action. History might often be written by the victors, but if nobody reads the history or is really interested in the often-complex details of the past, erecting a monument might be enough to make the history theirs.

NOTES

1. Petra Korn, "Jahrestagung in Quedlinburg Welterbe braucht auch den Tourismus." *Mitteldeutsche Zeitung*, accessed February 23, 2018, https://www.mz-web.de/mitteldeutschland/jahrestagung-in-quedlinburg-welterbe-braucht-auch-den-tourismus-599610.

2. The majority of monuments discussed in this essay have been visited several times by the author during his trips to Antarctica as a historic lecturer on expedition cruise ships since the 2012–2013 season. Comments on visitor experiences to these monuments are based on observation and communications with passengers during these cruises.

3. For a detailed description of the Imperial Trans-Antarctic Expedition compare, for example, Alfred Lansing, *Endurance: Shackleton's Incredible Voyage* (New York: Basic Books, 2014); and Ernest Henry Shackleton, *South: The Last Antarctic Expedition of Shackleton and the Endurance* (Guilford, CT: Lyons Press, 2008).

4. Ingo Heidbrink, "Claiming Sovereignty Where There Can Be No Sovereignty— Antarctica," *Environment, Space, Place* 8, no. 2 (2016): 99–121.

5. Ingo Heidbrink, "The Informal Open-Air Museum of Antarctic Transportation at Base Esperanza," *The Journal of Transport History* 37, no. 2 (2016): 258–62.

6. For the history of Operation Tabarin, compare Stephen Haddelsey and Alan Carroll with Andrew Taylor, Daniel Heidt, and P. Whitney Lackenbauer, *Operation Tabarin: Britain's Secret Wartime Expedition to Antarctica, 1944–46* (Stroud, Gloucestershire, UK: The History Press, 2016); Stephen Haddelsey and Alan Carroll, *Two Years Below the Horn: Operation Tabarin, Field Science, and Antarctic Sovereignty, 1944–1946* (Winnipeg: University of Manitoba Press, 2017).

7. United Kingdom Antarctic Heritage Trust, *Base "A" Port Lockroy Visitor Guide* (Cambridge, UK: United Kingdom Antarctic Heritage Trust, 2014).

8. For the development of the regulatory framework for the protection of historic monuments and sites in Antarctica, see R. I. Lewis Smith, D. W. H. Walton, and P. R. Dingwall, *Developing the Antarctic Protected Area System: Proceedings of the SCAR/IUCN Workshop on Antarctic Protected Areas*, Cambridge, UK, 29 June–2 July 1992. Gland, Switzerland: IUCN, 1994.

9. *The PM-3A Nuclear Power Plant: McMurdo Station, Antarctica* (Fort Belvoir, VA: US Navy, 1960); and M. E. Foster and G. M. Jones, *History of the PM-3A Nuclear Power Plant, McMurdo Station, Antarctica* (Port Hueneme, CA: Naval Energy and Environmental Support Activity, 1980).

10. Colin Michael Hall, *Tourism and Change in Polar Regions: Climate, Environment and Experiences* (London: Routledge, 2010).

11. British Antarctic Monument Trust, *The Antarctic Monument*, accessed February 23, 2018, http://www.antarctic-monument.org/index.php?page=monument.

12. Ibid.

CHAPTER 4

Phnom Penh's Independence Monument and Vientiane's Patuxai

Complex Symbols of Postcolonial Nationhood in Cold War–Era Southeast Asia[1]

ROGER NELSON

THE CONSTRUCTION OF MONUMENTS HAS BEEN A COMMON FEATURE OF URBAN modernization throughout Southeast Asia, as elsewhere. In capital cities, these monuments often function in part as symbolic articulations of nationhood. In this region, the formation of modern nation-states was inextricable from decolonization and shaped by the redeployment of premodern and prenational tropes as well as by pressures of the Cold War. This essay considers the Independence Monument in Phnom Penh, designed by Vann Molyvann around 1957 and inaugurated in 1961, and Patuxai in Vientiane, originally named the Monument to the Unknown Soldier, designed by Tham Sayasithsena in 1957 and completed a decade later. The designs of both structures combine specifically French architectural references with precolonial ornamentation that is generally understood as distinctly national, that is, specifically Khmer and Lao. In both monuments, we may discern two levels of redeployment: first, the use of both colonial and local architectural forms in the concrete articulation of postcolonial nationhood, and second, the shifting relationships of the monuments to their cities under successive political regimes with sharply differing ideologies. These processes of redeployment will frame what follows.

Phnom Penh and Vientiane, like the nations of which they are capitals—Cambodia and Laos, respectively—have endured a series of violent upheavals over the past half century. From the 1950s in Laos and 1966 in Cambodia until the 1970s, they were ravaged due to their proximity to the front lines of the global Cold War and, in its regional stage, the Second Indochina War. Both nations were subjected to "secret wars" waged by the United States in these bordering territories. Both nations suffered civil war, from the 1950s in Laos and 1970 in Cambodia until both were shaken by violent communist revolutions in 1975. More recently, in the second decade of the twenty-first century,

35

both cities have entered a new phase of transformation, their skylines rendered unrecognizable as a result of foreign (chiefly Chinese and East Asian) private investment in high-rises and other urban developments. These topographical changes in the cityscape have been matched by ideological shifts, from neutralism, to socialism, to postsocialist neoliberalism—with authoritarianism continuing throughout. The cities thus embody larger shifts that have occurred since the mid-twentieth century in Southeast Asia, and beyond.

Standing at the center of these cities, amid the surrounding turbulence, the Independence Monument in Phnom Penh and Patuxai in Vientiane may be viewed as synecdoches, bringing into view the irreducible complexity of broader cultural and historical forces shaping Southeast Asia's urban environments and national imaginaries (figures 4.1 and 4.2). Both monuments are contentious today largely because of their embodying the moments in which they were made. In what follows, we will thus focus on their designs and original functions and the relationships of these monuments to their cities from the time of construction until the revolutions of 1975. Interspersed throughout will be briefer reflections on the changing roles of both monuments in more recent years as their cities are transforming anew.

Figure 4.1. Independence Monument, Phnom Penh, Cambodia. To the left of the monument is Prime Minister Hun Sen's residence.
Photograph by Daniel Mattes, 2018.

Figure 4.2. Patuxai, Vientiane, Laos, while still under construction. Photograph 1966 by Robert Wofford.
Photograph by Terry Wofford, 1966.

Both Cambodia and Laos gained their independence in 1953, having formerly been protectorates within the Indochinese Union. The French had assumed control over Cambodia in 1863 and over Laos thirty years later. When Phnom Penh's Independence Monument was commissioned in 1957, its architect, Vann Molyvann, was personally selected and instructed on the design by Prince Norodom Sihanouk, who is regarded as the "father of independence" and ruled a nominally socialist government from 1955 to 1970. Construction was completed by 1960, and the Independence Monument was officially inaugurated in 1961.[2] Vientiane's monument was commissioned in 1957, its design by soldier, former journalist, and self-taught sculptor Tham Sayasithsena, having been selected from several others entered in a competition, under Prince Souvanna Phoumma's direction. It was not completed until 1968.[3] The intervening decade was one of civil war and political instability, with repeated coups d'etat—most with American backing—making Vientiane's postcolonial urban modernization more halting and uneven than Phnom Penh's.

Despite emerging in the same early postcolonial historical moment, Phnom Penh's Independence Monument and Vientiane's Patuxai are not alike in their overall outline. First, their axial orientations to the flat, former flood plains on which they sit are quite different. The monument in Phnom Penh is vertical in its thrust and rises to a single, tapered peak. Its shape is that of a *stupa*: a structure associated with funerary functions in the Theravada Buddhist tradition, usually conical in form. By contrast, Patuxai is more squat, comprising a cube topped by five towers, which usually appear to form a triadic peak that is more pyramidal in shape. These towers are also like *stupas*. The Vientiane structure's top-heavy ornamentation and bulky base tether it to the horizontal axis, much more than the shorter but slenderer tower in Phnom Penh.

Another key difference in the basic form of the two structures is their orientation to the spectator, which relates to each structure's siting. The Independence Monument rises from a roundabout at the meeting of two wide boulevards and is designed to be viewed from any angle along the five roads that approach and circumnavigate it. This is reinforced in photographs taken of the monument in the first years after its construction as well as in numerous films—including some directed by Sihanouk—in which the monument is filmed from moving vehicles, with other modern forms of transport, such as convertible sports cars and *cyclo* pedaled rickshaws, passing by.[4] The structure thus has a dynamic appearance, which is heightened by the lightness of the filigreed ornamentation protruding from its upper sections and the precise angling in the stepped corners of its rectilinear base. By contrast, Patuxai is sited on a single, straight road and, although visible from some distance, is primarily oriented to a singular view of it, being approached from either side of the long, straight Lane Xang Boulevard, which it sits astride. Patuxai therefore has a static appearance and is generally depicted from the same vantage point.

This discrepancy in the sophistication and dynamism of the structures could be seen as a reflection of differences in the two nations' respective regimes in the first years following independence and their ability to cohere a localized mode of postcolonial modernity. Cambodia enjoyed relative stability from independence until 1970, with Sihanouk a constant figurehead and political leader, whose power was largely uncontested at the time of the Independence Monument's commissioning and inauguration.[5] With the help of willing and well-trained collaborators, such as Vann Molyvann—who in addition to designing the monument also built dozens of other ambitious public works during the period—Sihanouk was able to deftly patronize a well-rounded and largely consistent image of the new, modernizing nation through transformations in many sectors, including urban environments. Laos, by contrast, went through a series of political changes during these years of civil war. Competing political players also had diverging views on how the nation should modernize. Moreover, some scholars have argued that "Lao-ness" was a more recent concept, fostered by the French.[6]

In the twenty-first century, a primary departure from these early postcolonial years is that the Laotian and Cambodian governments now exercise very little oversight over urban planning. Recent changes in Phnom Penh and

Vientiane are now chiefly shaped by private—and usually foreign, East Asian and Chinese—speculative capital. The Independence Monument and Patuxai remain fraught national symbols today, but their prominence within their rapidly transforming urban landscapes has decreased because they no longer function as focal points. Rather, these cities have become more multicentered and increasingly organized around commercial rather than civic zones.

Despite differences in the ways in which the postcolonial nations were articulated—including in spatial and architectural form—both Cambodia and Laos were defining their new independence in contradistinction to a shared colonial past. Thus, the presence of architectural features from the former French *metropole* is striking in both monuments. Patuxai directly refers to the Parisian Arc de Triomphe in its size and shape, whereas the Independence Monument utilizes Le Corbusier's system of proportion, known as *le modulor*, in the scaling of its lower section.

Moreover, both Cambodian and Laotian rhetoric announced the new nations to be derived from the ancient kingdoms of Angkor (ninth to fourteenth centuries CE) and Lan Xang (fourteenth to eighteenth centuries CE), respectively. Both monuments thus include design elements commonly understood as derived from Khmer and Lao "tradition."

Before turning to these aspects of the monuments' designs in more detail, it is helpful to identify two key reasons this redeployment of colonial and precolonial tropes is significant. First, this architectural and aesthetic syncretism is also a synthesis of the secular and the religious. Second, this conjoining of French and local forms places the monuments in a complex position in relation to the colonial past. Both Patuxai and the Independence Monument, after all, were commissioned to commemorate national independence, and yet they perform this celebratory role not only by signaling difference and implied distance from the colonial past but also by underscoring continuity. The late Grant Evans, preeminent cultural historian of Laos, observes that "for postcolonial nationalists it became *de rigeur* to de-emphasize connections between their project and the colonial state."[7] Yet these monuments instead emphasize continuing connections. They do this not only by explicitly referring to French designs but also in the very act of combining French architectural features with Khmer and Lao ones. This had also been a strategy employed by colonial authorities during the early twentieth century.[8] The early postcolonial governments' synthesizing of French, Khmer, and Lao design features is thus an act of double redeployment: it constitutes a return to or continuation of colonial modes of building.

Patuxai offers the more obvious case. The Lao name translates as "victory gate" or "victory arch," and many foreign observers refer to the structure as the "Arc de Triomphe." The resemblance to its counterpart in Paris is striking. The Arc de Triomphe is also solid and bulky in appearance, and its overall height—which is nearly identical to Patuxai's—is also mostly comprised of a base that is of equal width and height. Both structures are pierced by a similarly proportioned, arched opening. Both celebrate victories over enemies, and since 1920, the Arc de Triomphe has housed a Tomb to the Unknown Soldier, which was also the original appellation for Patuxai.

Given these similarities in shape, size, and function, Patuxai's references to the Arc de Triomphe are explicit. Patuxai's designer, Tham Sayasithsena, later affirmed in writing that "The monument has a form of a victory arch (similar to l'Arc de Triomphe in Paris). . . . The Arch in Vientiane has four archways—in Paris, two." He further suggested that the steeples crowning the structure "look like the apexes of the Taj Mahal."[9]

One key difference between Patuxai and the Arc de Triomphe is the siting of the monuments. The Paris structure is wider than it is deep; like the Phnom Penh Independence Monument, it sits at the intersection of several major boulevards and thus is intended to be viewed from numerous angles while approaching and encircling it. By contrast, Patuxai is cuboid and sits in the middle of a single boulevard, which runs in a long, straight line from it in both directions. This makes Patuxai different from the Arc de Triomphe in the way it appears and also in the way it is apprehended. The monument presents a single image of itself. In twenty-first-century tourism materials, it continues to be repeatedly pictured from the same frontal angle.

That Phnom Penh's Independence Monument utilizes Corbusier's *modulor* system of proportion would not be so evident to most viewers; however, its combination of a relatively unadorned, rectilinear base with an intricately decorated upper section nevertheless signals its synthesis of European and Khmer traditions. Despite this, it appears more Cambodian than French. This syncretic architecture was common at the time. Khmer novels from the 1960s include descriptions of buildings "with the grand, ancient [*purān*] style of the Cambodian heritage, combined very well with the most modern kind of international style that is popular all over the world today."[10] In the twenty-first century, with the appearance of the city's first high-rise apartment buildings, many built with foreign (chiefly Chinese and East Asian) capital, generic structures are often superficially ornamented with Khmer-style façades. The motivation for this now appears more commercial than ideological, and even with this decoration, the buildings appear very foreign in this context.

If Patuxai's adaptive redeployment of specifically French architectural form is obvious, where can we discern its use of design elements understood to be local and distinctly Lao? The answer requires three levels of analysis. In its surface decorations, crowning top structure, and siting in the city, Patuxai makes explicit claims to "Lao-ness," embodying what Oliver Tappe terms Laos's "national topography," which post-1975 simultaneously legitimizes the ruling Party-State.[11]

The interior of Patuxai's open archway is decorated with a temple-style painted mural and bas reliefs. These feature a repeated ornamental shape called *dokchan*, its form derived from a flower. Although also Khmer (and arguably Indic) in origin, the codified image is commonly found in the decoration of Lao temples and is perceived as "Lao." So too the decorative towers that crown Patuxai, which clearly resemble Theravada *stupas*. The siting of Patuxai places the monument in direct spatial dialogue with several much older *stupas* in the vicinity and is a third instance of the structure's redeployment of Lao tropes, in addition to French forms. Patuxai is located near the old center of Vientiane, where dozens of Lao temples attest to the city's ancient origins. The two oldest and most significant structures are also large *stupas*, named That Luang and That Dam. That Luang is believed in legend to have been founded by the Indic King Ashoka in the third century BCE and to have been endowed at that time with a relic of the Buddha. Its present structure dates to the sixteenth century, when the Lan Xang kingdom under King Setthathirath successfully fought off a Siamese invasion: it is thus also a kind of victory monument, like Patuxai.

Almost four decades after designing Patuxai, Sayasithsena still displayed an ambivalence toward this declaration of Lao-ness that also explicitly points to French sources. In the same text that concedes the monument's similarities to the Arc de Triomphe and Taj Mahal, quoted above, Sayasithsena writes that "None of [Patuxai's decorative features] are synthesized from foreign fine arts . . . because [Laos] is plentiful with various fine arts." This contradiction in Sayasithsena's account highlights the contradiction inherent in the structure's redeployment of the colonial trope of combining French and Lao forms.

It is worth noting that this reference to the classical French tradition places the structure at odds with the dominant architectural forms in Vientiane at the time. By 1960, the American government was investing heavily in Laos. When Patuxai was commissioned, the United States Operations Mission was just a dusty compound, dotted with humble wooden buildings. By the late 1960s, when the monument was completed, American facilities had been dramatically upgraded, with sleek, modern concrete designs.[12] In the intervening decade, America's "secret war" had begun in 1960, and Eisenhower had told Kennedy in 1961 that Laos was the single most important place on earth for the US Cold War strategy.[13] American investment thus escalated massively, despite widespread allegations of the misuse of aid. Indeed, Patuxai was unofficially known as the "vertical runway" due to rumors that it was built with concrete donated by the United States for airport construction.

Most other large public buildings constructed in Vientiane during the period, many of them sponsored and/or built by the Americans, were also rectilinear, modular, and flat roofed. Apartments, hotels, and offices began to reshape Vientiane, alongside the continuing presence of older, ramshackle and often informal settlements along canals and waterways.[14] Describing the transformations that took place in Vientiane during the 1950s and 1960s, historians have stressed the importance of American interventions in the urban landscape:

> In the 1960s and early 1970s, the modernization of Vientiane continued apace. While the core of historic Vientiane and the fundamental symbolic axes of the city (especially that leading to the That Luang) were the result of the French revival and consolidation of the pre-colonial city, the period of US influence established the basic morphology and appearance of the city that continues to characterize it today. In many ways contemporary Vientiane is more a creation of the two decades after 1954 than any other period in its history.[15]

Patuxai emerged amid this postcolonial and Cold War–shaped urban transformation, yet it did so by redeploying colonial and precolonial architectural forms diverging from the more explicitly modern styles that were otherwise proliferating. This contrast between the monument and the city in which it appeared makes its performance of continuity with the colonial past all the more striking. In the twenty-first century, superficial Lao-style ornamentation often adorns new government buildings, whereas many remaining colonial-era structures are being privatized and demolished.

While Patuxai was at odds with the predominant US-backed mode of architectural modernity in Vientiane during the 1950s and 1960s, the situation in Phnom Penh was quite different. The Independence Monument, with its combination of French and Khmer, classical and modern, epitomized the syncretic modern architecture being built across Cambodia at this time.

Several factors contributed to this cosmopolitan nature of modern architecture in Cambodia. One was the greater emphasis placed on design and construction by Sihanouk's postcolonial regime. Another factor was the vision of Cambodian architects, many of whom trained in France and elsewhere.[16] Yet the most significant explanation for the syncretic diversity of modern urban structures in Cambodia, as compared to in Laos, lies in their differing positions in the Cold War. The United States was overwhelmingly dominant in Laos from the late 1950s until the communist victory in 1975. In Cambodia, by contrast, American aid had to compete with assistance from many other countries. Being neutralist, or nonaligned, in the Cold War at that time, Cambodia was a key ideological battleground for powers from across the political spectrum. The writer Han Suyin characterized the situation well. Writing in

1960, she observed that "Being neutral, Cambodia gets help from *everyone*. The airport was French aid, the road was American; an enormous, dazzling white hospital was Russian, something else was Czech; three factories were given by China, the Japanese were taking out rusty water pipes and replacing the lot with Made-in-Japan plumbing; and so it went on."[17] Moreover, recent research reveals that at least twenty-three of Vann Molyvann's projects, of which the Independence Monument was one, involved collaboration with foreign experts of at least seven different nationalities.[18]

The Independence Monument's synthesis of diverse architectural sources, in other words, was much more in keeping with the norm in Phnom Penh, whereas in Vientiane, due to American dominance of urban development as well as politics, Patuxai's synthesis of the colonial and the local stood out as singularly unusual.

In both cities, while local ornamentation continues to appear on buildings constructed in more recent years, these are now usually constructed by foreign investors, with little if any governmental planning oversight.

The combination of French with Khmer and Lao design features in both monuments is also a synthesis of the religious and the secular. The *stupa* form, seen in the towers that crown Patuxai and in the overall form of the Independence Monument, had previously been usually reserved for Buddhist funerary functions. A *stupa* was, in other words, a signifier of religion in Theravada kingdoms.

By contrast, the original designation of Patuxai as the Monument to the Unknown Soldier situates it in a distinctly secular tradition, albeit one which Benedict Anderson has suggested effectively replaces religious affiliation with nationalist allegiance.[19] Sayasithsena writes about Patuxai in an extraordinary manner, at once narrating and performing this interlocking of the religious and the secular. He explains that the five steeples that crown the structure:

> politically denote the five precepts or the five peaceful coexistence principles which are followed by politicians the world over . . . which are the core directives in administering/governing/ruling the countries and the subjects, giving them happiness, security, rejoicing, justice. . . . They are the five principles of the administrations of the lands in accordance with the rules of Buddhist Dhamma, of the Middle Path.[20]

Here, modern nation-state political functions and Buddhist philosophies are poetically conjoined in a dazzling instantiation of multivocal, multilayered redeployment. That Patuxai's steeples have in recent years been appropriated for the new roof design at the nearby Presidential Palace—just one kilometer from Patuxai—suggests a continuing secularization of formerly religious architectural imagery in twenty-first-century Vientiane.

Phnom Penh's Independence Monument also mixes the religious and the secular in its design and especially in its siting. The ornamentation is based closely on the tenth-century temple Banteay Srei, although the overall *stupa* shape closely resembles that of the central towers of the twelfth-century temple Angkor Wat. The Independence Monument makes these previously exclusive royal-religious realms accessible to the mass of the population in the profane space of a traffic intersection. The siting of that intersection, which as with Patuxai connects the monument to symbolically loaded sites elsewhere in the city, similarly signals the Independence Monument's links to both the Buddhist and the secular. The monument is linked by a long, straight road named Norodom Boulevard to the Wat Phnom Hill temple, which was founded in the fourteenth century CE and from which Phnom Penh takes its name. This road also connects the monument with the Royal Palace and some of the city's oldest pagodas. Yet the other avenue that intersects with the monument connects it to two newer structures, both of which are associated with the modern nation-state rather than with ancient religious sites. These are the National Stadium, which would not be built until a few years later, in 1964, yet which was probably already being considered, and the Bassac Riverfront Complex, a housing and cultural precinct comprising exhibition halls, sports facilities, a theater, apartments, and other nonreligious structures.

These various secular sites were all constructed under Sihanouk's rule and today function as symbols for his regime, widely remembered or imagined as a "golden age" before the devastation of civil war and Khmer Rouge atrocities in the 1970s. The current prime minister, Hun Sen, who has held the position since 1985, is keen to downplay Sihanouk's importance and to distance the current regime from almost all of its predecessors. Hun Sen's spatial relationship to the Independence Monument is indicative of the fraught complexity of this position. His Phnom Penh mansion—backed by a private military compound, although rarely inhabited by the prime minister—is directly opposite the monument and rivals it in height. In the lead-up to the hotly contested 2013 national elections, Hun Sen declared that the auspicious location of his house guaranteed his political success, yet he specified that he was referring not to its proximity to the Independence Monument but rather to nearby Buddhist wats.[21] Echoing this displacement of the monument's symbolic power when political rallies gathered at the site during the 2013 election campaign, they faced toward Hun Sen's house, the privileged nexus of all political authority, and in so doing, literally turned their backs on the Independence Monument.[22]

With both Phnom Penh and Vientiane being presently remade according to the whims of speculative capital, the importance of the Independence Monument and Patuxai to their urban landscapes has significantly diminished. New monuments erected by the current postsocialist regimes have contributed to this.[23] Yet understanding the complex and often contradictory ideological negotiations of both colonial authority and Cold War power play has taken on a renewed relevance today as China openly vies for control over the region's cities and economies and the United States continues to engage in foreign combat using a template it developed during "secret wars" in Laos and Cambodia.[24] Phnom Penh's Independence Monument and Vientiane's Patuxai thus function as lessons in architectural and spatial syncretism and also shed light on broader shifts over the past half century in these contexts. In such rapidly and comprehensively transforming environments as these, it is clear that every turn is also a kind of return.

ACKNOWLEDGMENTS

This essay was developed from a lecture given at the symposium "Architecture and the Modern City: Knowledge and Social Memory of Modern Architecture" at Ilham Gallery, Kuala Lumpur, in January 2018. I thank the convenors, Simon Soon and Rahel Joseph, as well as fellow presenters Jiat-Hwee Chang, Thanavi Chotpradit, and Shirley Surya. I am also grateful to David Chandler for his generous and insightful comments on an earlier draft. This research and writing were mostly undertaken during a postdoctoral fellowship at Nanyang Technological University, Singapore. I thank Ute Meta Bauer for her support, and I thank Pen Sereypagna, Chairat Polmuk, Anna Koscheeva, Ashley Thompson, and others for conversations that have contributed to my thinking here.

NOTES

1. Phnom Penh's Independence Monument is known in Khmer as *vimān aekarāj*. Vientiane's Patuxai is also commonly romanized as Patouxay, Patuxay, and Patou Say and is also commonly referred to in Lao as *anousavaly*.
2. See Vann Molyvann, *Modern Khmer Cities* (Phnom Penh: Reyum, 2003), 157–60. Some secondary sources list the inauguration date as 1962; however, stamps commemorating the event were issued by the Royal Khmer Government in 1961.
3. See Grant Evans, *The Politics of Ritual and Remembrance: Laos Since 1975* (Chiang Mai: Silkworm Books, 1998), 119–26. See also Martin Stuart-Fox, *Historical Dictionary of Laos*, 3rd ed. (Lanham, MD, Toronto, and Plymouth, UK: Scarecrow Press, 2008), 249 and 341–42.
4. See, for example, the opening scenes of the film *Apsara*, written and directed by Norodom Sihanouk and released by Khemara Pictures in 1966. For an account of Sihanouk's cinema, see Eliza Romey, "King, Politician, Artist: The Films of Norodom Sihanouk," unpublished master's thesis, La Trobe University, Melbourne, 1998. For a discussion of the role of *cyclos* and other modern vehicles in Cambodian modernity, see Roger Nelson, "Introduction," in *A New Sun Rises over the Old Land: A Novel of Sihanouk's Cambodia*, ed. Suon Sorin, trans. Roger Nelson (Singapore: NUS Press, forthcoming).

5. Sihanouk's grip on power began to be seriously challenged only in the 1966 national elections, and until 1963, Cambodia enjoyed relative internal political stability. Stability, however, came at a price. See David Chandler, *The Tragedy of Cambodian History: Politics, War, and Revolution since 1945* (New Haven: Yale University Press, 1991), esp. 85–122.

6. See Søren Ivarsson, *Creating Laos: The Making of a Lao Space between Indochina and Siam, 1860–1945* (Copenhagen: Nordic Institute of Asian Studies, 2008).

7. Evans, *Politics of Ritual and Remembrance*, 125.

8. Phnom Penh's National Museum, for example, combined a plan and construction materials reminiscent of a French museum with ornamentation that drew on Khmer temples. It was inaugurated in 1920. Around the same time in Vientiane, French authorities actively sponsored and led the restoration of many important temples and religious-royal buildings, all of which had been destroyed in razings of the city by Siamese invaders in the century prior. See Penny Edwards, *Cambodge: The Cultivation of a Nation, 1860–1945* (Chiang Mai: Silkworm, 2007); and Ivarsson, *Creating Laos*.

9. Tham Sayasithsena, *Victory Arch: Construction, Significance, Prestige* (Nongkhai: Mtthai Press, 1995), 7–8.

10. Kim Set [*Gym Saet*], *Ae Naa Kūn Srī Khñum* [Where Is My Daughter?] (Phnom Penh: Srei Bunchan, 2004 [1962]), 1. Translation from Khmer is my own.

11. Oliver Tappe, "Shaping the National Topography: The Party-State, National Imageries, and Questions of Political Authority in Lao PDR," in *Changing Lives in Laos: Society, Politics and Culture in a Post-Socialist State*, ed. Vanina Bouté and Vatthana Pholsena (Singapore: NUS Press, 2017), 56–80, esp. 58.

12. See photographs in the Joel M. Halpern Laotian Slide Collection at the University of Wisconsin–Madison Libraries archive, accessed January 2018, https://uwdc.library.wisc.edu/collections/seait/laos/.

13. Joshua Kurlantzick, *A Great Place to Have a War: American in Laos and the Birth of a Military CIA* (New York: Simon & Schuster, 2016), 4.

14. Photographs of modern buildings in Vientiane are contained in the Joel M. Halpern Laotian Slide Collection. Photographs of informal settlements are contained in the Terry and Robert Wofford Laotian Image Collection, also at the University of Wisconsin–Madison Libraries archive. Accessed January 2018, https://uwdc.library.wisc.edu/collections/SEAiT/LaosImages/.

15. Marc Askew, Colin Long, and William Logan, *Vientiane: Transformations of a Lao Landscape* (London and New York: Routledge, 2010 [2007]), 138.

16. See Helen Grant Ross and Darryl Leon Collins, *Building Cambodia: "New Khmer Architecture" 1953–1970* (Bangkok: Key Publisher, 2006).

17. Han Suyin, "The Laughing Cambodians," *Eastern Horizon* 1, no. 1 (July 1960): 23–26 (24). Emphasis in original.

18. Masaaki Iwamoto, "The Roles of Foreign Experts in the Cambodian Modern Movement of 1950-60s: Focusing on the works of Vann Molyvann," *Proceedings of the 11th ISAIA*, September 2023, 2016, Miyakgi, Japan, 1185–89. Thanks to the author for sharing this document.

19. Cited in Evans, *Politics of Ritual and Rememberance*, 120.

20. Sayasithsena, *Victory Arch*, 19.
21. Neou Vannarin, "Hun Sen Says Mansion, Feng Shui Seal His Election Win," *The Cambodia Daily*, May 28, 2013, accessed January 2018, https://www.cambodiadaily.com/elections/hun-sen-says-mansion-feng-shui-seal-his-election-win-27253/.
22. See, for example, a photograph by Nick Axelrod depicting a Cambodian People's Party rally on July 26, 2013, accessed January 2018, https://www.gettyimages.com/event/final-day-of-campaigning-ahead-of-cambodian-poll-on-sunday-1744 81835#supporters-during-a-preelection-rally-for-the-ruling-cambodian-party-pic ture-id174462158. As early as 2001, gatherings of protestors were described as focused on the prime minister's residence, rather than on the Independence Monument, which the house faces. See Kay Kimsong, "Vendors Protest in Front of Hun Sen's House," *The Cambodia Daily*, March 28, 2001, accessed January 2018, https://www.cambodiadaily.com/archives/vendors-protest-in-front-of-hun-sens-house-20901/.
23. On a shift in emphasis away from Patuxai and toward new structures within the compound of the nearby That Luang, see Rafael Martinez, "Remembering within a Sacred Space in Vientiane," *The Journal of Lao Studies* 2, no. 2 (November 2011): 75–103. On the new focus on monuments glorifying the sixteenth-century Cambodian King Sdech Kân, see Astrid Norén-Nilsson, "Performance as (Re)incarnation: The Sdech Kân Narrative," *Journal of Southeast Asian Studies* 44, no. 1 (February 2013): 4–23.
24. Kurlantzick, *Great Place to Have a War*.

BIBLIOGRAPHY

Askew, Marc, Colin Long, and William Logan. *Vientiane: Transformations of a Lao Landscape*. London and New York: Routledge, 2010 [2007].

Chandler, David. *The Tragedy of Cambodian History: Politics, War, and Revolution Since 1945*. New Haven: Yale University Press, 1991.

Edwards, Penny. *Cambodge: The Cultivation of a Nation, 1860–1945*. Chiang Mai: Silkworm, 2007.

Evans, Grant. *The Politics of Ritual and Remembrance: Laos since 1975*. Chiang Mai: Silkworm Books, 1998.

Ivarsson, Søren. *Creating Laos: The Making of a Lao Space between Indochina and Siam, 1860–1945*. Copenhagen: Nordic Institute of Asian Studies, 2008.

Iwamoto, Masaaki. "The Roles of Foreign Experts in the Cambodian Modern Movement of 1950–1960s: Focusing on the Works of Vann Molyvann." *Proceedings of the 11th ISAIA*, September 20–23, 2016, Miyakgi, Japan, 1185–89.

Kimsong, Kay. "Vendors Protest in Front of Hun Sen's House." *The Cambodia Daily*, March 28, 2001. Accessed January 2018. https://www.cambodiadaily.com/archives/vendors-protest-in-front-of-hun-sens-house-20901/.

Kurlantzick, Joshua. *A Great Place to Have a War: American in Laos and the Birth of a Military CIA*. New York: Simon & Schuster, 2016.

Martinez, Rafael. "Remembering within a Sacred Space in Vientiane," *The Journal of Lao Studies* 2, no. 2 (November 2011): 75–103.

Molyvann, Vann. *Modern Khmer Cities*. Phnom Penh: Reyum, 2003. Nelson, Roger. "Introduction." In *A New Sun Rises over the Old Land: A Novel of Sihanouk's Cambodia*. Edited by Suon Sorin. Translated by Roger Nelson. Singapore: NUS Press, Forthcoming.

Norén-Nilsson, Astrid. "Performance as (Re)incarnation: The Sdech Kân Narrative," *Journal of Southeast Asian Studies* 44, no. 1 (February 2013) 4–23.

Romey, Eliza. "King, Politician, Artist: The Films of Norodom Sihanouk." Unpublished master's thesis, La Trobe University, Melbourne, 1998.

Ross, Helen Grant, and Darryl Leon Collins. *Building Cambodia: "New Khmer Architecture" 1953–1970*. Bangkok: Key Publisher, 2006.

Sayasithsena, Tham. *Victory Arch: Construction, Significance, Prestige*. Nongkhai: Mtthai Press, 1995.

Set, Kim [*Gym Saet*]. *Ae Naa Kūn Srī Khñum* [Where Is My Daughter?] Phnom Penh: Srei Bunchan, 2004 [1962].

Stuart-Fox, Martin. *Historical Dictionary of Laos*. 3rd ed. Lanham, MD, Toronto, and Plymouth, UK: Scarecrow Press, 2008.

Suyin, Han. "The Laughing Cambodians." *Eastern Horizon* 1, no. 1 (July 1960): 23–26 (24). Emphasis in original.

Tappe, Oliver. "Shaping the National Topography: The Party-State, National Imageries, and Questions of Political Authority in Lao PDR." In *Changing Lives in Laos: Society, Politics and Culture in a Post-Socialist State*. Edited by Vanina Bouté and Vatthana Pholsena, 56–80. Singapore: NUS Press, 2017.

Vannarin, Neou. "Hun Sen Says Mansion, Feng Shui Seal His Election Win." *The Cambodia Daily*, May 28, 2013. Accessed January 2018. https://www.cambodiadaily.com/elections/hun-sen-says-mansion-feng-shui-seal-his-election-win-27253/.

CHAPTER 5

Enshrining Racial Hierarchy through Settler Commemoration in the American West

CYNTHIA C. PRESCOTT

UPON HIS DEATH IN 1876, YANKEE-BORN CALIFORNIA SETTLER, philanthropist, and recluse James Lick bequeathed USD 100,000 (nearly $3 million in today's dollars) to erect statuary in downtown San Francisco "emblematic of the significant epochs in California history . . . from the early settlement of the missions" to his own.[1] Modeled after the elaborate monuments placed in Paris amid late nineteenth-century "statuomania,"[2] sculptor Frank Happersberger's 850-ton Lick Pioneer Monument (figure 5.1) combined sculptural portraits of famous white explorers, missionaries, and military leaders with scenes of frontier California and female allegories depicting Anglo-American civilization around a phallic stone pillar. And like contemporaneous monuments to Confederate soldiers erected across the American South and beyond, it declared white racial dominance. Read together, the various sculptural elements told a story that would have been familiar to its viewers, one of a Social Darwinist progression from wild American Indians to frontier racial mixing to civilized white society. Newspapers across the United States eagerly followed the monument's creation and celebrated its design. Over the next two decades, Western residents loudly objected to any deviations from the Lick Pioneer Monument's explicit depiction of racial progression in monument proposals for their own cities.

After World War I, Western pioneer statues abandoned such fin de siècle monuments' emphasis on Social Darwinism but continued to declare white cultural dominance. As white Americans grew increasingly confident about their dominance of Western lands, they stopped depicting supposedly disappearing Indians in pioneer-themed statuary. Instead, dozens of remarkably similar statues depicting an iconic white pioneer woman in a sunbonnet striding westward appeared throughout the United States in the 1920s and 1930s. This pioneer woman embodied white civilization and effectively erased the indigenous peoples whom she sought to civilize or displace. Similar imagery of white women carrying European culture to indigenous interior

49

Figure 5.1. Frank Happersberger, Lick Pioneer Monument, 1893, San Francisco, California.
Photograph by Lisa Allen.

peoples also appeared around that time in other settler societies—most notably the Afrikaner *volksmoeder* in South Africa.[3] But the impulse to erect a public statuary in honor of those women was particularly powerful in the United States, where it aligned with national agrarian myths.

Monuments to pioneer mothers—sometimes accompanied by their husband or children—would be erected in cities and smaller towns for the rest of the twentieth century and beyond. Although they did not explicitly depict a hierarchy of races or cultures in the manner of San Francisco's Lick Pioneer Monument, these pioneer mother and pioneer family memorials also celebrated white settler colonialism.[4] Deviations from the accepted image of a woman in a long prairie-style gown and wide-brimmed sunbonnet sparked public protest, such as those in Denton, Texas, in the 1930s, and Salem, Oregon, in the 1950s.

For most of the twentieth century, the Lick Pioneer Monument was largely forgotten by San Franciscans. Like many of the nearly two hundred pioneer monuments erected in the United States since the late 1880s, its urban location declined, and most people walked by the statue without paying it any attention. But plans to relocate the statue in the mid-1990s to accommodate a new city library sparked controversy. Preservationists opposed its relocation. Others wanted it removed altogether, decrying its depiction of white dominance over indigenous Californians. San Francisco's Art Commission compromised by installing a brass plaque beside the relocated statue acknowledging the devastating effect of white settlement on California's Native American population—from at least 300,000 in 1769 to 15,377 in 1900. But landscaping soon hid that plaque from the public eye.

In the early twenty-first century, scholarly discussions of US Confederate memory and commemoration[5] spilled over into public life. But white Americans remain far less willing to critically examine the nearly two hundred pioneer monuments in their midst. Whether they were erected—like most Confederate monuments—amid xenophobia and near-hysteria over women's changing social roles at the turn of the twentieth century or amid farm crises and debates surrounding multiculturalism at the turn of the twenty-first century, many Americans resist recognizing the racial subtext of statues to Western settlers.

Dozens of pioneer monuments erected from the 1880s through the 1930s commemorate the arrival of Euro-American "civilization" to "savage" native peoples.[6] In contrast, pioneer monuments erected after World War II tend to celebrate white settlers' persistence in an inhospitable landscape. While these more recent statues do not explicitly celebrate settler colonialism and a few seek to embrace cultural diversity by honoring the arrival of the dominant white culture, they indirectly commemorate Indian removal. Yet this racial subtext is rarely acknowledged, coming to light only when some aspect of the statue's design or placement sparks enough controversy to attract public and media attention. The nearly 200 pioneer memorials erected throughout the United States over the past 125 years are material manifestations of changing American ideas about race but also serve as a battleground on which racial hierarchies are both reinforced and challenged. Tracing changes over time in these monument designs and their public reception highlights the extent to which widespread faith in American agrarian ideals rests on a foundation of indigenous dispossession. More broadly, it reveals the ways in which racial hierarchies are subtly (and sometimes not so subtly) enshrined through the erection of statues commemorating founding fathers and self-sacrificing mothers.

TOWERS OF RACIAL PROGRESSION, 1890–1920

The earliest pioneer monuments, erected from the 1880s through the 1910s, emphasized the supposed cultural superiority of white settlers. For example, the Lick Pioneer Monument, discussed in the opening to this essay portraying the Americanization of California, was erected in front of San Francisco's new City Hall in 1894. The monument's central granite pillar features an honor roll of white explorers, missionaries, businessmen, and military and government leaders who brought Euro-American civilization to a supposedly savage land and people. The individuals thus honored represent two common forms of what Lorenzo Veracini calls settler colonial "screen memory": marking initial colonial exploration and nostalgic narratives of settler pasts.[7] Atop the central spire stand a bronze allegorical depiction of the spirit of white American California and a grizzly bear representing the US state. Female allegories of Plenty and Commerce on lower piers similarly declare the superiority of white American society.

Examining the episodes in California history and the specific individuals that sculptor Frank Happersberger (1858–1932) chose to honor in the Lick Pioneer Monument reveals late nineteenth-century white Americans' notions of their own cultural superiority. Happersberger traced California's history from its supposed discovery by European explorers in the sixteenth century to its annexation and incorporation into the American nation in the late nineteenth. The monument acknowledges California's indigenous peoples only in "Early Days" (a heroic-sized bronze grouping on one of the lower piers) and a relief depicting a white trapper trading with American Indians. In "Early Days," a late eighteenth-century Spanish Catholic missionary stands over an indigenous man who reclines at his feet. "On his face," *San Francisco Call* declared at the monument's dedication in 1894, "you may see the struggle of dawning intelligence."[8] Behind them, a *vaquero* (cowboy), representing California ranching culture under Mexican rule (1821–1848), throws a lasso, his upraised arm echoing the Spanish padre's raised arm and emphasizing their dominance over the indigenous figure. A trio of white Americans representing the sixty to seventy thousand miners who arrived in California during the 1849 Gold Rush balances "Early Days" and carefully erases the presence of Chinese, Mexican, and indigenous men and women in the mines.[9]

Happersberger constructed Anglo-American whiteness through his sculptural telling of the region's history. He placed Sir Frances Drake, who claimed the region for England in 1579, above Spanish soldier Juan Rodriguez Cabrillo, the first European to reach California. Spanish mission leader Junipero Serra and Swiss immigrant Johann Sutter (who relied on indigenous labor to build a private fiefdom before gold was discovered on his central California territory, sparking the 1849 Gold Rush) are the only non-Anglophones whom Happersberger honored with portraits alongside Drake, US explorer and infamous military leader John C. Frémont, and monument donor James Lick. Spanish and Mexican military leaders Gaspar de Portolá, José Castro, and Mariano Guadalupe Vallejo are named but not pictured; the indigenous peoples devastated by these white men are excluded altogether from Happersberger's honor roll.[10]

Salt Lake City, Utah, erected a similar pillar of white civilization shortly after San Francisco dedicated its Lick Pioneer Monument. And public outrage forced Frederick MacMonnies to replace a Plains Indian warrior with a white mountain man and Indian massacre leader Kit Carson to depict white cultural superiority in Denver, Colorado, in 1911. After World War I, communities abandoned Social Darwinist towers of white settlement—and Happersberger's elaborate combination of historic portraits and allegorical figures—in favor of a simpler heroic statuary mounted on a stone base. As white Americans grew confident in their conquest of native peoples, pioneer commemoration shifted toward gendered expressions of whiteness.

WOMEN CARRY WHITE CIVILIZATION WESTWARD, 1920–1940

Communities across the Western United States in the early twentieth century erected statues of generic white settlers. Forty-six pioneer monuments—one-quarter of all pioneer-themed monuments I have identified within the United States—were erected between 1920 and 1940. Iconography in those interwar pioneer monuments coalesced around remarkably similar depictions of a self-sacrificing Pioneer Mother carrying white civilization westward. Of the forty-six monuments erected during those two decades, forty-two (91 percent) focus explicitly on pioneer women. More pioneer *mother* monuments were erected in that period than were all pioneer-themed monuments erected between 1880 and 1920. Twenty depict pioneer women unaccompanied by men. While a few depicted older women in repose, their civilizing work done, most depicted a young woman in a long, simple dress and wide-brimmed sunbonnet carrying white civilization westward.

Yet even these impressive statistics understate the power of sun-bonneted Pioneer Mother imagery during the interwar period. The Daughters of the American Revolution (DAR) erected twelve identical manufactured stone *Madonna of the Trail* statues in states stretching from Maryland to California. Because these statues were highly publicized at the time and so many were installed across the country, they helped shape many Americans' mental image of frontier women. Meanwhile, wealthy oilman E. W. Marland sponsored a highly publicized competition to select a "Sunbonnet Woman" statue for his adopted hometown of Ponca City, Oklahoma.[11]

The twelve entries to Marland's design competition toured the country from New York and Boston to Minneapolis and Denver. A reported 750,000 Americans viewed the models and were invited to cast votes for their favorites.[12] According to the *New York Times*, "The exhibition included at least one figure to please almost every taste. And every great school was represented . . . from a figure suggesting the Greek [Arthur Lee's *Faithful*] to another embodying the last phase of modernism [Maurice Sterne's *Determined*]."[13] Despite these stylistic differences, the entries bear striking similarities: all twelve pioneer women are young, white women wearing long dresses. Nine wear sunbonnets. Ten hold babies. Those artists who deviated from popular Pioneer Mother imagery or from the Beaux-Arts style typical of early twentieth-century monumental sculpture were publicly mocked and soundly defeated. Bryant Baker's depiction of a young woman in a tailored gown and wide-brimmed sunbonnet guiding her young son westward, though dismissed by art critics, was the overwhelming public favorite. It received the most votes in eleven out of fourteen cities; nationwide, his design received 42,478 votes for first choice and a clear plurality overall with 123,000 total votes.[14] It was dedicated before a crowd of some 40,000 in 1930.[15]

Baker's winning *Pioneer Woman* carries a Bible in her right arm, reassuring viewers that this genteel young woman has braved dangers and endured hardships to spread white Christian civilization in a manner in keeping with 1920s' familial and civic maternalism.[16] Yet Ponca City's statue also memorialized the supposed disappearance of the region's native women and men. Where 1890s' monuments had explicitly depicted racial hierarchy, by the 1920s, Social Darwinist towers, such as San Francisco's Lick Pioneer Monument, were no longer necessary. Western Indians were presumed to have vanished, making way for civilized pioneer women, such as Ponca City's winning design. Even in Oklahoma, which had served as a destination for American Indians emigrating and being forcibly removed from the Eastern United States throughout most of the nineteenth century and where native populations persisted, sculptural depictions of indigenous peoples gave way to celebrations of white settlers claiming Indian lands. The scale and popularity of Marland's competition ensured that Ponca City's winning design—like the DAR's twelve *Madonna of the Trail* statues stretching from coast to coast—would linger in the American imagination and heavily influence the design of later monuments.

WHITE SETTLERS CAME TO STAY, 1975–2000

Interest in erecting pioneer monuments declined dramatically after World War II, as national attention shifted from assimilating American Indians in the West to challenging—or defending—segregation in the South. Then, as identity politics and the "Culture Wars" of the 1980s and 1990s sparked public debates about multiculturalism in the nation's progressive coastal cities, rural peoples in the interior of the country facing corporatization and crippling debt embraced pioneer monuments as a means to mark local centennials. These centennial monuments emphasized early settlers' successful use of Euro-American technology, such as steel plows to survive and thrive in harsh Western environments. By constructing bronze and stone narratives of pioneer persistence and dominance of the land, however, these statues also celebrated white dispossession of native peoples stretching back to Thomas Jefferson's vision of a nation of small farms owned by white farmers.

Greg Todd's They Came to Stay—which was erected on the grounds of the Sherman County courthouse in Goodland, Kansas, to mark the county's 1987 centennial—celebrated white persistence on native lands particularly clearly

Figure 5.2. Greg Todd, They Came to Stay, 1987, Goodland, Kansas.
Photograph by the author.

(figure 5.2). A white man clad in late nineteenth-century work clothes and a wide-brimmed hat squats down in his field, holding the rich soil in his proper right hand. Beside him stands his young wife; the wind sweeping the high plains blows her long skirt and apron. Her right hand rests gently on her husband's shoulder, indicating her reliance on his strength. Her left holds tightly to one handle of their prominently featured walking plow. Her posture makes clear that she does not manage the plow herself but reserves that physically demanding task for her strong husband. His hard work and ingenuity—and that of other white men like steel plow inventor John Deere—make it possible for them to survive and thrive, transforming tough Kansas sod into the good land celebrated in the town's moniker. But the pioneer woman's presence ensures—like the female allegories of American Progress in San Francisco's Lick Pioneer Monument—that this is no boomtown populated by unattached men seeking to get rich and move on quickly. She relies on her husband and his plow for physical sustenance, but their community relies on her reproductive labor and nurturance for its survival. Together—sculptor Greg Todd and his hometown of Goodland declare—they built a community that survived a century of hardship and would persist in the face of depopulation and crippling agricultural debt.

Western cities a century earlier had declared white American cultural supremacy, seeing modern cities as the pinnacle of human evolution. By the 1980s, smaller farm towns sought to forestall further evolution. Resisting urbanization and the rise of corporate agriculture, they gazed longingly back to a time when the only technology required to support their family was a horse-drawn walking plow. But just as Ponca City, Oklahoma's *Pioneer Woman* celebrated the arrival of white civilization at the expense of American Indians, by commemorating their ancestors' persistence in harsh environments, the Goodland statue and nine similar statues erected on the Great Plains in the 1980s and 1990s also marked native dispossession. And while they do not depict native peoples, six others erected to celebrate Oklahoma centennials since the 1980s—including *Brand New State*, Oklahoma City's forty-five 150-percent-sized bronze figures depicting the 1889 land run—explicitly celebrate whites claiming Indian lands. White settlers "came to stay" on land that they made "good" by removing indigenous peoples, exterminating bison herds, and tearing up native grasses to plant European crops. By erecting and maintaining monuments like Greg Todd's in Goodland, white Westerners choose to remember white settlers who arrived a century earlier and to forget those who had lived on and shaped that landscape for thousands of years. These monuments naturalize and reinforce white cultural dominance.

ATTEMPTED INCLUSIVITY, 1990–2018

In the early twentieth century, monuments that failed to sufficiently celebrate white supremacy sparked public protest. By the 1990s, however, many Americans viewed such depictions of native conquest as culturally insensitive. San Francisco's acclaimed Lick Pioneer Monument—the benchmark against which other early monuments had been judged—became controversial due to its depiction of white dominance, as did efforts to erect new statues to generic white settlers in several other communities. Since that time, a few communities, including Broken Arrow, Oklahoma, have erected pioneer-themed monuments that seek to tell more culturally inclusive stories. Instead of erasing peoples of color, these monuments include them. Avoiding the San Francisco Lick Pioneer Monument's lessons in Social Darwinism, they depict Native Americans or Hispanics alongside white settlers. Yet even these seemingly inclusive new statues reproduce earlier monuments' narrative of progression from primitive indigenes to advanced white society and erase white violence against native peoples.

As scholars and native activists challenged 1990s plans to celebrate the 500th anniversary of Christopher Columbus's supposed discovery of the New World, protestors in San Francisco who associated the Lick Pioneer Monument with cultural humiliation and genocide splashed it with gallons of red paint. They singled out the monument's "Early Days" bronze grouping depicting a Mexican *vaquero* and a Spanish Franciscan missionary towering over a submissive indigenous Californian as particularly offensive. The city sought to balance the demands of Native activists, preservationists, the Roman Catholic Church, the Spanish government, and diverse other groups by erecting a plaque explaining the history depicted in "Early Days"—a compromise that satisfied no one.[17]

The dozen recent centennial monuments erected in Oklahoma reveal particularly clearly the persistence of racial hierarchies even in seemingly inclusive monuments. While a few of these memorialize settler persistence, most explicitly celebrate whites claiming Indian lands. In response to native activists' protests, Ponca City stripped the title *This Land Is Mine* from its 1993 centennial statue but remained determined to erect the bronze depiction of a white man staking a claim to former Indian lands about a mile from its famous *Pioneer Woman* monument and accompanying museum. Other, supposedly more inclusive, Oklahoma monuments include native peoples as a starting point from which a more successful and whiter society has emerged—thus replicating in a more subtle manner the logic of Social Darwinism.

Broken Arrow, Oklahoma's 2002 centennial monument depicts what appears at first glance to be yet another pioneer family monument celebrating early settlers' persistence in an unforgiving land. Indeed, local residents—including the artist—refer to the piece as *Pioneer Family*. David Nunneley's grouping features a young boy standing in front of his parents, prepared to lead them into the future. The Centennial Commemorative Statue Committee selected the piece because it "combined all the things that have made Broken Arrow a booming community—family, tradition, farming, heritage and hard work"—and even included a nod to the area's Native American heritage.[18]

However, closer examination reveals the ways that Nunneley's piece reinforces white domination even as it celebrates cultural inclusivity. Nunneley's grouping for Broken Arrow depicts a rangy white man united by marriage to what the *Tulsa World* described as a "lithe Indian maiden."[19] A union between a native man and a white woman would raise the specter of American Indian captivity narratives. In contrast, wedding a meek Indian maiden to a strong white farmer gives an illusion of equality, while actually depicting the white takeover of native lands and cultures. The large book that the native woman carries suggests her embrace of the twin blessings of Euro-American education and Christianity carried West by white pioneer women like those still celebrated in Bryant Baker's heroic statue in Ponca City. Yet her knee-length, fringed buckskin dress and moccasins and the two braids hanging down below her shoulders mark the limits of her assimilation. In contrast, her husband's cowboy boots and hat demonstrate his hardy white masculinity. Rather than embracing one another in marital unity, they stand apart, their arms crossing behind the boy as each separately guides their young son forward. The ripe peaches in the father's bucket and the robust rooster in the boy's arms symbolize local white agricultural industries. The boy's Euro-American features, clothing, and hairstyle assure viewers that white culture will dominate indigenous influences. Only the boy's bare feet call into question his degree of civilization. But viewers clad in modern sneakers or cowboy boots are more likely to view his shoelessness—like his pet rooster—as a nostalgic sign of rural freedom than as a challenge to past or future white supremacy.

RACIAL HIERARCHIES REMAIN

Today, frontier imagery remains powerful in American culture. While many decry Confederate memory as racist, most Americans remain hesitant to recognize the ways in which pioneer monuments also memorialize their nation's racial hierarchy. As several cities voted to remove monuments to Confederate leaders and protestors in Durham, North Carolina, tore down their local Confederate soldier monument, activists once again called for the removal of San Francisco's divisive Lick Pioneer Monument. Apparently swayed by shifting public opinion nationwide, the city's Art Commission voted in late 2017 to remove the controversial "Early Days" grouping. Yet even if the city does remove the Spanish padre, Mexican *vaquero*, and prostrate Indian from one of four bottom piers, placing "Early Days" in storage and leaving an empty pedestal, questions of how to interpret the remainder of the massive monument remain. The central granite pillar with its hierarchical honor role (including the newly sainted Junipero Serra); its heroic grouping of white Forty-Niners; and its allegories of American Commerce, Plenty, and California statehood will remain in place, just as the racial hierarchy that the 1894 statue celebrated remains carved in stone in American society and is continually reinforced by the bronze statues commemorating its arrival across the Western American landscape.

NOTES

1. Quoted in San Francisco Civic Art Collection Staff, "Pioneer Monument Staff Report," October 2, 2017, http://sfgov.org/arts/sites/default/files/100217_Pioneer_Monument_Staff_Report.pdf.
2. Sergiusz Michalski, *Public Monuments: Art in Political Bondage, 1870–1997* (London: Reaktion Books, 1998).
3. Anne McClintock, *Imperial Leather: Race, Gender and Sexuality in the Colonial Contest* (New York: Routledge, 1995), 378–79.
4. On settler colonialism, see Lorenzo Veracini, *Settler Colonialism: A Theoretical Overview* (New York: Palgrave Macmillan, 2010); and Patrick Wolfe, "Settler Colonialism and the Elimination of the Native," *Journal of Genocide Research* 8, no. 4 (December 2006): 387–409.

5. Kirk Savage, *Standing Soldiers, Kneeling Slaves: Race, War, and Monument in Nineteenth-Century America* (Princeton: Princeton University Press, 1997); Cynthia J. Mills and Pamela H. Simpson, eds., *Monuments to the Lost Cause: Women, Art, and the Landscapes of Southern Memory* (Knoxville: University of Tennessee Press, 2003); Paul A. Shackel, *Memory in Black and White: Race, Commemoration, and the Post-Bellum Landscape* (Walnut Creek, CA: Altamira Press, 2003); Catherine W. Bishir, "Landmarks of Power: Building a Southern Past, 1885–1915," *Southern Cultures* 1 (1993): 5–45; Karen L. Cox, *Dixie's Daughters: The United Daughters of the Confederacy and the Preservation of Confederate Culture* (Gainesville: University Press of Florida, 2003).

6. On cultural constructions of civilization and savagery, see Gail Bederman, *Manliness and Civilization: A Cultural History of Gender and Race in the United States, 1880–1917* (Chicago: University of Chicago Press, 1996).

7. Veracini, *Settler Colonialism*, 90.

8. "It Is Realized," *San Francisco Morning Call*, November 30, 1894.

9. Susan Lee Johnson, *Roaring Camp: The Social World of the California Gold Rush*, reprint ed. (New York: W. W. Norton & Company, 2000), 59.

10. Benjamin Madley, *An American Genocide: The United States and the California Indian Catastrophe, 1846–1873*, reprint ed. (New Haven: Yale University Press, 2017).

11. John Joseph Mathews, *Life and Death of an Oilman: The Career of E. W. Marland* (Norman: University of Oklahoma Press, 1951), 179–80.

12. "Pioneers," *Time*, January 2, 1928.

13. "Pioneer Woman Seen in Bronze: Twelve Sculptors Show Their Models for the Proposed Monumental Statue to Be Erected in Oklahoma—Other States to See Them," *New York Times*, March 20, 1927.

14. "Bryant Baker 'Pioneer Woman' Art File" 1927, Kansas City Public Library; "Pioneers (Arts)," *Time* 11, no. 1 (1928): 20.

15. "The Pioneer Woman," *New York Times*, April 29, 1930.

16. Rebecca Jo Plant, *Mom, The Transformation of Motherhood in Modern America* (Chicago: University of Chicago Press, 2010).

17. San Francisco Civic Art Collection Staff, "Pioneer Monument Staff Report."

18. Becky Clark, "Centennial Committee Chooses Sculptor for Historical Statue," *Tulsa World*, June 19, 2002, sec. Broken Arrow Community world.

19. Tim Stanley, "Centennial Souvenirs," *Tulsa World*, June 18, 2003, accessed December 25, 2018, http://www.tulsaworld.com/archives/centennial-souvenirs/article_631c692d-7b89-58e1-aecf-bcaf41d64742.html.

CHAPTER 6

In Defense of Historical Stains

How Clean Approaches to the Past Can Keep Us Dirty

Dan Haumschild

In Berlin, Germany, the Topography of Terror Documentation Center attempts to represent the crimes of Nazism at the former site of its disciplinary nexus, the Reich Security Main Office. The Topography of Terror is situated on the grounds where men like Heinrich Himmler and Reinhard Heydrich oversaw all the operational facets of the SS and the Gestapo. The terrain that a visitor encounters at the site today looks markedly different than it would have in 1944, however. The building that held the offices of some of the most infamous criminals in human history was mostly destroyed by Allied bombing near the end of the war, and according to James E. Young, was little more than a pile of rubble between 1949 and 1981.[1] When the ruins of the Gestapo headquarters were unearthed by accident in 1985, debate about what to do with the space was brought into the limelight,[2] and after a lengthy and complex process, Topography of Terror debuted in 1987. It first appeared as a temporary exhibit and then later as a permanent installation in a new building that anchors the present site's extensive landscape.[3]

Today, visitors are ushered around the sleek, well-manicured grounds of the former Gestapo headquarters. The terrain, architecture, and display of artifacts adopt the minimalism that has become "the dominant visual style for memorials around the world."[4] Often, memorials to genocide focus on the tragedy of victimization, but at the Topography of Terror, perpetration takes center stage and visitors are asked to consider the experiences of Nazis and bystanders. The clean documentary nature of the exhibit is accentuated by the utilization of photographs as a primary artifact within the Center itself. Undermining the truths evinced by the photographs, docents engage visitors in an examination of what exists beyond the frame of the photo in terms of both composition and the historical and social context. Situated in and contributing to postmodern Berlin, the exhibit calls into question our knowledge of the crimes of Nazism, our capacity to know, and even "the city's past repression of memory."[5]

The Topography of Terror Documentation Center has been the focus of criticism since its finalization in 2010. Indeed, upon its grand reopening, Layla Dawson published a scathing commentary in *Architectural Review*. She describes the building as a "grey, horizontal gash in the landscape" and the excavated Gestapo headquarters as being "sanitized, as if for military inspection."[6] The lack of focus on victimization and the conceptual destabilization of evil that is tied into the postmodern minimal approach seem to constitute Dawson's main objection to this form of memorial display: "The imprisoned, tortured and murdered, once held in the cellars, have been relegated to minor roles. However well-meaning its intentions, the architecture projects an obsession with order, control and, ultimately, a lack of humanity."[7] Near the end of Dawson's single-page review, she prompts the reader with a question that motivates the present examination: "Should a 'dirty' history be cleaned up to this extent?"[8]

As someone who has spent considerable time in Rwanda, Dawson's contention brings to mind representations that are at the opposite end of the spectrum, and I question whether their "dirtiness" is more or less appropriate to the task of memorialization.

For example, at the Ntarama Genocide Memorial Center, the primary memorial artifacts are the skeletal remains of genocide victims. The memorial is situated in a former church, an hour south of the capital of Kigali, where nearly five thousand people were massacred during the 1994 genocide. The "cleanest" part of the exhibit is in the main building. There, the visitor will see bloodstained clothes hung from the trusses or piled in massive heaps along the pews. In one corner, cups, sandals, glasses, and dolls intermingle in a great mound, which gives the visitor a glimpse into the personal nature of the tragedy. Additionally, the skeletal remains of victims are categorized by type and stacked together to give a sense of the magnitude of the slaughter—a shelf full of femurs is juxtaposed to an equally large shelf of skulls. These artifacts are contextualized by the national story that is rendered by the textual display in the church's nave. As such, the remains of these victims are meant to prompt inductive reasoning about other churches across the country.

Moving into even dirtier territory, the outbuildings of Ntarama confront the visitor with the memorial's most dramatic element. When I first visited the site in 2008, I felt a sense of relief upon entrance to a small nearby classroom, for the space seemed to be devoid of the morbid evidence that is predominant throughout the rest of the grounds. I expected to use the quietude of the partially destroyed building to gather myself. But as I gazed toward my feet, I realized that the dirt floor was strewn with a variety of items, including small shards of bone. To my own shame, I noticed that my foot was pressing a human vertebrae further into the soft floor. With horrified vigilance, I tiptoed about the space, seeing a child-sized ribcage, a shard of a humerus and countless other unidentifiable bones scattered everywhere.

Leaving Ntarama, my shirt had acquired the distinct smell that accompanies an unknown tonnage of blood-stained clothes. My shoes and pants were covered in the dust of Ntarama's floor and whatever had been ground into it during the fourteen-year interval between the genocide and my own presence at the site. In short, I left the space literally carrying the detritus of the genocide and reckoning with the realities of this acquisition in all of its manifestations.

OVERCOMING THE COMPARATIVE CHASM

The question that grounds this examination is whether Ntarama's representation of genocide is any more appropriate or more "humane" than the Topography of Terror. Of course, given the significant differences between these two historical events, it is not surprising that their memorial representations would be divergent. Moreover, in attempting to provide a comparative analysis of these two sites, it must be noted outright that these efforts are beset by the social and cultural gap between Germany and Rwanda—both historically and contemporarily.

Moreover, it should be acknowledged that my own cultural and academic lens might limit my ability to evaluate these two memorials in equal light. As Nicholas Mirzoeff has suggested, the standard for representation in Western society is abstraction, whereas in non-Western societies, direct representation remains at the forefront.[9] Even when we maintain "unquestionably good intentions," we may become "entangled in the difficulties of using Western-based art practice to represent subaltern culture."[10] In short, the way that Europeans are trained and interested in thinking about genocide lies in stark contrast to the training and interest of non-Europeans. Indeed, as Mirzoeff suggests, we must recognize "that the extremity of the genocide has made visible the incommensurability of Western visual practice, on one hand, and subaltern life, on the other, within the frames currently offered."[11] Perhaps I too will get entangled in the chasm of incommensurability simply by virtue of the fact that I am trained in a Western tradition. The challenge, of course, is to keep the divide between Rwanda and Germany in mind while finding a bridge between them that makes comparison plausible.

So rather than using standards of "visual practice," which are determined almost exclusively by cultural values, I propose comparing these memorials on their relative departure from forms of representation that were predominant during the genocide in question. This seems to be a fair point of contact between Ntarama and the Topography of Terror. Both are invested in the goal of a society that "never again" commits genocide; they are thus committing these forms of representation to the work of social transformation. Within the context of a memorial, social transformation can be accomplished only by altering the way a community receives and is empowered to interpret information. Certainly, both memorials bring us closer to an understanding of genocide, but which practice of representation distinguishes itself more distinctly, those that were manifest during the genocide? Is the sanitized nature of Topography of Terror recapitulating the methodologies of Nazi representation; does the dirty ground of Ntarama cleanse Rwanda of the era of genocide? And which memorial is more effectively prompting its viewers to both never forget the hideous past and never again fall into the social practices that led to these events? It appears that by comparing the relative transformation of representation, we can highlight where each memorial effects the humane work desired by Dawson, me, and others.

'HUMANE' WORK

While the contexts are vastly different, both posit a positive relationship between never forgetting and never again committing such crimes. To that end, it will be useful to address the particularities of this humane work that observers are hoping to see expressed in public history spaces.

According to Roger I. Simon, memorials to genocide are tasked with producing "futurity," or a "break from the endless repetition of a violent past."[12] This is an eloquent and concise way of accounting for the never again half of the aforementioned couplet. However, Simon is highly critical of the popular conceptualization of what it means to never forget because the tactics that have been taken almost never result in the production of futurity.

Simon writes:

> Public history must provide something more than a version of the past that functions as a fragile "post-it" note placed on the refrigerator to remind us of our obligation and values—a note that is always on the verge of falling off or getting lost amid the clutter of other reminders of the pressing concerns of daily life.[13]

This Post-it style of remembrance is flawed in two ways. First, it adds additional stress to a system that is already tasked with remembering thousands of other pieces of information that are required simply to survive the trials of daily life. Second, the Post-it approach assumes "a self-evident and measurable usefulness"[14] contained by the memories we choose to represent and repeat. This is a problem because our memories and histories of the past—especially the traumatic past—are neither fully knowable nor fully transferrable. Both the Rwandan genocide and the Holocaust are events that, in many ways, escape comprehension, and when we consolidate this fragmentary knowledge into a truncated story that can easily be adhered to the next visitor, we provide a false sense of closure around the subject. Representing the past in this way promotes the idea that the story as it is told contains all the secrets of the tragic past and, therefore, by simply keeping the Post-it safe, social transformation will naturally occur.

Because this form of historical acquisition does not challenge visitors to reconsider their own role in history or a necessary continuous relationship to it, it will not result in futurity. Instead, this form of historical representation, which "presume[s] a simple one-way 'listen and learn' pedagogy anchored in the notion of the museum as an authoritative legislator,"[15] will merely charge the visitor with acquiring and admiring[16] seemingly accessible and self-contained pieces of information.

Futurity is accomplished through an inheritance of the past rather than simply an acquisition of knowledge. Inheritance entails a relationship with history in which the recipients of its representation are compelled to question "not what they must remember in order to be, but what it means, in light of the experience of the past, to be what they are now."[17] A way of representing the past that encourages inheritance would (1) address the event itself and (2) acknowledge that the event is not yet, and perhaps never can be, fully known or knowable. The admission of unfinished history by the memorial itself demonstrates an open-ended relationship to the past that encourages a visitor to likewise engage. A memorial constructed in this manner invites visitors to participate in the ongoing struggle to understand and, in so doing, demands that they develop their own sense of the past's meaning.[18]

In this constellation, the memorial both initiates and invites the visitor to join the "interminably unfinished project of democracy."[19] It is worth noting that Simon's conception of democracy is decidedly postmodern, derived from the philosophy of Emmanuel Lévinas and Jacques Derrida, among others. So the term democracy here is not what might immediately come to mind—European and American forms of neoliberalism. Instead, democracy is a practical antidote to totalitarianism and fascism insofar as it is constituted by the activity of participatory, critical, community building. In short, democracy is a verb. And in the memorial context, democracy is initiated by the "premise that we have not yet understood how to face the realities of a genocidal fascism in a way that makes possible a hopeful relation between the past and future."[20] This subtle shift encourages the visitor to partake in the ongoing project and provides a clear image of what is at stake.

DIRTY OR CLEAN?

To return to the comparison, we can say with certainty that if either Rwanda's Ntarama or Germany's Topography of Terror accomplished the task set forth by Roger I. Simon, it would be departing dramatically from the forms of representation that were prevalent during each country's era of genocide. For while the differences between the Holocaust and the Rwandan genocide are too exceptional to enumerate here, both of them were also notable for totalizing ideologies, strong propaganda programs, and a culture of terror that coerced everyday individuals to obey a murderous authority or to look the other way. Simon's vision of democracy, therefore, is useful for imagining futurity in either context. He establishes an ideal on a distant horizon toward which every memorial should aim.

In an attempt to establish a fair bridge between Ntarama and Topography of Terror, we must not evaluate them on their relative proximity to Simon's ideal, steeped as it is in a culture that favors the German example. Rather, we must see to what degree each memorial generates a representation of history that departs from the representations that dominated the genocidal eras. Asked another way, how far have they come toward futurity from their starting points? This orientation requires a brief review of the way that the genocide was represented in each context at the moment it was occurring. Thereafter, we can briefly return to the memorials themselves to garner a view of how they distinguish themselves from the era they historicize.

Here again, Nicholas Mirzoeff provides an excellent entry point to the Rwandan case. He situates the Rwandan genocide as "a form of mediated representation."[21] This is not to take away from the reality of the event but to suggest that "it was also symbolic in form and practice."[22] The brutality and exceptional pace of violence during the one hundred-day span of the genocide were not exclusively the result of historical conditions. Hutu fear and anger were expressed through the close-range decimation of their enemies. Moreover, the propaganda machine of the time, Radio Télévision Libre des Mille Collines, promoted visible and visceral forms of rape, assault, and murder. According to Mirzoeff, "the manual labor of the genocide was not a sign of Rwanda's primitivism but a symbolic act. The genocide was presented throughout as 'work,' and machetes and firearms were used as 'tools.'"[23] In 1994, the goal of umuganda, the Kinyarwanda word and long-standing tradition of "communal work," was the creation of a new and safe Rwanda.[24] For this work to be deemed complete, it had to be verifiable by the corpses of Rwanda's mortal enemy, Tutsis. From the moment it began, there was no secrecy about the genocide. As violence spread and bodies began piling up, those who were ordering the massacres paid no mind to covering their tracks. This was not an error or a miscalculation; on the contrary, "the genocide was drawing a 'world picture,' or engaged in 'world making,' creating a world that was now visibly different because it was ethnically the same."[25] The indisputable death of the "Others," represented by their mutilated and lifeless bodies, was a requirement of the genocide's intended work. If we employ the language of Simon here, we could say that the génocidaires promised futurity through the visible death of the enemy, keeping the massacre before the eyes of both the victor and the not yet vanquished.

By utilizing the bodies of the slain in their genocide memorials, the Rwandan government employs a similar representational method to their genocidal predecessors. At memorials like Ntarama and Murambi—wherein the mummified corpses of victims lie accessibly strewn about the rooms where they were slain—the Rwandan government represents the genocide by preserving the scenes of the crime. As it was in 1994, the genocide remains "unavoidable" precisely because the authority has made the choice to leave visible its destructive traces. As Mirzoeff suggests,

> In these "cities of the dead," the departed remain in all senses, for they are not segregated from the living, in the manner of the cemetery, but have taken over key venues of civil society such as churches and schools. They are not gone in order not to be forgotten.[26]

As I have argued elsewhere,[27] the utilization of death and the dead constitutes a form of what Achille Mbembe calls necropolitics. Bodies[28] are left to mark the spaces of a sovereign's influence, to represent both the fact of an authority's existence and give weight to the cost of contending with that authority. Rwandan memorials complicate Mbembe's definition, but when "everyday experience constantly offers the possibility of the recurrence of genocide,"[29] the representational overlap is made uncomfortably clear.

In its dirty memorialization of the genocide, the Rwandan government leaves little space for visitors to reckon with their inheritance of a historical stain. Ntarama's dust was instead stuck to me like a Post-it. It confronted me directly, but rather than asking me to engage, it simply demanded that I receive. Furthermore, the shame associated with the direct encounter with death is the government's method for generating futurity. But shame reinforces an edict of prohibition "that reduces the significance of this history to 'we must not let the past be repeated.'"[30] Furthermore, it binds the visitor to the authoritative account that is presented rather than encouraging each individual to inherit the task of remembrance. Ironically, the dirtiness of the exhibit cleanses the story that it represents by cutting off the visitor's access to elements of the past that are not consolidated by the bodies of victims and the accompanying state-sponsored story.

During the Holocaust, the intention was to completely burn, or eradicate, all traces of the Nazi enemy. Though in the open during its early stages in Poland, the Holocaust receded further and further from the public eye as it intensified. Those who ordered the murder, those who carried out the orders, and those who were killed were all enveloped by a "secret art"[31] that rendered bodies invisible and displaced culpability. The Holocaust was not addressed directly but euphemistically through catch phrases that further disrupted one's capacity to understand the realities of the ongoing slaughter. Despite the intentionally vague rhetoric about the means of dealing with the "Jewish problem," a unifying national story was available in print, on the radio, and in film; these stories promised futurity through ideological alignment and social, political, and racial homogenization.

At the Topography of Terror, the era of Nazism and the Holocaust is represented through expositional photographs. As an exposition, the memorial antagonizes the modus operandi of the Nazi era. Rather than secrecy and allegiance, it shows both the veil and the people behind it. The memorial challenges visitors to design their own conclusions about the meaning of each artifact, for it is not heavy-handed and docents generate enough space to encourage each visitor to "read" the photographs before revealing facts about the image. Even when they expose elements of the photo or its context that would be invisible to the untrained eye, docents encourage an "open-ended interrogation . . . in which one's thinking is never just a conversation one has with oneself but a speaking and listening within which others are needed."[32]

The visitor is therefore called upon to wrestle with history's gray areas: to see the laughing Nazis as human beings while attending to the evil they stood for and enacted. Photographs hang in space rather than being plastered to the walls. They sway and shift with the drafts and are occasionally bumped by the crowds. Even in this subtle way, they interact with the present, momentary environment. Furthermore, photos are positioned in such a way that in some sight lines, one will catch the legs of another visitor occupying the space where Heinrich Himmler's ought to be. Thus, while the exposition attests to the fact of mass murder, it also encourages visitors to think beyond the frame and draw their own conclusions about each artifact's meaning. The Topography of Terror promises futurity through each visitor's active attempt to reconcile humanity with evil. The clean lines and minimalist form may indeed replicate the coldness of an industrial killing machine. Representationally, however, the exposition of the human faces that breathed life into this machine and the unequivocal illustration of murderous intent work in opposition to the Nazi order. The call for each individual to reckon with the Holocaust on his or her own terms is clearly a deviation from Nazi representations of history that were absolutist in nature. Ultimately, then, the cleanliness of the Topography of Terror invites the visitor to interact with a dirty, messy past that it deems to be not fully known. The indelible historical stain is represented with both depth and dimension that demand further examination, enticing visitors to inherit the past rather than simply tack it to their memory.

Layla Dawson's concerns about the sterilization of history are fair and seem derived from a genuine concern for keeping the past situated in a context that represents something true. However, as a space for public history, the memorial is tasked with providing an educational rendering of the past that can be accessed by visitors in a way that allows them to inherit the past. Perhaps in Dawson's mind, the Holocaust should rightly be represented as a bloody horror show. But at Ntarama in Rwanda, we see that by confronting the visitor with death and its subsequent shame, the Rwandan government replicates forms of representation that dominated during the era of genocide. If the ultimate goal of the memorial is to participate in a project of futurity—which is to say, the enduring attempt to never again commit such crimes—models of representing the past that were employed for evil purposes should at least be complicated if not directly antagonized. Through this brief comparison to dirtier forms of representation, we must acknowledge that the Topography of Terror actually instantiates an enduring confrontation with the past precisely through its cleanliness. I believe that, in due time, Rwanda will begin to feel comfortable with transitioning away from displays like Ntarama. Rwandans have had fifty fewer years to deal with the consequences of the genocide than their German counterparts, and their most pressing concern remains proving that it happened rather than opening up conversations about why it happened and what it means. If they intend to move on from the genocide, however, they will need to generate their own versions of memorialization that distinguish themselves from representational models that were employed by those who pursued genocidal aims.

NOTES

1. James E. Young, *The Texture of Memory: Holocaust Memorials and Meaning* (New Haven: Yale University Press, 1993), 86.
2. Young, *The Texture of Memory*, 88.
3. See ibid., chapter 3, for a lengthier rendition of the site's history.
4. Nicholas Mirzoeff, "Invisible Again: Rwandan and Representation after Genocide," *African Arts* 38, no. 3 (2005): 47.
5. Young, *The Texture of Memory*, 89.
6. Layla Dawson, "Berlin, Germany—Topography of Terror Has Washed Away Too Much Dirt in Presenting Nazi History," *Architectural Review* 227, no. 1361 (2010), 29.
7. Dawson, "Berlin, Germany," 29.
8. Ibid.
9. Mirzoeff, "Invisible Again," 87.
10. Ibid.
11. Ibid., 89.
12. Rodger I. Simon, "Museums, Civic Life, and the Educative Force of Remembrance," *The Journal of Museum Education* 31, no. 2 (2006), 120.
13. Simon, "Museums, Civic Life, and the Educative Force of Remembrance," 116.
14. Ibid.

15. Ibid.
16. Ibid., 115.
17. Ibid., 119.
18. Ibid., 118–19.
19. Ibid., 114.
20. Ibid., 118.
21. Mirzoeff, "Invisible Again," 37.
22. Ibid.
23. Ibid., 39.
24. Ibid., 39. See also Mahmoud Mamdani, *When Victims Become Killers: Colonialism, Nativism, and the Genocide in Rwanda* (Princeton: Princeton University Press, 2001).
25. Mirzoeff, "Invisible Again," 87.
26. Ibid., 90.
27. See Daniel Haumschild, "Inappropriate Transgressions: Reanimating Necro-politics via Memorialization in Rwanda," in *Transitional Justice and Education: Engaging Young People in Peacebuilding and Reconciliation*, ed. Clara Ramírez-Barat and Martina Schulze (Göttingen: V&R Academic 2018), 143–58.
28. See Achille Mbembe, "Necropolitics," trans. Libby Meintjes, *Public Culture* 15, no. 1 (2003): 11–40.
29. Mirzoeff, "Invisible Again," 90.
30. Simon, "Museums, Civic Life, and the Educative Force of Remembrance," 118.
31. Mirzoeff, "Invisible Again," 87.
32. Simon, "Museums, Civic Life, and the Educative Force of Remembrance," 119.

CHAPTER 7

Repairing and Reconciling with the Past

El Ojo que Llora and Peru's Public Monuments

Ñusta Carranza Ko

THE LOCK THAT HOLDS THE DOORS TO PERU'S PUBLIC MEMORIAL EL OJO QUE LLORA (The Eye That Cries),[1] inside the park El Campo de Marte in the Lima neighborhood of Jesús María, is one of the many reminders of the difficult political history the memorial has endured since its opening for public viewing in August 2005. From the vandalism that took place on September 23, 2007, where several pebbles of the memorial were displaced and covered in orange paint, a color coincidentally of former Peruvian President Alberto Fujimori's political party,[2] to the most recent attacks on February 28, 2017, El Ojo que Llora has undergone moments of resistance and challenge. Walking along the garden area that leads to the central piece of the memorial, the "eye" that sheds "tears," the director of Institutional Projections of the Asociación Pro-Derechos Humanos (APRODEH), Rosario Narváez, explained how "the site has been in function for about twelve years, eight of which have been like rowing against the current," confronting the indifferences of the local and state authorities to the vandalisms and attacks against the memorial.[3] The damages to the memorial were reflective of the continuous struggle that Peruvian society has in reconciling with the historical truth about the internal armed conflict (1980–2000), specifically the responsibility of the state and guerilla groups for human rights violations.

According to Peru's Comisión de la Verdad y Reconciliación (CVR: Truth and Reconciliation Commission), a total of 69,000 Peruvians were killed or disappeared during the internal armed conflict. The state was responsible for 37 percent of the deaths and disappearances.[4] In states transitioning from such authoritarian pasts of human rights violations to a democracy, policies of memorialization play a unique role in the process of societal reconciliation. Particularly, memorialization practices that include the construction of sites of memory and memorials complement transitional justice policies of truth-seeking, prosecutions of human rights criminals, and medical and financial reparations that "confront wrongdoings of repressive predecessor regimes."[5] The goal of reparations in this context is to provide victims with the most tangible manifestation of state policy to remedy the violations they suffered. Specifically, symbolic reparations constitute "official apologies, rehabilitation, the change of names of public spaces, the establishment of days of commemoration, the creation of museums and parks,"[6] including memorials. The Peruvian memorial *El Ojo que Llora* is a form of symbolic reparation and serves this function as a site of production of collective memory that provides recognition for victims and their family members. However, it has also been a place of struggle for the truth between the sectors of society who prefer to forget the official truth from the CVR and others who want to remember the past.

This chapter examines Peru's *El Ojo que Llora*—one of the few national memorials that is not physically confined to the site of conflict and serves as a performance of memory. The majority of the deaths and disappearances from the internal armed conflict took place disproportionately in poor rural areas,[7] whereas the memorial is situated in Lima's urban middle-class neighborhood. From the framework that regards public memorials as instruments of reparations that keep the past visible, this study analyzes *El Ojo que Llora* as an active symbolic reparative tool for victims and their family members and society's reconciliation efforts. As Gisela Ortiz, a human rights victims' family member notes, *El Ojo que Llora* has been the subject of the "battle for memory between the victims" who want to remember and "others who are opposed" about the official memory of the internal armed conflict.[8] From the victims' perspective, the memorial is an empirical "real and live" recognition of what happened, one that has served to unify the victims to feel recognized by society and receive symbolic reparations for their sufferings.[9] And it has become a "meeting point" for families of victims and human rights groups to commemorate communities and the disappeared.[10] Using interviews from nongovernmental human rights organizations managing the memorial and a victim's family member, the chapter examines the memorial from the victim's perspective of what the memorial is and where it is currently situated in the political discourse of Peruvian politics on memory and symbolic reparations. The chapter finds that *El Ojo que Llora* represents a step toward active commemoration and collective memory building involving contested interpretations about Peru's recent past and facilitates the healing of Peruvian society in transition as a public space that binds the narratives of violence from the past with the present through allegorical portrayals of victims and their lives.

SITUATING THE MEMORIAL IN POLITICS

After an abrupt democratic transition with President Alberto Fujimori's resignation in 2000 and the following interim transition government of Valentín Paniagua (2000–2001), an interinstitutional group led by jurist

Diego García Sayán was set up under Supreme Resolution 304-2000 tasked with developing a thoughtful response for victims of the armed conflict. Out of this initiative, the working group recommended the establishment of a truth commission, which would investigate the truth about human rights violations during the period from 1980 to 2000. The *Comisión de la Verdad* (Truth Commission) was created on June 4, 2001, and was shortly after replaced with the CVR via Supreme Decree No. 101-2001-PCM on September 4, 2001, with the new administration of Alejandro Toledo (2001–2006). The work of the CVR finished with the Final Report released in 2003, in which the commission issued a set of recommendations for the state to consider. Namely, they were in the form of transitional justice policies of criminal prosecutions and the creation of integral reparations programs, including symbolic reparations.

The symbolic reparations recommended by the CVR were the state's public apology of wrongdoings and creation of places of memory, museums, and publications honoring victims of human rights violations.[11] The earliest specification of this memorialization was the CVR's recommendation for the state to create a space for the viewing of the photo exposition of *Yuyanapaq* (to remember). The exposition assisted in commemorating the investigations of truth, provided recognition for victims, created a temporal space for remembrance where the exhibition took place, and generated conversations about the representation of reality and collective memory.[12] Nonetheless, *Yuyanapaq* did not create a permanent physical space of memory.

El Ojo que Llora was the first site of memory, the first memorial, which was created out of a private civil society–driven initiative by sculptor Lika Mutal. The memorial, which was opened for public viewing in August 2005, was envisioned as part of a series of the *Alameda de la Memoria* (promenade or avenue of memory), which would incorporate a state-funded memory project—*Yuyanapaq*—and another civil society–led commemorative venture—*El Quipu de la Memoria* (Quipu of Memory). The *Quipu* project retrieved a tradition of communication from the Incas where knots were made in ropes as codes for a message, and using the same idea, knots were tied to ropes to represent victims of political violence. The project was first elaborated at the site of *El Ojo que Llora* in 2005 with the participation of nongovernmental organizations and victims' family members who created knots to remember those who had fallen.[13] Like the *Quipu* project formed out of a bottom-up movement, *El Ojo* also received domestic nongovernmental organizations' support and even funding from private corporations. And initially, the memorial's construction was also supported by the Municipality of Jesús María. Mutal "intended the memorial to commemorate all the victims of the violence," including members of leftist guerrilla group *Sendero Luminoso* who had been killed during the internal

Figure 7.1. *El Ojo que Llora*, Lika Mutal, Lima, Peru, December 20, 2017
Photograph by the author.

armed conflict.[14] Each victim's life would be reproduced with the inscription of names on stones along with the years of births and deaths laid out circularly orbiting the center sculpture representing *Pachamama* (Mother Earth; figure 7.1). All the victims' names were provided by the CVR. And unintentionally, they included the names of forty-one *Sendero* members who were convicted criminals in the Miguel Castro Castro prison who had been killed by Peruvian National Police and Peruvian military personnel in 1992.[15] Due to the commemoration given to guerrilla groups, particularly the convicted criminals of the Castro Castro prison, the Municipality of Jesús María ultimately withdrew its financial support for *El Ojo*, and the memorial has become a politicized space seen as sympathizing with terrorist causes and vandalized on multiple occasions, most recently on February 28, 2017.[16]

EARLIER WORK
The scholarship that examines *El Ojo que Llora* commonly agrees on the importance that the memorial holds for memory and societal reconciliation in Peru. In her work on memory, Hite provides an overview of the emergence of *El Ojo que Llora* and the politics of commemoration exploring how "particular memories of struggle, war, conflict, and violence" have

emerged stronger today and what they represent for the society undergoing transition.[17] Hite discusses the role that *El Ojo* represents in Peru's history, in sparking a series of reflections of who constitutes a victim or a perpetrator of human rights violations.[18] Hite[19] also points to the symbolism the memorial holds for the victims and their families, as a reminder of the ongoing struggle for accountability. Such views are also noted in Macher's work[20] that studies the status of the CVR's recommendations related to memory. Macher reiterates Hite's view on how *El Ojo* has come to embody the politics of contrasting memory, referring to examples of attacks against the memorial from President Alberto Fujimori's supporters. These individuals saw *El Ojo* as defending "terrorists,"[21] contrary to Mutal's vision of honoring all victims and their memories.

The battle of narratives is also present in Milton's research,[22] where she focuses on the challenges this public space of memory has faced in Peru. Rather than approach the attacks against the memorial as violence and vandalism, Milton documents the divisions of interpretations of memory and discusses how competing groups have used the memorial to exhibit their "own interpretation of the past," one which ultimately has had the effect of suppressing the victim and repressing memories.[23] Similar observations are made by Drinot, who characterizes these competing interpretations related to *El Ojo* as the binary polemic between those who regard the memorial as a site that pays homage to "terrorists" who were solely responsible for triggering the conflict and others who point to the structural problems in Peruvian society that instigated the violence from 1980 to 2000.[24] Drinot argues that the continued existence of such strong opposing views may reflect the limits of memory projects in bringing about reconciliation in Peru.[25]

Other scholarship has carried the idea of the politics of memory further by focusing on the political framing of memory. Milton's recent work explores the question of to whom all the memory work is speaking and "how effectively this message is getting across" to those who wish to forget or not know of the past human rights abuses.[26] She explains various memory initiatives in Peru to discuss the framing of memory, such as the Itinerant Museum, *El Ojo que Llora*, Houses of Memory, and the Scarf of Hope and how each may be subject to the "pitfalls of memory," where art or formations of art are shaped often by the artist-survivor's intentions to tell a particular story,[27] one which might be subjective. The framing of memory is explored in a different way by Saona,[28] who uses the esthetics of *El Ojo* or the physical object of the stone and the sculpture to illustrate the structuring of memory. Particularly about the stone engravings, Saona notes how the inscription of each victim's name and the dates of births and deaths re-create the temporality of the victim's life and evokes a notion of collective loss for those visiting the memorial.[29]

This chapter takes a slightly different approach while adding to the conversation on *El Ojo que Llora* from other scholars. It explores the narratives from victims and nongovernmental organizations in examining the performative role of the memorial in keeping the past alive. The narratives are not limited to reiterating the victims' family members' view on the "dignifying satisfaction" *El Ojo* provides for them.[30] Here, I discuss the administrative difficulties the memorial has faced and argue how notwithstanding the challenges to the memorial, *El Ojo* continues to be an effective instrument of symbolic reparations that serves to preserve the memory of victims and past repression, reinvigorates new memory, and has helped bind competing narratives of violence from the past with the present. These ideas are built on the understanding that memory initiatives do have the power to transform contested interpretations about Peru's recent past and can reconcile a divided society.

KEEPING THE MEMORY ALIVE

Unknown to the public, from the beginning of the creation of *El Ojo que Llora*, the memorial was managed privately by a group of volunteers who formed a part of the *Asociación Caminos de la Memoria* (Association Routes of Memory). The group was spearheaded by Francisco Soberón, the founder of APRODEH and a human rights defender. The associated members of the *Caminos de la Memoria* included members from nongovernmental organizations and individuals such as Gisela Ortiz, who was a family member of a victim of human rights violations. Gisela's brother, Luis Enrique Ortiz, was one of the students from La Cantuta University who was forcibly abducted and executed by state-sponsored death squads on July 18, 1992. Because there was no legislation to financially support sites of memory, except for the *Lugar de la Memoria, la Tolerancia y la Inclusión Social*, which was created after an "international scandal" that began with the donation from the German government to the Peruvian state for the creation of a museum of memory,[31] *El Ojo que Llora* has had to be self-financed and administered. Each member of the *Caminos de la Memoria* made his or her contribution to a common fund, and the association also accepted individual donations. The funds have been just enough to be able to hire Mr. Clodoaldo Huanca, a part-time gardener for 400 SOL per month ($US~122.33), and only recently, the association had enough funds to install electric outlets and lights at the memorial.[32] Along with the self-financing status, the attacks against the memorial forced the members of the *Caminos de la Memoria* to put a lock on the doors leading to the site. The closure of the doors restricted public access and resulted in a greater reliance on volunteers from the association who were needed to unlock doors and provide a guided tour of the memorial.

Despite the financial and administrative difficulties in maintaining the memorial and relying on volunteers, *El Ojo que Llora* has still been actively used as a space to keep the past alive and create new forms of memory. The association organizes yearly commemorations on August 28, the date of the CVR's submission of the final report, to pay respect to the students who were killed or disappeared by leftist guerilla groups and the armed forces. Annual celebrations are also organized on November 1, the day of the dead, when families of victims come together in an act of remembrance and memory to the memorial.[33] Along with activities that evoke memories of political repression, the association has also taken up a new set of efforts to keep the past alive. Most recently, the members of the *Caminos de la Memoria* have registered the association in the public registry, a move that reflects the organization's will to systematize commemoration. As a publicly registered group, Soberón explains that the association would have the resources to provide more guided tours, hire full-time personnel to manage the site, apply for funds from international human rights organizations to sustain the memorial, and open a bank account to manage the finances.[34] Such decisions would help keep the functions of *El Ojo*. The memorial was a form of symbolic reparation recommended by the CVR, one that recognized that an international harm had been committed. And with the individualized memory emblems in the form of stones with victims' names, it also was a "space for truth-telling," which also sparked some contestation.[35] Given that recognition to victims is the goal of all transitional justice measures (i.e., truth seeking, prosecutions, and reparations).[36] The existence of the memorial and its structure, including the individual victims' names inscribed to each stone, served to acknowledge the identity of the victims and preserve the memory of the violation alive. Hence, the process of registering the association, which would administer the memorial and continue to propagate the memory of all the victims of the violence with guided tours to the public would help continue the recognition.

Preserving the memory, specifically the official memory reflecting the Final Report of the CVR, has not been the only function of *El Ojo que Llora*. The memorial has reinvigorated new memory, one that has brought together various human rights violations, victims, and even victims' family members from different periods of time. Narváez recalls how the sculptor Lika Mutal envisioned the memorial not as a perfectly tended garden but more in the form of an open field.[37] Following these views and commemorating Mutal's death in 2016, the *Caminos de la Memoria* used its funds to create an area of remembrance in the same park area as *El Ojo que Llora*. Trees native to the Andes, trees that bear different fruits, medicinal plants, and flowers were planted around several tree trunks, and a series of individual altars were placed with the names of Pilar

Figure 7.2. Rose Garden in *El Ojo que Llora*, Caminos de la Memoria, Lima, Peru, December 20, 2017.
Photograph by the author.

Col, Carlos Iván Degregori, Javier Diez Canseco, Margarita Patiño, Lika Mutal, *Angélica* Mendoza de Azcarza (Mamá Angélica; figure 7.2), and Rosa del Águila García.[38] All the individuals, who had distinct identities and were active in different periods in Peru's political history, were selected for their work on defending human rights and the impact they had on society. For instance, Mamá Angélica was the mother of Arquimedes, who was forcefully disappeared by the military on July 3, 1983; became a symbol of the battle for justice in Peru; and founded the human rights organization ANFASEP, the National Association for Families of the Kidnapped, Detained, and Disappeared in Peru. The identity of Rosa del Águila was distinct to that of Mamá Angélica because Rosa herself had been the victim of an extrajudicial execution on August 12, 1993. And in her case, the crime was committed by *Sendero* and not the state.[39] In a different role, neither that of a victim or a victim's family member, Degregori was a scholar, activist, and former CVR member who wrote on human rights, the debates between *Sendero* and the state during the internal armed conflict, and on memory and political violence.

The different profiles of those who were being remembered in the new altar area and the period of their work signaled the addition of new layers of remembrance and memory creation associated with the memorial. First, the new altars' memories accompanying *El Ojo que Llora* overcame political differences of whether the state or leftist guerilla groups were responsible for human rights violations. Mamá Angélica and Rosa del Águila's altars adjacent to one another broke the dichotomy that existed between the two competing narratives of memory of state versus *Sendero* responsibility. Second, no longer was *El Ojo* responsive exclusively to the memory of the victims from the internal armed conflict. Degregori's presence made it possible to envision the area holistically as reflecting a memory of victims, their family members, and even Peruvian society. In such ways, the new area reflected the original idea of Lika Mutal on recognizing all victims of political violence, which in this case transcended time periods to encompass all those whose rights were violated and who were trying to defend the rights. Third, the new altars, along with the plants and trees, further transformed the area surrounding *El Ojo* into a family friendly picnic leisure area. It became a place where victims' family members or visitors to the memorial could spend a day with tree trunks to sit on, remembering the past. Simultaneously, while continuing the remembrance, visitors and family members could also celebrate the new forms of life, with the new vegetation surrounding the area. As Narvaez explains, "the planting of flowers, trees, and medicinal plants was built on the idea of how people return to the mother earth in death, which protects us, and gives us new forms of life with fruits that nourish the body, plants that cure us, and flowers that give joy to sight."[40] In metaphorical terms, the vegetation was a symbol of the victims of human rights, who in death were being reborn into a new form of life. Through this process, the memorial area transitioned from being a traditional place of mourning, one that "evoked the memories" of victims' suffering and injustice,[41] to a new space of memory, one that celebrated life and united the past and the present.

CONCLUSION

On December 24, 2017, Alberto Fujimori received a humanitarian pardon from President Pedro Pablo Kuczynski (2016–2018). The pardon overturned the sentence of Fujimori on crimes against humanity for the massacre in Barrios Altos and La Cantuta University, ruled by the Inter-American Court of Human Rights (2001 and 2006) and once again reaffirmed in 2009, during the sentencing of Fujimori. Roughly a month later in response to the state's decision, victims' family members gathered at *El Ojo que Llora* with yet another reproduction of memory, a new mural with the faces of victims from La Cantuta and Barrios Altos.[42] The memorial provided the victims and their family members a space to once again remember, fight back against the injustice, and create a new memory for the future.

There is still much more to be done. As both Narváez and Ortiz note, not many people know of *El Ojo que Llora*.[43] The people attending the events are either scholars, members of nongovernmental organizations, or victims and their family members. However, it is also important to recognize the advances that resulted from the initiatives surrounding *El Ojo* and the groups that have promulgated the causes. In August 2013, *El Ojo que Llora* was declared by the ministry of culture as a "cultural heritage" site of Peru.[44] The state's recognition of the memorial as a cultural patrimony was a step toward reconciling the narrative struggle, which pitted the state against the victims and the memories that each group wanted to preserve and remember. The memorial was emblematic of this conflict because it was constructed with private funding and not supported by the state, although the CVR's recommendations on symbolic reparations were directed toward the state. Hence, *El Ojo* represented a measure of reparation that the state could not guarantee for the victims of the internal armed conflict and a controversial space of memory for those who wanted to remember a selective version of history different to that of the CVR's official account. Knowing these discordances that originally plagued the memory debate, the 2013 declaration reflected the extent to which the competing narratives had come to reconcile matters. And even with the vandalism that has continued in 2017, the memory initiatives that developed in the surrounding areas of *El Ojo* in 2017 and the 2018 mural have created layers of new memory that recognizes a broader group of victims. In this process, *El Ojo que Llora* as the central piece of symbolic reparations for victims of human rights violations has reshaped the politics of memory in Peru.

NOTES

1. Throughout the chapter, the memorial will be interchangeably referred to as *El Ojo que Llora* or *El Ojo*.
2. Alberto Fujimori (1990–2000) was the first democratically elected president to be tried for human rights violations and was convicted for twenty-five years on April 7, 2009, for crimes against humanity, the forced disappearance and extrajudicial execution of students and one professor from *La Cantuta University* (July 18, 1992), *Barrios Altos* massacre of fifteen civilians (November 3, 1991), and the kidnapping of journalist Gustavo Gorriti and the businessman Samuel Dryer (April 1992).
3. Author's interview with Rosario Narváez, director of Institutional Projections, Asociación Pro-Derechos Humanos, December 18, 2017, Lima.
4. Transfer Commission of the Truth and Reconciliation Commission of Peru, *Hatun Willakuy: Abbreviated Version of the Final Report of the Truth and Reconciliation Commission* (Lima: Transfer Commission of the Truth and Reconciliation Commission of Peru, 2014), 12.
5. Ruti G. Teitel, *Transitional Justice* (New York: Oxford University Press, 2000), 69.
6. Pablo De Greiff, "Introduction: Repairing the Past: Compensation for Victims of Human Rights Violations," in *The Handbook of Reparations*, ed. Pablo De Greiff (New York: Oxford University Press, 2006), 453.

7. Transfer Commission of the Truth and Reconciliation Commission of Peru, *Hatun Willakuy*, 12.

8. Author's interview with Gisela Ortiz, director of Operations and La Cantuta victim family member, Equipo Peruano de Antropología Forense, January 4, 2018, Lima.

9. Ibid.

10. Cynthia E. Milton, "Introduction: Art from Peru's Fractured Past," in *Art from a Fractured Past: Memory and Truth-Telling in Post-Shining Path Peru*, ed. Cynthia E. Milton (Durham: Duke University Press, 2014), 12; and Sofía Macher, *¿Hemos avanzado? A 10 años de las recomendaciones de la Comisión de la Verdad y Reconciliación* (Lima: Instituto de Estudios Peruanos, 2014), 167.

11. Comisión de la Verdad y Reconciliación, *Informe Final: Tomo IX* (Lima: CVR, 2003), 79, 116–19.

12. Margarita Saona, *Los mecanismos de la memoria: Recordar la violencia en el Perú* (Lima: Fondo Editorial PUCP, 2017), 31–64; and Iván Carlos Degregori et al., *No hay mañana sin ayer, batallas por la memoria y consolidación democrática en el Perú* (Lima: Instituto de Estudios Peruanos, 2016), 47–48.

13. La República, "La sociedad civil teje el Quipu de la memoria," published August 5, 2005, accessed December 26, 2018, http://larepublica.pe/sociedad/295971-la-sociedad-civil-teje-el-quipu-de-la-memoria.

14. Katherine Hite, *Politics and the Art of Commemoration: Memorials to Struggle in Latin America and Spain* (New York: Routledge, 2012).

15. Paulo Drinot, "*El Ojo que llora*, las ontologías de la violencia y la opción por la memoria en el Perú," *Hueso Húmero* 50 (2007): 55–59.

16. La República, "*El Ojo que llora*: Monumento fue atacado nuevamente y familiares exigen major seguridad," published March 3, 2017, accessed December 26, 2018, http://larepublica.pe/politica/853467-el-ojo-que-llora-monumento-fue-atacado-nuevamente-y-familiares-exigen-mayor-seguridad.

17. Hite, *Politics and the Art of Commemoration*, 1.

18. Ibid.; and Katherine Hite, "The Eye That Cries: The Politics of Representing Victims in Contemporary Peru," *A Contra corriente* 5, no. 1 (2007): 108–34.

19. Hite, *Politics and the Art of Commemoration*, xx.

20. Macher, *¿Hemos avanzado?*, xx.

21. Ibid., 167.

22. Cynthia E. Milton, "Defacing Memory: (Un)tying Peru's Memory Knots," *Memory Studies* 4, no. 2 (2011): xx.

23. Ibid., 192.

24. Drinot, "*El Ojo que llora*," xx.

25. Drinot, "*El Ojo que llora*," 73.

26. Milton, "Introduction: Art from Peru's Fractured Past," 12.

27. Ibid., 18.

28. Saona, *Los mecanismos de la memoria*, xx.

29. Ibid., 112.

30. Ortiz, interview.

31. Saona, *Los mecanismos de la memoria*, 37.
32. Ortiz, interview.
33. La República, "Familiares de desaparecidos visitaron '*El Ojo que llora*' en el día de los muertos," published November 1, 2016, accessed December 26, 2018, http://larepublica.pe/politica/817403-familiares-de-desaparecidos-visitaron-el-ojo-que-llora-en-el-dia-de-los-muertos-fotos.
34. Author's interview with Francisco Soberón, president, Asociación Pro-Derechos Humanos, December 18, 2017, Lima.
35. Milton, "Defacing Memory," 200.
36. De Greiff, "Introduction: Repairing the Past," 42.
37. Narváez, interview.
38. Ibid.
39. LUM, "Caso: Rosa del Águila García, testimonio: José Soto del Águila," accessed December 26, 2018, http://lum.cultura.pe/cdi/foto/caso-rosa-del-%C3%A1guila--garc%C3%ADa-testimonio-jos%C3%A9-soto-del-%C3%A1guila.
40. Narváez, interview.
41. Hite, *Politics and the Art of Commemoration*, 43.
42. La República, "Develan mural con rostros de víctimas en rechazo al indulto a Fujimori," published February 9, 2018, accessed December 26, 2018, http://larepublica.pe/politica/1191646-develan-mural-con-rostros-de-victimas-en-rechazo-al-indulto-a-fujimori-fotos.
43. Narváez, interview; and Ortiz, interview.
44. Peru21, "Declaran Patrimonio Cultural del Peru *El Ojo que Llora*."

BIBLIOGRAPHY

Comisión de la Verdad y Reconciliación. *Informe Final: Tomo IX*. Lima: CVR, 2003.

Degregori, Iván Carlos, Tamia Portugal Teillier, Gabriel Salazar Borja, and Renzo Aroni Sulca. *No hay mañana sin ayer, batallas por la memoria y consolidación democrática en el Perú*. Lima: Instituto de Estudios Peruanos, 2016.

De Greiff, Pablo. "Introduction: Repairing the Past: Compensation for Victims of Human Rights Violations." In *The Handbook of Reparations*, edited by Pablo De Greiff, 1–20. New York: Oxford University Press, 2006.

Drinot, Paulo. "*El Ojo que llora*, las ontologías de la violencia y la opción por la memoria en el Perú." *Hueso Húmero* 50 (2007): 53–74.

Hite, Katherine. "The Eye That Cries: The Politics of Representing Victims in Contemporary Peru." *A Contra corriente* 5, no. 1 (2007): 108–34.

Hite, Katherine. *Politics and the Art of Commemoration: Memorials to Struggle in Latin America and Spain*. New York: Routledge, 2012.

La República. "Develan mural con rostros de víctimas en rechazo al indulto a Fujimori." Published February 9, 2018. Accessed December 26, 2018. http://larepublica.pe/politica/1191646-develan-mural-con-rostros-de-victimas-en-rechazo-al-indulto-a-fujimori-fotos.

La República. "*El Ojo que llora*: Monumento fue atacado nuevamente y familiares exigen major seguridad." Published March 3, 2017. Accessed December 26, 2018. http://larepublica.pe/politica/853467-el-ojo-que-llora-monumento-fue-atacado-nuevamente-y-familiares-exigen-mayor-seguridad.

La República. "Familiares de desaparecidos visitaron '*El Ojo que llora*' en el día de los muertos." Published November 1, 2016. Accessed December 26, 2018. http://larepublica.pe/politica/817403-familiares-de-desaparecidos-visitaron-el-ojo-que-llora-en-el-dia-de-los-muertos-fotos.

La República. "La sociedad civil teje el Quipu de la memoria." Published August 5, 2005. Accessed December 26, 2018. http://larepublica.pe/sociedad/295971-la-sociedad-civil-teje-el-quipu-de-la-memoria.

LUM. "Caso: Rosa del Águila García, testimonio: José Soto del Águila." Accessed December 26, 2018. http://lum.cultura.pe/cdi/foto/caso-rosa-del-%C3%A1guila-garc%C3%ADa-testimonio-jos%C3%A9-soto-del-%C3%A1guila.

Macher, Sofía. *¿Hemos avanzado? A 10 años de las recomendaciones de la Comisión de la Verdad y Reconciliación*. Lima: Instituto de Estudios Peruanos, 2014.

Milton, Cynthia E. "Defacing Memory: (Un)tying Peru's Memory Knots." *Memory Studies* 4, no. 2 (2011): 190–205.

Milton, Cynthia E. "Introduction: Art from Peru's Fractured Past." In *Art from a Fractured Past: Memory and Truth-Telling in Post-Shining Path Peru*. Edited by Cynthia E. Milton, 1–34. Durham: Duke University Press, 2014.

Peru21. "Declaran Patrimonio Cultural del Peru *El Ojo que Llora*." Published August 24, 2013. Accessed December 26, 2018. https://peru21.pe/lima/declaran-patrimonio-cultural-peru-ojo-llora-121343.

Saona, Margarita. *Los mecanismos de la memoria: Recordar la violencia en el Perú*. Lima: Fondo Editorial PUCP, 2017.

Teitel, Ruti G. *Transitional Justice*. New York: Oxford University Press, 2000.

Transfer Commission of the Truth and Reconciliation Commission of Peru. *Hatun-Willakuy: Abbreviated Version of the Final Report of the Truth and Reconciliation Commission*. Lima: Transfer Commission of the Truth and Reconciliation Commission of Peru, 2014.

CHAPTER 8

Ruptures and Continuities in the Post-Apartheid Political and Cultural Landscape

A Reading of South African Monument Culture

RUNETTE KRUGER

CONTESTATIONS

THE #RHODESMUSTFALL CAMPAIGN WAS LAUNCHED IN MARCH 2015 WHEN, in an "unusual act of defiance," a student threw excrement at the statue of Cecil John Rhodes installed on the terraces of the University of Cape Town.[1] The act refocused the national movement to decolonize universities and the broader South African landscape, and the #FeesMustFall movement, which rapidly developed out of the successful campaign to remove the statue, still dominates higher education in South Africa three years later. The Rhodes campaign also resonated with global communities—at the University of Oxford's Oriel College, where Rhodes studied, a similar student protest movement agitated for the removal of a statue of Rhodes adorning its façade but was unsuccessful. At Oxford, the fear of damaging the institution's standing (and alumni funding) triumphed.[2] The stark terms in which the dispute at Oriel College was framed have furthermore come to define monument contestation activism in its many current forms. Protesters were accused of a countercivilizing desire to erase history and destroy culture, comparable to the actions of the Islamic State in its demolition of cultural landmarks, while, in turn, Rhodes came to be described as the "Hitler of southern Africa."[3] In less extreme but equally polarized terms, those in favor of removing the monument were accused of politically correct moral vanity, while the protesting students challenged the institution to live up to its official stance on inclusivity and equality.[4]

Similar clashes have erupted in the United States. A December 2017 open letter by artists and scholars called for the removal of statues of Christopher Columbus, J. Marion Sims, and Theodore Roosevelt from New York City public spaces.[5] The letter was published after a series of five Mayoral Advisory Commission public hearings in which New Yorkers had the opportunity to argue for or against the removal of these monuments. Proposals to remove the monument to Christopher Columbus, particularly, stirred strong divisions.[6] As with Rhodes, the controversy came to revolve around opposing perceptions regarding the cultural significance of a particular historical figure. The final recommendation regarding the monuments in question, published on January 12, 2018, stipulates the removal of the statue of Sims from its architectural plinth in East Harlem, Upper Manhattan, for relocation to Green-Wood Cemetery, Brooklyn. The plinth is to remain in place, with additional plaques to "contextualize" Sims's historical significance.[7] The monuments to Columbus and Roosevelt are to remain in place and an "additive" approach will be taken: new works will be commissioned to honor underrepresented communities in the city, and the Ford Foundation will establish a grant toward creating a New York City Public History Project to address the "shared past of New Yorkers."[8]

In South Africa and, more specifically, its capital, Tshwane/Pretoria,[9] almost identical disputes have ensued around the statue of Paul Kruger on Church Square.[10] On April 5, 2015, the statue was doused in green paint, reportedly by members of the Economic Freedom Fighters (EFF). The statue has subsequently also been stoned (April 2015) and set alight (November 2016) by EFF members.[11,12] The EFF has clashed with the ruling party over what it considers to be the slow pace of transformation regarding racial equity, land rights, and socialist economic reform. EFF spokesperson Mbuyiseni Ndlozi called for the removal of the statue and for it to be replaced by a more appropriate monument.[13] The call sparked counterprotests on April 8 at Church Square by Afrikaner/white rights advocates centered around far-right Afrikaans celebrity Steve Hofmeyr. Amid a crowd of a few hundred protesters, fellow stalwart of Afrikaner self-determination, Sunette Bridges, chained herself to the statue in a symbolic gesture of defiance. The flag of the nineteenth-century *Boer* republic (the *Zuid-Afrikaansche Republiek,* or *ZAR*), of which Kruger was president for four consecutive terms, featured prominently. In the aftermath, political organization AfriForum, established in 2006 to promote Afrikaner culture (see Afriforum.com), blamed the ruling party for the ongoing attacks on the statue and for stigmatizing the Afrikaner community, which no longer feels "welcome in the country."[14]

A main rallying point for the various pro-Afrikaner groups, besides self-determination, and one raised once more at the April 8 rally, is the call for the government to take action against farm murders (notably, thus, crime against white Afrikaans farmers/landowners). At similar rallies, crime against other sectors of society is never raised as an issue. In an unusual twist to the April 8 highlighting of farm murders, a lone white Afrikaans protester held up a sign that read "Farm murders and township murders are equal!" Though well meaning as a humanizing call for social equality, the irony of still being able to designate farm owners as a group of specifically white landowners and of being able to refer collectively to black South Africans as township dwellers is palpable. Agitating for equality in death still ignores lingering stark social inequalities along a racial divide in life.

These examples, and the sociocultural and political background against which they are unfolding, are detailed here in order to interrogate the question of how to proceed amidst such implacable positions on the preservation or removal of monuments to historical colonial figures and what these developments mean for the future of monument culture itself. What is being contested in these protests and protests against protests is history and memory: the creation of monuments is about the institutionalization of particular versions of history. Contestation of the right of existing monuments to be honored thus indicates a drive toward changing the official version of history, notably by sectors of society who have historically been excluded and marginalized (and who in some cases continue to be) or who feel themselves to be marginalized in comparison to the unchallenged authority they have enjoyed (as I argue is the case with Afrikaner groups who feel themselves to be culturally under threat).

The demands and counterdemands around the Kruger monument currently circulating include suggestions by the EFF to relocate it to a designated museum, which would function similarly to the Apartheid Museum.[15] Although the statue has been targeted on several occasions, there are no official calls for its permanent destruction. The Afrikaner organizations and groups who oppose its removal refuse to even entertain the thought of change. Bridges notes: "[W]e will not stand for the destruction or even discussions about the removal of the statue of Paul Kruger from Church Square."[16] For Bridges, Hofmeyr, and the Afrikaner groups who feel represented by them, the call for removal of this and other statues associated with the Apartheid era is conflated with a lack of respect for Afrikaner communities and history and with loss of land[17] or the perceived threat of the loss of land. Statements such as "we want our land back"[18] are potentially mystifying because despite a change in dispensation, no exchange in ownership of actual land has occurred that would substantiate such a demand. However, it is possible to contend that what such claims actually signify is a hankering for the unquestioned authority enjoyed by Afrikaners under Apartheid.

There are in addition to these opposing stances, more reconciliatory views regarding the ongoing contestations. Calls for education regarding intersecting histories and the deracialization of South African society are central to moderate views around the issue.[19] However, deracialization (or a kind of color-blindness) is argued here to be untenable against a background of continued stark disparity in access to education, employment, and health care along a racial divide that cannot merely be wished away. The causes of such lingering inequality need to be actively addressed. On the other hand, heightened knowledge of diverse histories is a valuable project. The government's official stance has been one of "reconciliation, nation building and social cohesion"; that vandalism of the statues is a criminal act in contravention of the country's constitution; and that due process, as outlined in the National Heritage Resources Act of 1999, needs to be followed in the contestation of existing monuments.[20,21] The Act states that "heritage resources have the capacity to promote reconciliation, understanding and respect. . . . Heritage resources form an important part of the history and beliefs of communities and must be managed in a way that acknowledges the right of affected communities to be consulted and to participate in their management."[22]

Amid continued frustration around the fate of the Kruger statue, to date the only recourse has been to fence it off with barbed wire. It remains in place, and one does not perceive a sense of urgency in addressing the matter. If monuments are a "constant, public reminder of the foundation[al] values of the state and those in power,"[23] merely preventing further opportunities for protest does not seem to constitute sufficient political will toward sociopolitical redress, regardless of official rhetoric. On February 23, 2018, at a briefing on the twenty-one resolutions that were the outcome of a national consultative task-team convened in 2015, the first ministerial-level announcement on the issue in three years clarified that the Kruger statue would remain in place but would be accompanied by other monuments and artworks.[24] Notably, a statue of Kgosi Mampuru II would be installed. Mampuru is a Bapedi leader who was hanged in 1883 (the year Kruger was first elected president of the ZAR) for refusing to recognize the republic and pay taxes to it.[25]

POSSIBILITIES

This brief review of current monument contestation, ultimately a political endeavor, reveals that the actual removal of monuments is rare, particularly because consensus around the negative reading of a particular monument (or regime and its body of monuments) is exceptional. In instances of large-scale, government-backed monument removal or destruction, political will is in line with official rhetoric (as has happened under drastic regime changes or, for instance, in the aftermath of the Holocaust). In South Africa, which has had a clear regime change from a broadly reviled Apartheid system to a democratic dispensation very widely embraced by the majority of South Africans (particularly initially), the lack of political will to actively address monument contestation seems anomalous.

Instead (as in the United States, particularly in New York), an additive approach has been adopted, where current monuments will be augmented by commemoration of important historical figures quashed or demonized under Apartheid. However, a new project to redress the marginalization of significant South African historical figures has taken shape as an ambitiously scaled monument: the National Heritage Monument, situated on the outskirts of Tshwane/Pretoria. It is a recently constructed monument dedicated to the history of indigenous struggles and, particularly, the bitter struggle for liberation under Apartheid.

The minutes of the parliamentary interrogation of the 2013 Annual Report of the South African Department of Arts and Culture provides some insight into the early stages of conceptualization of the project: four hundred to five hundred life-sized bronze figures of notable leaders "from the 1600s up to 1994" would be commissioned and installed on land provided by the City of Tshwane.[26] The report contextualizes the rationale for creating the vast monument against the 1993 findings of the National Monument Council that "at that time, 99% of South African heritage was about white experiences, white stories and white figures of history."[27] The National Heritage Monument was thus poised to redress a lingering imbalance in representation. The necessity for the monument was furthermore related to key national concerns, such as economic development and national unity: the vast scale of the project would provide much-needed employment in the creative industries as well as construction workers, initially, and later, workers at the site's visitor center and in the envisaged expansion of the monument complex. The scale of the project was calculated to instill national civic pride and to promote "social cohesion and reconciliation."[28] The name of the monument, Long March to Freedom, refers to the similarly titled autobiography *Long Walk to Freedom* (1995) by South Africa's first president under democracy, Nelson Rolihlahla Mandela.[29] The project was, lastly, envisaged to become in the global imaginary what the Giza Pyramids are for Egypt and the Eiffel Tower is for France.[30] This somewhat overblown vision connotes underlying sociopolitical problematics addressed below.

The figures immortalized in bronze and walking in purposeful procession in the direction of "four pillars of the fight for liberation," namely, armed struggle, underground political movements, international solidarity, and mass mobilization (http://www.nhmsa.co.za/monument.html#!Heroes), are certainly inspiring. By April 2016, fifty-six of the (by then narrowed down) total of four hundred envisaged figures had been created and installed on-site, including those of Chief Kgamanyane Pilane (circa 1820–1871), who became leader of the Bakgatla-Baga-Kgafela in 1848; Clements Kadalie (1896–1951) of South Africa's first black national trade union in the early twentieth century; Zainunnisa Gool (1897–1963), founder of the National Liberation League; and human rights agitator and feminist author Olive Schreiner (1855–1920).[31]

As part of the overall National Heritage Monument project, a mentorship program involving the third-year sculpture students of the Department of Fine and Applied Arts of the Tshwane University of Technology was launched in April 2016. It entailed collaboration between the department (represented by sculpture lecturer and project leader Carol Kühn) and the National Heritage Project Company (NHPC), created to drive the overall National Heritage Monument project to completion. The program involved mentoring of the third-year students by industry specialists for the duration of the project and frequent feedback by the main client (the NHPC). The students' fees and materials were also sponsored by the NHPC with funding sourced mainly from the Department of Arts and Culture. The students initially created fourteen maquettes (small-scale representations) of struggle heroes associated with the 1956 Treason Trial. The trial itself was the culmination of the arrest of 156 leaders of the liberation struggle in a predawn raid. The stalwarts were detained in several communal cells, resulting in what Mandela[32] came humorously to describe as "the largest and longest unbanned meeting of the Congress Alliance in years."[33] Out of the fourteen maquettes, three figures, namely those of Duma Nokwe, Frances Baard, and Dorothy Nyembe, were chosen to be sculpted to life size by the students (figure 8.1).[34] These sculpted figures were subsequently cast in bronze (at an external foundry with sufficient capacity) and joined the total of one hundred figures installed at the Heritage site by the end of 2017.[35]

RUPTURES AND CONTINUITIES

Although this epic vision is still unfolding, it can be interpreted as already partially successful in achieving its primary goals, namely, representation of a counterhistory, sociocultural unity and addressing problems arising from South Africa's flagging economy. The embodiment of a crowd of heroes whom one walks among while confronting a disturbing history could work toward dispelling widespread denialist amnesia among South Africans about our shared brutal inheritance as the descendants of either settler communities or colonized communities. This amnesia takes many forms, such as a presumably nihilist sense of defeat on the part of the oppressed in the face of ongoing social inequity, on the one hand, and a persistent lack of knowledge of black history by notably white sectors of society, on the other, who then nevertheless dismiss reference to the incalculable violence of the past as exaggerated. A further layer of the disavowal that arguably characterizes the current South African imaginary might also be ascribed to the deep-seated need to believe that sufficient change is imminent or has materially already occurred.

Countering such resistance to engagement with history and its current effects, the Monument Project concretizes historical figures previously demonized as terrorists, assumed guilty of mere savage and unprovoked violence—terms in which the liberation struggle has been, and in some cases still is, conceptualized. The figures depicted are humanized as we interact

Figure 8.1. *Figure of Frances Baard* in The Long March to Freedom, part of the National Heritage Monument, Fountains Valley Resort, Groenkloof, City of Tshwane. Modeled by Kgaogelo Mashilo, assisted by Sello Letswalo and Ivan Mostert, 2015–2016.

Image copyrighted to the National Heritage Monument and used with permission.

with them on their march. Thus, although the medium (bronze) and the style (realistically depicted figures) conform to the Western canon of monument production, the life-sized scale of the individual characters and their placement on the ground in procession—their accessibility—works to disrupt traditional manifestations of monument culture. In honoring ordinary people distinguished only by their courage and defiance under dehumanizing circumstances, dominant colonial and Apartheid narratives are challenged. Performatively interactive rather than spectacularizing and authoritarian, the monument can be interpreted as a memorial to the politically minoritarian rather than as a monument to past or present figures of power or, alternatively, as an unusual hybrid memorial monument.[36] The observation of detail that has gone into the depiction of each one of the figures (such as Mrs. Baard's spectacle frames and hair ornament) is endearing, or certainly so for the current author, without detracting from her bravery. Such personalization embedded in the particular has the potential to destroy the mental and physical violence that is the outcome of abstracting an "other." That the march is continuously joined (for now) by more figures and the figures themselves are unremittingly under way to some hopeful destination also invokes a sense of unfolding newness and futurity rather than of a lifeless past. The overall sense created by the figures in procession is celebratory, and a ruthlessly one-sided history is contested upon learning about them.

Dozens of young artists and students in South Africa have also unquestionably benefited from the frenetic creation of the bronze figures, and the mentorship program in particular has enabled transferal of skills from established to emerging artists. However, closer scrutiny of the Monument Project reveals aspects of the deep structure of South African society that stubbornly persist. For instance, thirty of the thirty-three artists acknowledged on the official National Heritage Monument website are white, of which twenty are male, reflecting ongoing class division along a racial axis and lack of gender representation in the art industry. The grand scale of the overall project, positioned to rival the pyramids, also paints a picture of hubris emanating from a lingering sense of exceptionalism in tandem with a need for validation. South African exceptionalism, which under Apartheid manifested as a narrative of a chosen *volk* (nation), lives on in an arrogant sense of superiority over "other" African nations and, chillingly, as xenophobia—that most unattractive expression of revanchist nationalism. The archetype of Apartheid might be said to be continually replicated in new forms.

The complex will, furthermore, include the largest water amusement park in Africa in an officially water-scarce country and in an ecologically fragile region. As such, the project openly privileges commercial over ecological considerations. Lastly, the project entails immense expenditure in a country struggling to provide adequate education, health services, and employment to the poor. Transparency over how the proceeds of such a venture might benefit ordinary citizens (specifically workers and the unemployed) on an ongoing basis would legitimize the project from a broadly human rights perspective but would still fail to alleviate ecological concerns. A further possible critique is that the monument can be interpreted as a manipulative hyper-commodification of liberation rhetoric—the endorsement of rebellion and political struggle that the text on the National Heritage Monument website suggests is belied by ongoing attempts to repress current sociopolitical dissent and discredit it as mere ill-discipline amidst the ruling party's ongoing factional struggles. From this perspective it is, lastly, not a far cry to suggest that South Africa is still ruled by an elite that breezily sacrifices the rights and basic chances of economic survival of its citizens as it jostles to serve its own interests. Let the people eat bronze.

CHANGE

This reading of South African monument culture has attempted to trace ruptures and continuities in a post-Apartheid society still riddled by inequality. Disputes about removing or maintaining in place monuments such as the Kruger statue arc back and forth across a history in which changes are discernible but which also highlights disconcerting continuities. The South African currency code is currently still *ZAR*—a telling economic marker in a country where vast mineral resources are yet to sufficiently benefit its workers who, in certain cases, pay with their lives for dissent against economic exploitation (Marikana being a case in point).[37] Nestled in the hills of Tshwane not far from the *Voortrekker* Monument, the National Heritage Monument promises to reignite postliberation civic pride and address economic hardship while state departments squander and misappropriate public funds (the parliamentary interrogation of the 2013 Department of Arts and Culture annual report referred to earlier is revealing in this regard). Thus, although a regime change has brought the universal right to vote—a significant victory—political will to enable actual equality has seemingly stagnated. Such dynamics are revealed in a country's monument culture, as this analysis has attempted to show: change promised by governments and professed through their commissioned monuments does not necessarily translate as change in lived experience for broader society.

The National Heritage Monument almost fulfills its exciting potential to foreground what Philo,[38] with reference to Foucault, describes as bellicose history, or the narrative that "is interested in defining and discovering, beneath the . . . order that has been imposed, the forgotten past of real struggles, actual victories, and defeats which may have been disguised but which remain profoundly inscribed. [Bellicose history] is interested in rediscovering the blood that has dried in the codes." A truly living monument could take the form of commitment to ongoing dissent against crushing power and exploitation and as an unremitting struggle for lived equality—values that cannot be captured by sentimentalizing and commodifying struggle icons. A truly new monument culture would also include the forgotten narratives of noncitizens—a growing demographic made up of migrant workers and refugees. It remains to be seen whether such (bellicose) monument culture can find expression in brick and mortar.

Declaration of interest: the NHPC has collaborated with the Department of Fine and Applied Arts of the Tshwane University of Technology in the production of three of the sculptures installed at the National Heritage Monument. This collaboration took the form of a mentorship project with the students. The students' fees and materials for 2016 were covered by funds sourced by the NHPC, and the department received funding to upgrade its sculpture studio.

NOTES

1. Norimitsu Onishi, "Students in South Africa Protest Slow Pace of Change," *New York Times*, September 8, 2015, https://www.nytimes.com/2015/09/09/world/africa/student-protests-in-south-africa-highlight-dissatisfaction-with-pace-of-change.html.
2. Stephen Castle, "Oxford University Will Keep Statue of Cecil Rhodes," *New York Times*, January 29, 2016, https://www.nytimes.com/2016/01/30/world/europe/oxford-university-oriel-college-cecil-rhodes-statue.html.
3. Richard Garner, "Oxford University Risks 'Damaging Its Standing' If It Pulls Down Cecil Rhodes Statue, Warns Tony Abbott," *Independent*, December 23, 2015, http://www.independent.co.uk/news/education/education-news/oxford-university-risks-damaging-its-standing-if-is-pulls-down-cecil-rhodes-statue-warns-tony-abbott-a6784536.html.
4. Ibid.
5. "Letter from Scholars to the Mayor's Commission on Monuments," December 1, 2017, https://hyperallergic.com/414315/over-120-prominent-artists-and-scholars-call-on-nyc-to-take-down-racist-monuments/
6. Ibid.
7. New York City, "Mayor de Blasio Releases Monuments Commission's Report, Announces Decisions on Controversial Monuments," Published January 12, 2018, http://www1.nyc.gov/office-of-the-mayor/news/030-18/mayor-de-blasio-releases-monuments-commission-s-report-decisions-controversial.
8. Ibid.
9. Calls for a name change of the city from Pretoria to Tshwane intensified in 2015 after the success of the #RhodesMustFall campaign. In 2016, then mayor of Tshwane/Pretoria, Kgosientso Ramokgopa, declared that the name of the capital

would change to Tshwane for the sake of "social cohesion" (Karabo Ngoepe, "Pretoria Name Change Will Go Ahead—Ramokgopa," News24, published April 22, 2016, https://www.news24.com/SouthAfrica/News/pretoria-name-change-will-go-ahead-ramokgopa-20160421).

However, no official name change occurred. On February 23, 2018, then minister of arts and culture, Nathi Mthethwa, announced that the city will still officially be known as Pretoria, a decision made "in the interest of reconciliation" (James Mahlokwane, "Mthethwa at Provincial Consultation on the Transformation of the National Heritage Landscape," IOL News, published February 23, 2018, https://www.iol.co.za/pretoria-news/mthethwa-at-provincial-consultation-on-the-transformation-of-the-national-heritage-landscape-13447690).

The use of either Pretoria or Tshwane currently hinges on personal preference.

10. Kruger was elected president of the Republic of South Africa (*ZAR*) in 1883. He was subsequently reelected for three consecutive terms, ending in 1902 with the defeat of the Republic in the Second Boer War (1899–1902), which rendered it a British colony once more.

11. Alex Mitchley, "EFF Members Allegedly Throw Stones at Kruger Statue," *The Citizen*, April 13, 2015, https://citizen.co.za/news/south-africa/361794/eff-members-allegedly-throw-stones-at-kruger-statue/.

12. Rapula Moatshe, "EFF Brings Pretoria CBD to Standstill," IOL News, November 3, 2016, https://www.iol.co.za/dailynews/news/eff-brings-pretoria-cbd-to-standstill-2086320.

13. Amanda Khoza, "Paul Kruger Statue in Pretoria Vandalised Again," News24, April 11, 2015, https://www.news24.com/SouthAfrica/News/Paul-Kruger-statue-in-Pretoria-vandalised-again-20150411.

14. "Zuma to Blame for Attacks on Statues—AfriForum," News24, April 13, 2015, https://www.news24.com/SouthAfrica/News/Zuma-to-blame-for-attacks-on-statues-AfriForum-20150413.

15. Kristian Meijer, "Heavy Police Presence at EFF Statue Protest," *Pretoria East Rekord*, April 11, 2015, https://rekordeast.co.za/47959/heavy-police-presence-at-eff-statue-protest/.

16. Alex Mitchley, "Tshwane Won't Bow to EFF Pressure on Kruger Statue," *The Citizen*, April 10, 2015, https://citizen.co.za/news/south-africa/359804/tshwane-wont-bow-to-pressure-on-kruger-statue/.

17. Austil Mathebula, "'Boer People Want Their Land Back.'" *The Citizen*, November 28, 2016, https://citizen.co.za/news/south-africa/1358931/boer-people-want-land-back/.

18. Ibid.

19. Ockert De Villiers, "Statues Are Not about Black, White—PE Resident," News24, April 13, 2015, https://www.news24.com/SouthAfrica/News/Alleged-Gandhi-statue-vandal-released-on-bail-20150413.

20. Mitchley, "Tshwane Won't Bow."

21. Adam Wakefield, "Statue Vandalism Is a Criminal Act—Mapisa-Nqakula," News24, April 14, 2015, https://www.news24.com/SouthAfrica/News/Statue-vandalism-is-a-criminal-act-Mapisa-Nqakula-20150414.

22. National Heritage Resources Act, South Africa, *Government Gazette* #19974, Vol. 406, 1999.

23. Mahlokwane, "Mthethwa at Provincial Consultation on the Transformation of the National Heritage Landscape."

24. James Mahlokwane, "Pretoria's Name and Oom Paul's Statue to Stay in Place," IOL News, February 24, 2018, https://www.iol.co.za/news/politics/pretorias-name-and-oom-pauls-statue-to-stay-in-place-13465261.

25. Ibid.

26. "Dali Tambo on National Heritage Monument Project," Parliamentary Monitoring Group, published October 14, 2013, https://pmg.org.za/committee-meeting/16534/.

27. Ibid.

28. Ibid.

29. Nelson R. Mandela, *Long Walk to Freedom: The Autobiography of Nelson Mandela* (Boston: Little, Brown, 1995).

30. "Dali Tambo."

31. Mathe, "The Iron Guard."

32. Mandela, *Long Walk to Freedom*.

33. A complete list of the original 156 arrested Alliance members and information on their background and struggles is available at http://www.sahistory.org.za/topic/treason-trialists-1956 and on the official National Heritage Monument website at http://www.nhmsa.co.za/sculptures.html.

34. The three teams responsible for the life-sized modeling of the chosen figures were Paballo Majela, assisted by Sipho Ntjie and Kamogelo Makwela (Duma Nokwe); Kgaogelo Mashilo, assisted by Sello Letswalo and Ivan Mostert (Frances Baard); and Mamphuti Mabotja, assisted by Lindokuhle Khatide (Dorothy Nyembe).

35. "Welcome to the National Heritage Monument," National Heritage Monument, accessed December 27, 2018, http://www.nhmsa.co.za/index.html#!Introduction.

36. The term *minoritarian* here is used not in the sense of referring to a minority stance politically (that is, as a political view held by a relatively small group of people) or to a group of people merely less numerous than a "majority" against which it would be measured. The term is used in the way that Deleuze and Guattari (1993) employ it to refer to those who do not hold overt sociopolitical power. In South Africa, for instance, a group comprising a physical minority of white people held absolute political power under Apartheid. From this perspective, they were politically "majoritarian," and, it could be argued, still are (Gilles Deleuze and Félix Guattari, *A Thousand Plateaus: Capitalism and Schizophrenia*, trans. Brian Massumi [Minneapolis: University of Minnesota Press, 1993]).

37. On August 16, 2012, thirty-four miners working in the Lonmin-owned Marikana Platinum mine in Rustenburg, South Africa, were killed by members of the South African Police Service in an effort to quell a strike at the mine. The miners were earning an average salary of US$500 per month working at one of the richest platinum mines in the world and went on strike on August 10 for higher salaries and better living conditions. The current (2018) president of South Africa, Cyril Ramaphosa, was on the board of Lonmin at the time and pressured the South Afri-

can Police Service to end the strike, which he rejected as "criminal." The Marikana Massacre, as it has come to be referred to, has been described as "Zuma's Sharpeville," referring to the Sharpeville Massacre of 1960, and the event is regarded as a turning point in the contemporary political landscape of South Africa. See "South Africa's Lonmin Marikana Mine Clashes Killed 34," BBC News Africa, August 17, 2012, http://www.bbc.com/news/world-africa-19292909; "Lonmin an Example of Exploitation," IOL Business Report, August 17, 2012, https://www.iol.co.za/business-report/companies/lonmin-an-example-of-exploitation-1365221#.UCw5d1lS19; Malala Justice, "The Marikana Action Is a Strike by the Poor against the State and the Haves," *The Guardian*, August 17, 2012, https://www.theguardian.com/commentisfree/2012/aug/17/marikana-action-strike-poor-state-haves; Nick Davies, "Marikana Massacre: The Untold Story of the Strike Leader Who Died for Workers' Rights," *The Guardian*, May 19, 2015, https://www.theguardian.com/world/2015/may/19/marikana-massacre-untold-story-strike-leader-died-workers-rights; Paul Trewhela, "Marikana—Zuma's Sharpeville," Dispatch Live, October 30, 2013, http://www.dispatchlive.co.za/news/2013/10/30/marikana-zumas-sharpeville/; and William Gumede, "South Africa: Marikana Is a Turning Point," *The Guardian*, August 29, 2012, https://www.theguardian.com/commentisfree/2012/aug/29/marikana-turning-point-south-africa.

38. Chris Philo, "'Bellicose History' and 'Local Discursivities': An Archaeological Reading of Michel Foucault's Society Must be Defended," in *Space, Knowledge and Power: Foucault and Geography*, ed. Jeremy W. Crampton and Stuart Elden (Aldershot, Hampshire: Ashgate, 2012), 341–67.

CHAPTER 9

Beyond Ruins

Borgoño's Barracks and the Struggle over Memory in Today's Chile

Basil Farraj

La estrella de la esperanza continuará siendo nuestra.

—Víctor Jara[1]

TWENTY-EIGHT YEARS FOLLOWING ITS RETURN TO DEMOCRACY, STRUGGLES over memory are ongoing and in full force in Chile. Since 1990, numerous initiatives, state-sanctioned and otherwise, have taken place toward accounting for the violence committed during Augusto Pinochet's bloody seventeen years in power.[2] These initiatives include work done by the multiple national truth commissions, the placement of memorials and placards in public spaces, the construction of Santiago's Museum of Memory, and ongoing initiatives by relatives of the executed and disappeared. Additionally, the fight for transforming into sites of memory many of the dictatorship's former detention and torture centers has long been one important arena for dealing with the violent past and its ongoing effects in present-day Chile.

Rising to power following the US-supported military overthrow of Salvador Allende's democratically elected government, Pinochet's regime was categorized by the violence it carried against those designated as enemies. This violence was intended to erase the political project of Salvador Allende and to inscribe the norms of a restructured society over the bodies of those at the receiving end of violence. The massive violence—at times selective, at others systemic—unleashed against opponents included kidnappings, executions, forced exile, imprisonment, torture, and enforced disappearances. As Teresa Macias writes, the dictatorship's social reordering project "required the violent elimination of the socialist project through the planned and systemic identification of internal enemies, their deliberate elimination through execution and disappearance, and their subjugation through torture."[3] The detention centers used by the military regime were one of the locations from which this violent reordering took place.

According to the National Commission on Political Imprisonment and Torture—the Valech Commission, as it is more commonly known—the dictatorship's regime employed a network of 1,132 detention centers spread across the country at various stages of its years in power.[4] Years following Chile's political transition, activists, civil society members, former political prisoners, and families of the executed and disappeared began their fight for gaining access to a number of those centers and toward incorporating them within Chile's geographies of memory. A few have successfully been transformed into sites of memory and are open to the public while a few others are at various stages of this struggle for access and over discourse. These struggles have been referred to as processes of recuperation, from the Spanish verb *recuperar*. The use of this particular term already points to the heavily charged act of restoring and bringing to life that which has long been lost and silenced.

This chapter deals with the ongoing work toward recuperating el Cuartel Borgoño "Borgoño's Barracks," one of the dictatorship's former centers of detention and torture, and transforming it into a site of memory. It is argued here that tracing the work to recuperate this particular location of past violence is illustrative of current struggles over memory in present-day Chile. The cuartel reveals the multiple processes of erasure and denial carried out during and after Pinochet's regime and, similarly important, reveals responses to those erasures and denials twenty-eight years following the end of the dictatorship. What do these recent struggles tell about the location of past violence in today's Chile? And how can these struggles and tensions be understood within Chile's context?

Drawing upon fieldwork conducted in Chile,[5] I center this essay on a visit conducted to the cuartel alongside members of *la Corporación Memoria Cuartel Borgoño 1470*. The corporation consists of a number of former prisoners and their family members and activists who have been working toward recuperating this location and transforming it into a site of memory. I trace the location's usage before, during, and after the dictatorship and discuss the particularity of the cuartel as one of the military regime's long-hidden and important detention centers. Referring to aspects of the visit and to conversations held with former prisoners and activists, I describe memory of the cuartel as persistent, despite new constructions and the ruins and rubbles that lay within its walls.

ENCOUNTERING THE CUARTEL

I was in a state of anticipation because the corporation had set the date of our visit to the complex where the notorious Cuartel Borgoño once stood. By that time, I had been attending several of the corporation's meetings and had met a number of former prisoners who were, as part of their journey to multiple imprisonment and torture centers, once held in that fortified site of horror. I was told that the location now hosts offices of the Investigations Police of Chile (PDI).

On an early April morning, I met up with Victoria, a daughter of a former prisoner and a member of the corporation, in Barrio Quinta Normal, blocks away from Chile's acclaimed Museum of Memory. We had met a month before at a memory event held at Santiago's National Stadium, another location where thousands of prisoners were imprisoned and tortured during the first months of the dictatorship. After having breakfast, we headed to a nearby shop to buy packets of flour. Carrying six packets, along with our cameras and a tripod, we made our way to the other side of the Mapocho River in Independencia. It was my first and the corporation's second visit to the cuartel. This visit was intended to collect further evidence, search for traces of the past, and converse with PDI agents. Using flour, the corporation had also intended to mark the physical limits of the location where bodies were once tortured and disappeared.[6]

Awaiting the arrival of other members of the corporation, Victoria and I sat on a bench outside a gate bearing the number 1154 (figure 9.1). The complex had an imposing structure, large gates, and high walls. Victoria began to narrate ways in which the dictatorship worked to occult the presence and usage of this location. It seems strange how such an inescapable location would be hidden from the public, though this should not come as a surprise. Many of the dictatorship's detention and torture centers were able to fully function treading a line between visibility and invisibility: highly visible and centrally located yet maintaining secrecy and invisibility.[7] The rest of the team arrived shortly afterward. Besides Victoria and me, present were three former prisoners (Luisa, Gabriela, and Victor) and two archaeologists.

A few minutes later, four PDI agents, working at the Human Rights Division, arrived and accompanied us to the main entry. We submitted our documents, and following receipt of entry approval, we began our tour in the PDI complex alongside the four agents. At first sight, nothing can possibly allude to the horrors that have occurred within the complex's walls over forty years ago.

FROM PUBLIC FUNCTION TO A FORTIFIED LOCATION OF HORROR
Prior to August 1977, the complex, consisting at that time of five buildings located between *Avenida Santa María* and *Calle General Borgoño*, had served multiple public functions. At distinct periods, the complex hosted the Institute of Hygiene, the Institute of Public Health, and the National Health Service. In August 1977, following the dissolution of the dictatorship's National Intelligence Directorate (DINA), the five-building complex was usurped by the newly formed security agency: Central Nacional de Informaciones (CNI).[8] The formation of the CNI marked a change in the dictatorship's repressive

Figure 9.1. The cuartel's main gate. Notice the number on the gate, 1154. It used to be 1470. Photograph taken by author on April 18, 2017, in front of the Cuartel Borgoño, Santiago, Chile.

strategies. Differing from the DINA, the CNI attempted to institutionalize and systematize state terrorism and aimed to completely dismantle movements of resistance and military rebellion that were emerging against the dictatorship. In particular, the highly specialized CNI worked to eliminate the Revolutionary Left Movement (MIR), the Manuel Rodríguez Patriotic Front (FPMR), and the Popular Unity Action Movement (MAPU) that launched well-organized campaigns against Pinochet's regime.[9]

For eleven years (i.e., until 1988), the complex functioned as a fortified detention center through which thousands of prisoners passed and from which at least eight persons were last seen and thus count among Chile's *detenidos desaparecidos*.[10] The exact number and details of prisoners, as well as the previous usage of the site as a detention center, are not well known due to the lack of archives and to the subsequent demolishing of parts of the complex's buildings. Survivors' testimonies and the work done by the corporation, however, identify the basement and ground floor of a currently nonexistent building, referred to as the bacteriological, as the location of past violence. These two floors, previously dedicated to questions of public health and hygiene, were thus transformed into well-secured locations of horror, violence, and death.

At the cuartel, prisoners were kept blindfolded and naked. They were subjected to electric shocks, suffocation, loud music, death threats, and various other methods of torture. In a published testimony, one of the prisoners recalls being led to the underground floor and hearing blows and hammer noises coming from the upper floor.[11] In another anonymous testimony published in the Valech report, a prisoner describes a close encounter with death. Arriving at the cuartel at night, the prisoner was given a shovel and forced to dig his own grave. He was told that he would not be killed if he would share all that he knew. Responding that he had nothing to tell, he was asked to lie down in the pit he had dug. A gun was loaded and placed on his forehead. After a while, the agents removed him from the pit and escorted him to a military vehicle, handcuffed, blindfolded, and shackled.[12] While not executed, this prisoner's testimony shows that death was always there—at times as a threat and at other times as an act.

In 1988, two years before the country's political transition, the CNI passed the five buildings' cuartel to the PDI and changed the numbers of the main entrance from 1470 to 1154 as a way of erasing the place's history. This strategy of hiding the past was not restricted to the cuartel. In reality, attempts at erasing the past were systematically carried out by the military regime and continued, to varying extents, following the Chilean political transition.[13]

In 1997, the bacteriological building identified by survivors as the main location of detention was demolished in order to construct the PDI's new building. Two additional buildings were demolished to make way for the construction of a large parking lot. Recently, in April 2016, neighbors noticed demolition of the only two remaining buildings and alerted survivors, who in turn organized themselves to save the site. Following organizing efforts, demolition processes ceased, leaving some of the structures of the buildings intact.[14] In June 2016, the National Monuments Council of Chile declared the Cuartel Borgoño as a national monument, thus protecting the location from any further modifications.[15] This can be seen as the first step not only toward monumentalizing the location and its history but also toward constituting it as a site to be constantly revisited.

SEARCHING FOR THE TRACE: *EL SUBTERRÁNEO*

Walking around the complex, the three former prisoners were attempting to recall characteristics of the basement, *el subterráneo*, where they were held over thirty-six years ago. The following is part of a conversation that took place between them and a PDI agent.

> Gabriela: The point is, today, we can't recall the building in which we were held because we never saw it. It, perhaps, is the sensation that guides our remembrance. I obviously did not see the building when I was held there—it was my senses telling me where I was walking then.

Victor: In my case, I only saw the building once: from the second floor . . . when I was in the basement, they took me to a bathroom on the second floor and I was able to peek and look at the surroundings—there was a yard, and there were a number of CNI agents there.

Luisa: They took you to a bathroom located on a second floor?

Victor: This is what . . . as I was in the basement, they took me to the first or second floor . . . but in any case, I saw the yard from the bathroom. There were agents: relaxing, talking, men and women, there, yes, so . . .

Gabriela: It might have been the first floor . . .

Victor: Yes, it might have been. I don't know. I remember going up stairs different to those leading to the basement. Another stairs. Also, this bathroom was high, very high.

PDI agent: It might have been a second floor, then.

Gabriela: Yes, it might have been.

As this conversation was taking place, the three former prisoners were standing in front of an entirely new building built on top of the location of their past imprisonment. It had no resemblance to the old bacteriological building. Nonetheless, they were attempting to locate the past and search for its trace knowing that, once, the complex looked and felt differently. Prisoners were blindfolded throughout their detention period, and they have no visual memory of the building or the basement. The only reference to the location of their imprisonment was through a couple of old photos they had found and printed in an attempt to imagine the cuartel's previous existence. Indeed, the conversation above points to the difficulty of recalling the past. Yet memory was somehow fully alive and present during this visit.

Following nearly thirty minutes during which the archaeologists and the rest of the team were searching for material traces that might have survived demolition, we made our way to the PDI building's basement. As we descended, Gabriela, Luisa, and Victor were discussing among themselves, trying to recall their arrival to the *subterráneo*; the doors they might have been brought from; and their descent, blindfolded, to the cells where they were held and tortured for days. This was the first time they had entered this part of the PDI building. They commented on the difficulty of descending to the basement and began walking around and examining the basement, in silence.

In her critique of Chilean transition politics and official memory, Nelly Richard writes:

Tribunals, commissions, and monuments to human rights regularly quote memory (they mention her) but leave aside from their diligent wording all the wounded substance of remembrance: the psychic density, the magnitude of the experience, the emotional wake, the scarring of something unforgettable that resists being submissively molded into the perfunctory forms of judicial procedure or inscription on an institutional plaque.[16]

This short journey, descending down from the PDI building's ground floor toward the basement, powerfully points to the "unforgettable," and "wounded substance of remembrance" that persists many years after imprisonment and after numerous attempts at reckoning with the violent past. It was the act of descending, charged with violence and its memory, that forcibly brought the past into the present and where the past through its besiegement, enclosure, and violence can be located.

TRACES, RUINS, AND THE CHALLENGE OF MEMORY

Leaving the basement in silence, we began to walk around the exterior of the buildings. A few moments later, one of the archeologists stopped in front of a street sign bearing the name *Coronel Lopez de Alcazar*. Holding an old map, he tried to locate, to the closest extent possible, where the bacteriological had once existed. We all gathered around, the four police officers and the rest of the team. This sign had survived demolition and erasure. The former prisoners began to narrate other aspects of what they recalled: the sound of the Mapocho river, the long drive to the cuartel, their arrival, the sensation of hearing a door open to allow passage for military vehicles, and hearing heavy street movements from their confinement in the *subterráneo*.

The sign was pointing to a nonexistent street. But that did not matter. While not representing a material trace of past violence or a re-creation of it, the street sign invoked remembrance of the past and brought forward memories of past incarceration and violence. Perhaps, forty years ago, military vehicles carrying soon-to-be tortured prisoners had to cross this street on their way to the cuartel's gates. This might also not be the case. But during this memory-charged visit, the street sign formed an essential part of the work toward constructing a narrative of the past and of the cuartel.

Near the end of our visit, we headed toward the two buildings that, to an extent, survived last year's demolition attempts. The corporation is demanding complete access to these two buildings in order to have a physical place of memory in ways mirroring that of other centers of detention turned places of memory. For the moment, it is not demanding the recuperation of the entirety of the PDI complex nor the location where prisoners were previously incarcerated and tortured.

These two buildings were in an utter state of ruin. Parts of the walls had been knocked out; it appeared that windows and doors had been removed and replaced with wooden objects; shards were lying all around; and the outer stair steps were similarly destroyed. Since the buildings were closed, we were not able to enter and examine them. However, a few moments later, one of the former prisoners managed to find a hole through which we were able to view the interior of one of the buildings: it, similarly, was in a state of ruin.

Upon leaving the cuartel, Gabriela, Luisa, and Victor commented on how strange it was saying good-bye to the PDI officers who were accompanying us and to leave the cuartel as they did: freely walking out of the main door. The buildings in ruins do not stand in the exact location of past violence and torture. Yet the former prisoners and activists were closely examining them as if they were. Similar to the way the basement was examined, they were searching for any trace that might have survived. What explains this interest in two destroyed buildings full of shards and wood?

FORCING THE PAST INTO THE PRESENT

The search for traces of the past and the fight against official erasures form part of the symbolic and material effects of the original violence, which continues to this day. The visit to the cuartel brings forward the impact of the prisoners' experience, its invisible traces, and the difficulties of remembering the violent past. The afterlife of past violence is present in attempts at transforming this location into a place of memory where the past is dealt with and brought forward.

The visit and the ongoing work of the corporation have successfully marked the entire PDI complex with the past violence and torture that once took place within its walls. The basement does not hold any physical trace of past violence; the sign that potentially points to a street marking the physical territory of the cuartel and the ruins have all been forcibly inscribed as part of the memory of past violence. While the functioning of the cuartel had changed, it has been, and still is, marked as a space where well-calculated and systematic violence took place and where memory practices continue to evoke the past and its pain.

The work toward monumentalizing the cuartel is the former prisoners' and activists' response to this resistant afterlife of past violence. Through the corporation's struggle and that of others, Chile's violent past will continue to be forcibly brought into the present as a reminder that much work still needs to be done and that the past can't easily be subjected to erasure and silence.

NOTES

1. Víctor Jara, Chilean singer, poet, and theater director, was imprisoned, tortured, and later executed by the military regime on September 16, 1973.
2. Accounting for the violence carried out by the dictatorship's regime from September 11, 1973, until March 1990, has been a long process, and the numbers of those affected are continuously debated, added to, and contested. The multiple truth commissions and works by activists and scholars reveal varying aspects of the ways in which thousands of victims were subjected to torture, imprisonment,

executions, and enforced disappearances. Consult the Retting and the Valech Commission for an official accounting of the violence. See, inter alia, Steve J. Stern, *Reckoning with Pinochet: The Memory Question in Democratic Chile, 1989–2006* (Durham: Duke University Press, 2010); and Macarena Gómez-Barris, *Where Memory Dwells: Culture and State Violence in Chile* (Berkeley: University of California Press, 2009), for an extensive discussion on the dictatorship's violence and its relation to struggles over memory.

3. Teresa Macias, "'Tortured Bodies': The Biopolitics of Torture and Truth in Chile," *The International Journal of Human Rights* 17, no. 1 (2013): 114.

4. Comisión Nacional sobre Prisión Política y Tortura, *Informe de La Comisión Nacional Sobre Prisión Política y Tortura*, La Nación S.A, 261, https://www.indh.cl/bb/wp-content/uploads/2017/01/informe.pdf.

5. The fieldwork was carried out in Santiago and in a number of other cities and towns between February and June 2017. To protect the identity of contacts, the names mentioned here have been anonymized.

6. This visible intervention in the location did not occur because PDI agents preferred for it to take place on a different day. However, the idea can be thought of as an attempt by the corporation to mark the space of past violence and to visibly invoke memory of past violence.

7. Other examples include Londres 38, Chile's National Stadium, Chile's Stadium (now named Victor Jara's Stadium), and Clínica Santa Lucía.

8. Red Metropolitana de Sitios de Memoria, *20 Años de Lucha y Resistencias por la Recuperación de Sitios de Memoria*, Consejo Nacional de la Cultura y las Artes, 2016, 135.

9. Ibid., 136.

10. Ibid., 140.

11. Clara de las Mercedes Maldonado Herrera, Testimonio en Vida," in *Cien Voces Rompen el Silencio: Testimonios de ex presos políticos de la dictadura militar en Chile (1973–1990)*, ed. Wally Kunstman Torres and Victoria Torres Ávila (Santiago: Ediciones de la Dirección de Bibliotecas, 2008), 320.

12. Comisión Nacional sobre Prisión Política y Tortura, 239.

13. For instance, following the dissolution of the DINA, the property of Villa Grimaldi, another center of detention and torture, was first passed to the CNI and then, to a construction company. Similarly, property of Londres 38 was passed to the O'Higgins Institute, and the street direction was changed from thirty-eight to forty for many years. As is well known, struggles by former prisoners and activists managed to restore both locations and convert them into a site of memory.

14. Red Metropolitana de Sitios de Memoria, 140.

15. Camila Medina, "Ex Cuartel Borgoño es declarado Monumento Histórico Nacional," Diario y Radio Uchile, June 9, 2016, http://radio.uchile.cl/2016/06/09/ex-cuartel-borgono-es-declarado-monumento-historico-nacional.

16. Nelly Richard, *Cultural Residues—Chile in Transition* (Minneapolis: University of Minnesota Press, 2004), 18.

BIBLIOGRAPHY

Comisión Nacional sobre Prisión Política y Tortura. *Informe de La Comisión Nacional Sobre Prisión Política y Tortura.* La Nación S.A. https://www.indh.cl/bb/wp-content/uploads/2017/01/informe.pdf.

Gómez-Barris, Macarena. *Where Memory Dwells: Culture and State Violence in Chile.* Berkeley: University of California Press, 2009.

Macias, Teresa. "'Tortured Bodies': The Biopolitics of Torture and Truth in Chile." *The International Journal of Human Rights* 17, no. 1 (2013): 113–32.

Maldonado Herrera, Clara de las Mercedes. "Testimonio en Vida." In *Cien Voces Rompen el Silencio: Testimonios de ex presos políticos de la dictadura militar en Chile (1973–1990)*, edited by Wally Kunstman Torres and Victoria Torres Ávila, 317–21. Santiago: Ediciones de la Dirección de Bibliotecas, 2008.

Medina, Camila. "Ex Cuartel Borgoño es declarado Monumento Histórico Nacional." Diario y Radio Uchile, June 9, 2016. http://radio.uchile.cl/2016/06/09/ex-cuartel-borgono-es-declarado-monumento-historico-nacional.

Red Metropolitana de Sitios de Memoria. *20 Años de Lucha y Resistencias por la Recuperación de Sitios de Memoria.* Consejo Nacional de la Cultura y las Artes, 2016.

Richard, Nelly. *Cultural Residues—Chile in Transition.* Minneapolis: University of Minnesota Press, 2004.

Stern, Steve J. *Reckoning with Pinochet: The Memory Question in Democratic Chile, 1989–2006.* Durham: Duke University Press, 2010.

CHAPTER 10

Iconoclasm and Imperial Symbols

The Gough and Victoria Monuments in Ireland and the British World, 1880–1990

Derek N. Boetcher

THE CURRENT MONUMENTAL LANDSCAPE IN DUBLIN, IRELAND, IS MUCH different than the one an Irish citizen would have encountered in the early twentieth century. Several monuments commemorating British monarchs and military figures have been destroyed, and the statues of General Gough (erected 1880) and Queen Victoria (erected 1908) have been moved out of the country. All of these monuments experienced acts of iconoclasm. An examination of the migration of imperial symbols is important because this movement of commemorative objects can be viewed as a form of iconoclasm that goes beyond the traditional definition of physical attempts at image-breaking. The statues of General Gough and Queen Victoria that were removed from Dublin and are currently residing in Northumberland, England, and Sydney, Australia, respectively, have represented the British Empire for over a hundred years and generated wide-ranging responses to the idea of imperial belonging. These commemorative artworks, along with others erected in Ireland and the Dominions in the late nineteenth and early twentieth centuries, have changed sites in response to these countries gaining independence from the empire. In this essay, I apply an expanded definition of iconoclasm to the migration of these monuments and then examine these acts of iconoclasm in reference to imperial and postimperial representations of power, symbolism, identity, and memory in connection to the British Empire and Ireland's relationship with it.

The traditional definition of iconoclasm is the breaking, or often, the destruction, of physical icons or symbols. The most common reason to destroy monuments, according to Leslie Brubaker, "is to annihilate the belief system that they are thought to embody."[1] To consider the destruction of such monuments an act of iconoclasm, the individuals involved must have acted intentionally, although Fabio Rambelli and Eric Reinders contend that such intentions can be either positive or negative. Further, and more importantly for the present analysis, Rambelli and Reinders view iconoclasm as a series of actions, not just a single destructive incident, that influence the physical state, context, or meaning of the object. Thus, iconoclasm can be acted out within a variety of contexts, including the physical migration of a controversial monument from its original to a new site. This applies to both cases examined here. Over several decades, the Lord Gough monument experienced multiple physical attacks and governmental attempts to remove the statue before its eventual movement out of Ireland. The statue of Queen Victoria was also moved several times in Ireland, and its fate was debated throughout the twentieth century before it finally migrated to Australia.

Moreover, the fragmentation, mutilation, or at times, the complete removal of a monument may not necessarily be successful in destroying the belief system to which it is supposedly connected. Taking up an argument by Megan O'Neil, I contend that the sites of either damaged or destroyed monuments can be viewed as often retaining their symbolic potency and connections to both their pasts and presents. The sites where Lord Gough and Queen Victoria once stood in Dublin are intriguing examples of all these concepts of iconoclasm since these artworks and their meanings still inform, if not haunt, the city's landscape. But these works also retain their symbolic vitality since they continue to exist in new locations with imperial and postimperial pasts and presents. A potentially useful way to assess this form of iconoclasm through migration is to consider Dario Gamboni's suggestion that iconoclasm is not only about the meanings destroyed monuments have for their former sites but that their destruction may stimulate the production of new objects, particularly ones that are intended "to proclaim their differences from their predecessors."[2] In this case study, I am expanding Gamboni's approach to iconoclasm by considering the meanings migrated monuments have for their original sites as well as the symbolic differences that these objects project at their new sites.

Field Marshall Viscount Gough (1779–1869) was a British military officer who commanded in more general actions than any other officer except Wellington during his era. In 1814, following his services in China, he was created a baronet and made commander-in-chief in India. In 1815, he was knighted for having distinguished himself in the Peninsula War. Although he had an overall excellent military reputation, it was tarnished a bit in 1849 following a pyrrhic victory over the Sikhs at Chillanwallah. This action led to his being given the nickname the "Hammer of the Sikhs," but his victories in India nonetheless resulted in Britain's annexation of the Punjab. The statue of Gough presents an interesting wrinkle in the saga of iconoclasm, in its traditionally understood forms, in Ireland. Iconoclastic acts in Ireland have typically been committed against monuments to British royals or British-born military figures, such as the statues of King William III, King George II, or Admiral Lord Nelson. But Gough was an Irishman born in County Limerick, and he had lived in his native country whenever he was not on military service within the empire. Although the Gough statue did not seem to illicit similar bad feelings about an imperial subject having been commemorated in Dublin, it still experienced attacks and was eventually sold and moved to England.

The idea of erecting a statue to commemorate Gough followed his death on March 2, 1869, when his friends, viewing him as an upstanding Irishman, contended that a monument funded by public subscriptions should be placed on a prominent site in Dublin. On May 21, 1869, Gough's friends formed a memorial committee and offered the commission for the monument to the Irish-born sculptor J. H. Foley. Having been granted the metal for the statue by the British government, Foley began a slow process of designing and casting the work. Foley was unable to complete the statue before dying in 1874, but he declared in his will that his leading pupil, Thomas Brock, take over the work. Although Brock sculpted most of Gough's figure, a shortage of funds forced him to use a mold of the horse Foley designed for his renowned 1858 statue of Viscount Hardinge in Calcutta. Even so, the *Irish Times* asserted at the unveiling of the statue that it was "a fine specimen of Mr. Foley's genius. Lord Gough is represented on horseback in his uniform of Colonel of the Guards at a review of the regiment. His head is bare, and in his right hand he holds the baton of his rank as Field Marshal, while the various decorations and medals he received are depicted on his breast" (figure 10.1).[3] The newspaper also noted the British Parliament's grant by explaining that the bronze for the equestrian statue had been cast from "fifteen tons of gun metal from cannon captured by Lord Gough, principally in China."[4]

Although the memorial committee made its decision to erect a monument to Lord Gough in 1869, it took several years to select a site for the statue. In 1872, the Dublin Corporation granted a site in Foster Place for the monument, but Foley and the memorial committee did not view this as a prominent enough place to honor Gough. The memorial committee in 1878 suggested placing the statue on the south side of the new Carlisle Bridge on the River Liffey. Some members of the Dublin Corporation were amenable to granting this new site to the memorial committee, but nationalists on the O'Connell monument committee objected to it. These nationalists had erected a monument to the memory of Daniel O'Connell (1775–1847), the nineteenth-century Irish nationalist leader and important figure in Catholic emancipation, on the north side of Carlisle Bridge. They argued that a statue with Gough's imperial connections should not be in such close proximity to their nationalist hero and pressured the Dublin Corporation to deny the site on the south side of the river in July 1879. A location for the Gough statue was eventually decided upon on the main road in Phoenix Park, on the west side of Dublin. It was unveiled on February 21, 1880.

Figure 10.1. Lord Gough Monument, John Henry Foley, completed by Thomas Brock, 1880. Bronze equestrian statue, Phoenix Park, Dublin, Ireland.
Image Courtesy of the National Library of Ireland.

The statue of Gough was intended to commemorate an Irishman, but from the outset, some observers saw it as a celebration of empire. In fact, the *Irish Times* made note of the monument's imperial status in the newspaper's assessment of the statue's unveiling. The article published on February 23, 1880, states that

> The occasion was even one of more than national importance. In many lands— in every quarter of the globe—the soldier whose name and fame were being commemorated had been the instrument of the Empire's policy, the pioneer of British interests, and many nations will now learn that the seal of approval has been put by his native country to the work of the Irishman who, in so many hard-fought fields, led the armies of England to victory.[5]

Further, some attendees believed that the monument would have been more appropriate for a site in London since so many British soldiers were present at the ceremony that the Duke of Marlborough, Lord Lieutenant of Ireland, mentioned that the park looked like the Champs de Mars of Dublin.[6]

Irish observers may not have been pleased with the Gough monument's imperial status, but the statue escaped being vandalized or subjected to acts of iconoclasm for several decades. This was not the case for quite a few other monuments in Dublin, especially by the early twentieth century. Although vandalism of monuments with imperial connections occurred throughout the period of British rule in Ireland, radical nationalists did not engage in more significant acts of iconoclasm until after the 1916 Easter Rising and the establishment of the Irish Free State in 1922. After 1922, iconoclastic actions occurred in Dublin with greater frequency. By this time, as Yvonne Whelan argues, "when Ireland stood on the cusp of independence, the symbolic fabric of the capital had come to embody and reflect the struggle for superiority, victory and ultimately power, that persisted between Britain and one of its kingdoms."[7] The statues of King William III in College Green (1701) and King George II in St. Stephen's Green (1758) were bombed on Armistice Day in 1928. It is not stated who ordered or conducted repairs to the monument to King George II following the 1928 attack, but the restored statue was significantly damaged by another explosion in 1937 and was removed from St. Stephen's Green. In 1958, the statue of the Earl of Carlisle was bombed. This work was located in the Phoenix Park on the western side of Dublin, not far from the site of Lord Gough's monument. The Irish government and Irish press often quickly accused the republican movement of these bombings, but the Irish nationalists began to distance themselves from these incidents by declaring that they were concerned with contemporary political issues, not symbols of the past.

The view that the Gough monument positively promoted the British Empire eventually led to the work being attacked on multiple occasions in the mid-twentieth century. On Christmas Eve 1944, the figure of Gough was beheaded and his sword was removed.[8] In October 1956, paint was poured over the statue.[9] In November 1956, the horse's right hind leg was blown off.[10] Then, at 12:45 a.m. on Monday, July 23, 1957, a group of French bombing experts associated with the IRA set off a large explosion that knocked the entire statue from its base. Added to the 1956 damage that had not yet been repaired, two more of the horse's legs were severed and its belly had a large hole in it, and the tail, ears, stirrups, reins, and head were cracked. Gough's head was blown off the statue, and one boot, epaulette, and the baton were damaged.[11] The Office of Public Works removed the severely damaged statue from Phoenix Park and placed it in storage for the next twenty-nine years at the Royal Hospital, Kilmainham, which at that time was being used as a storage location for property belonging to the National Museum of Ireland. Although various interested groups and citizens suggested that the plinth, which remained in the park, should have a new statue of possibly St. Patrick or Thomas Davis placed on it, the Irish government directed the Board of Works to remove the granite base in 1962.[12]

Whereas the 1966 destruction of Nelson's Pillar was either celebrated or not lamented, the acts of iconoclasm against the Gough monument were condemned and regretted—at least from an artistic if not an imperial or post-imperial perspective. In a 1962 piece in *The Irish Times*, a commentator argues that "the Gough statue was politically obnoxious only to lunatics; in itself, it was a thing of beauty."[13] In 1966, an art lecturer at the Dublin Municipal Gallery declared that the destruction of the Gough monument was a regrettable act.[14] John Armstrong, the news editor for *The Irish Times*, asserted in a 1969 commentary that the removal of the Gough monument from the landscape of Dublin was a considerable artistic loss.[15] These critiques did not lead to the statue being restored, and little more was spoken about the artwork until the 1980s, when its migration from Ireland was conducted.

Taking up once again the concept that iconoclasm is a series of actions against an object, such as the Gough monument, the Fianna Fáil government's 1967 contention that Ireland needed to dispose of "this embarrassing piece of sculpture" was an iconoclastic act that influenced the statue's meaning and eventually its physical state and context.[16] While the primary iconoclastic acts against the statue of Lord Gough had been the physical attacks in the 1940s and 1950s that led to its removal from the Phoenix Park, the Fianna Fáil declaration further diminished Irish opinion of the imperial symbol of Gough and ultimately led to its migration to England. This declaration was not followed up on until August 1986, when the art collector Robert Guinness of Straffan, County Kildare, purchased the statue of Lord Gough from the Irish government for less than £1,000. The condition that the artwork be removed from Ireland was still valid since the government had never formally rescinded it. Guinness did not immediately take the statue out of the country; rather, in 1988, he sold it to a distant relative of Gough, who had it restored by the Newcastle blacksmiths, J. S. Lunn and Sons, and in 1990 erected the newly refurbished monument at his home, Chillingham Castle in Northumberland, England. Thus, the migration of the statue of Gough to England can be seen as a final act of iconoclasm against the monument since its physical location and context were changed. No longer would it reside on Irish soil and be seen as a symbol of British imperialism; rather, it could now be viewed as a memorial to a family member in a pastoral setting on English land.

However, not everyone was content with the sale and removal of this imperial symbol. For example, Teachta Dála (TD) Ruairi Quinn, the Minister for Public Service and then the deputy leader of the Labour Party, during a series of parliamentary sessions between 1987 and 1991, inquired about the possibility of having the statue returned to Ireland and re-erected in a public place in Dublin, such as Mountjoy Square, which was near where the sculptor Foley had lived. Nothing came of these inquiries, and the Gough monument continues in its place at Chillingham Castle to this day.

Figure 10.2. Queen Victoria Monument, John Hughes, 1908. Bronze, on marble pedestal with bronze figures, Leinster House lawn, Dublin, Ireland.
Image Courtesy of the National Library of Ireland.

As with the series of iconoclastic actions that resulted in the migration of a controversial imperial symbol out of Ireland as demonstrated by the case of the Gough monument, a similar migratory, albeit less destructive, case of iconoclasm can be made with Dublin's statue of Queen Victoria. In 1900, following Queen Victoria's visit to Ireland, the Royal Dublin Society met and approved the erection of a statue in her honor in front of their headquarters at Leinster House (figure 10.2). On February 15, 1908, the memorial by the Irish sculptor John Hughes was unveiled at a festive ceremony. Leinster House at the time was the headquarters of the Royal Dublin Society, but the building became the parliament house of the Irish Free State in 1922. This led to the Irish expressing discomfort about the statue's position. During the next twenty-six years, Parliament and the press carried out a lengthy debate over the statue's fate. This debate can be viewed as an extended iconoclastic act since the commentary routinely featured language that worked to dismantle the positive imperial symbolism embodied by a royal statue. A common sentiment, as proclaimed in *The Irish Times* in 1929, was that the continued presence of the statue in front of Leinster House was "repugnant to national feeling, and that, from an artistic point of view, it disfigures the architectural beauty of the parliamentary (Oireachtas) buildings."[17] In 1933, members of Fianna Fáil expressed their frustration that "this relic of imperialism should still disgrace the precincts of our Parliamentary institution."[18] However, in 1948, the statue was still standing in front of Leinster House. In a parliamentary debate that summer, TD Con Lehane declared that "the national feelings of the majority of Irishmen are outraged by the failure to remove the statue of a foreign monarch from the Quadrangle at Leinster House."[19] Finally, in July of that year, the Irish parliament ordered that the statue be transported to the grounds of the Royal Hospital Kilmainham in western Dublin. The official reason for finally moving the statue from in front of Leinster House was that a car park was to be developed on the site. This was little more than a diplomatic statement intended to make the statue's removal seem apolitical to prevent dissent from any sympathetic Irish or British groups.

Despite the statue's removal to a less central and symbolic location in Dublin, the Irish government was interested in completely abolishing Victoria from the country. But the desire to eliminate the monument from Ireland did not result in physical attacks on the artwork; rather, the Irish government entertained offers to purchase the monument and move it to another country. In the late 1940s and early 1950s, various cities in Canada, including London, Peterborough, and Victoria, voiced interest in purchasing the statue but were unable to gather the funds necessary to ship the work. In the early 1980s, Frank Atkinson, the director of the Beamish North of England, Open Air Museum, inquired about moving the statue to England in anticipation of a royal visit to the museum. Atkinson suggested that the statue could be unveiled "as the formal monument in the visit."[20] No deal was made to send the statue to England since it was determined that the artwork was too big for its intended exhibition space at Beamish.

When restoration work on the Royal Hospital began in 1980, the statue was moved out of Dublin to the grounds of a former children's reformatory in Daingean, County Offaly, where it sat in an overgrown yard near other works held by the National Museum of Ireland. The refurbished hospital was opened in May 1991, as the Irish Museum of Modern Art, but the statue of Queen Victoria does not seem to have been included in any plans for bringing it back to the hospital grounds as part of a sculpture garden. Instead, the Irish government continued to field offers for an interested group to remove this imperial symbol from the country.

Finally, in 1983, the city of Sydney, Australia, asked about purchasing the statue to position in front of its restored Queen Victoria Building (QVB). The QVB had originally been commissioned in 1892 as a grand new market building to complement the adjacent Town Hall, which was regarded as a Victorian masterpiece. Although the QVB was considered by many to be Sydney's architectural masterpiece upon its opening in 1898, successive city councils saw the building primarily as a financial liability. During its early existence, the building was a vibrant market, but as the twentieth century progressed, it fell into disuse and disregard. Restoration work on the QVB began in 1983. As the renovations progressed over two years, Neil Glasser, the director of promotions for the QVB, visited several countries to inquire about the possibility of gaining possession of one of several different Queen Victoria monuments before finding success in Ireland. Although there was some opposition in both countries to moving the statue, including from some Australians with republican sympathies, the Irish government proceeded to donate the monument in August 1986 as a "permanent loan" to the people of Sydney in a "spirit of good will and friendship."[21] This agreement between Ireland and Australia can be seen as a positive reinforcement of the relationship between two former British colonies; however, it should not be forgotten that the result was Ireland's ability to shed itself of a "repugnant" imperial symbol by effectively giving it to a postimperial entity interested in embracing and celebrating a statue with imperial associations. As if the iconoclastic action of migrating the statue of Queen Victoria out of the country was not enough for Ireland, the government added a stipulation that the monument not be recognized as an imperial symbol. As Martina Droth explains, "the gift of the statue came with a crucial condition. The monument was not to be understood as celebrating Australia's bicentennial year in 1988; the gift from the Irish people was not to be implicated in British colonial history. As such, the unveiling ceremony took place in advance of the bicentennial. The Irish ambassador was not present."[22] Even so, the newly placed statue of Queen Victoria was unveiled in Sydney on December 20, 1987, by Sir Eric Neal, chief commissioner. Further, the building and the monument were visited by Queen Elizabeth II on May 4, 1988, during Sydney's bicentenary celebrations. Thus, the decades-long iconoclastic odyssey of the Queen Victoria statue ended with its placement in a major urban center of a former dominion, allowing it to continue to project imperial symbolism in a new, and seemingly more appreciated, postimperial setting.

Ultimately, this analysis has demonstrated that iconoclasm is intimately connected to the reception and treatment of imperial monuments over time. But, as has been argued, an expanded definition of iconoclasm is needed to account for the migration of controversial or "outdated" monumental artworks. Also, by accepting the movement of monuments as iconoclastic in a way that allows for the evolution of the objects' symbolism, and not just available as a destructive act, these artworks can still hold meaning in new locations. Further, by constructing a history of connections focused on acts of iconoclasm performed against monuments, the formation of a nation can be reframed from being merely the ascendancy of national history to imagining an empire that was being remade to incorporate a variety of political entities. This approach can demonstrate how the settler colonies represented and remembered their positions and interactions *within* the webs of empire and Commonwealth over time. On an experiential level, the erasing of these imperial symbols can be recognized as having broken both horizontal and vertical connections between Ireland and the former component parts of the British Empire. The physical symbols of Lord Gough and Queen Victoria no longer stand in Dublin to provoke in the viewer of the statues memories and an identity that once connected them to both Britain and the individual colonies throughout the empire. But, instead of resulting in a mesh of imperial connections that was completely broken because of the destruction of its nodes, the statues of Lord Gough and Queen Victoria that sat in prominent locations in Dublin continue to exist in the postimperial Irish imagination and can add nuance to our understanding of how the empire's citizens negotiated and renegotiated their relations with the metropole and each other over time.

NOTES

1. Leslie Brubaker, "Making and Breaking Images and Meaning in Byzantium and Early Islam," in *Striking Images, Iconoclasms Past and Present*, ed. Stacy Boldrick, Leslie Brubaker, and Richard Clay (Surrey, England: Ashgate, 2013), 13.
2. Anne McClanan and Jeff Johnson, "Introduction: 'O for a muse of fire. . . . ,'" in *Negating the Image: Case Studies in Iconoclasm*, ed. Anne McClanan and Jeff Johnson (Aldershot: Ashgate, 2005), 6.
3. "Statue of Lord Gough," *The Irish Times*, October 15, 1878, 8.
4. Ibid. Also, see "London, Saturday, July 23, 1870," *The Times*, July 23,1870, 8.
5. "Unveiling the Gough Memorial," *The Irish Times*, February 23, 1880, 6.
6. "Unveiling of the Gough Statue," *The Irish Times*, February 28, 1880, 2.
7. Yvonne Whelan, "The Construction and Destruction of a Colonial Landscape: Monuments to British Monarchs in Dublin before and After Independence," *Journal of Historical Geography* 28, no. 4 (2002): 512–13.
8. See "Gough Statue Beheaded," *The Irish Times*, December 27, 1944, 2; and Quidnunc, "An Irishman's Diary: The Headless Horseman," *The Irish Times*, December 29, 1944, 3.
9. See "Memorandum for the Government: The Gough Statue in Phoenix Park," September 3, 1957, NAI TSCH/3/S16307 A.
10. See "Gough Monument Damaged," *The Irish Times*, November 6, 1956, 1.
11. See "Gough Monument Wrecked by Explosion," *The Irish Times*, July 23, 1957, 1.
12. See "Cabinet Minutes—Gough Statue, Phoenix Park: Removal of Base," October 6, 1961, NAI TSCH/3/S16307 B/61; "Memorandum for the Government: The Gough Statue in Phoenix Park," September 27, 1961, NAI TSCH/3/S16307 B/95; and "No Bronze Horse in the Land of Horses," *The Irish Times*, April 5, 1962.
13. "Horseman, Pass By," *The Irish Times*, April 5, 1962, 7.

14. See "Demolition of Gough Statue Regrettable," *The Irish Times*, October 19, 1966, 8.

15. See John Armstrong, "Dublin's Vanishing Statues—1," *The Irish Times*, November 26, 1969, 12.

16. Frank McDonald, "Gough Statue May Return Home," *The Irish Times*, September 10, 1986, 1.

17. "Queen Victoria Statue," *The Irish Times*, August 9, 1929, OPW/9/A25/16/1/37. Ernest Blythe, the Irish Minister of Finance, also stated that "the statue in question is not regarded as a valuable or attractive work of art" Irish Parliamentary Debates, Ceisteanna, Questions—Oral Answers—Queen Victoria Statue, 36, no. 10 (December 11, 1930), 6.

18. "Queen Victoria Statue," *The Irish Times*, February 20, 1933; also, see "Statue of Queen Victoria Outside Leinster House," *The Irish Press*, February 8, 1933.

19. Irish Parliamentary Debates, Ceisteanna, Questions, Oral Answers—Queen Victoria Statue, 111, no. 13 (June 30, 1948), 3.

20. "Letter from Frank Atkinson, Museum Director, Beamish North of England, Open Air Museum to Attracta Halpin, Arts Adviser, Department of the Taoiseach," July 12, 1984, National Archives of Ireland, 2014/105/25: Queen Victoria Statue, Leinster Lawn, Removal.

21. Whelan, "The Construction and Destruction of a Colonial Landscape, 524–27.

22. Martina Droth, Jason Edwards, and Michael Hatt, *Sculpture Victorious: Art in an Age of Invention, 1837–1901*. (New Haven: Yale Center for British Art in Association with Yale University Press, 2014), 145. Also, see City of Sydney Archives, Y03-00790: Queen Victoria Statue, Official Unveiling, December 20, 1987.

CHAPTER 11

Monuments of Refugee Identity

Pain, Unity, and Belonging in Three Monuments of Cappadocian Greeks

ZELIHA NILÜFER NAHYA AND SAIM ÖRNEK

DURING THE CONFERENCE OF LAUSANNE (1922–1923), TURKEY AND GREECE signed the Agreement on the Exchange of Populations. Nearly 1,500,000 Greeks and 500,000 Muslims left their homelands. While Muslims settled in different parts of Turkey, Greeks mostly settled into different parts of Northern Greece. Many of these Greeks and Muslims built new villages and houses in their new countries.[1] In other words, they created new lives.[2] Today, immigrant Greeks are called refugees (πρόσφυγες) in Greece. They constitute a refugee identity constructed among the regions from which they migrated, including the Greeks of Eastern Thrace, called Thracians, and the Pontiacs of the Black Sea region, a coastal and inner region of Asia Minor.[3] One of these refugee groups calls themselves "Cappadocian Greeks/Rums" (Ρωμιοί της Καππαδοκίας) and are known as *Karamanlı* or *Karamanlides* in literature.[4] Like other refugees, they sometimes shared their new settlements with local Greeks or established new villages with other refugee groups.

The focus of this paper is on three monuments in three Cappadocian Greek villages. Multiple meanings of the monuments representing their Cappadocian and refugee identity are evaluated. Some interviews and observations were also used in monument descriptions. Indeed, this paper is based on research conducted in two fieldworks between August 13 and September 10, 2016, and later, from July 20 to September 5, 2017, in some of the Cappadocian Greek villages. Since the broader aim of the research was the identity construction and belonging among Cappadocian Greeks, their monuments were included in the research.[5]

THE MONUMENT OF THE SAINT: RELIGION, NATIONALISM, AND REFUGEES

Vounena (Βούναινα) is a Cappadocian Greek village in Larrisa in Northern Greece. These refugees migrated from Sulucaova, Niğde, to this small area and established their own village. The monument of St. Chrysostomos Kalafatis was erected by Vounena villagers in 2015.[6] St. Chrysostomos Kalafatis, the Archbishop of Izmir, was killed during "the fire of Izmir/Smyrna" in 1922. He was named a saint in 1993. The monument displays the front half of the saint's sculpture in front of a wall. Both figures are made of white marble. Since the top of the back wall appears broken, the monument looks like a piece carved out from a larger monument telling a bigger story. This gives the impression of a missing piece of history of the refugees. Holding his crosier referring to his religious rank and authority, the monument of St. Chrysostomos Kalafatis stands alone on a stone base. Only his name is inscribed near his statue on the wall behind him.

Similar to the following two monuments, the monument of St. Chrysostomos Kalafatis stands in the middle of Greek and Patriarchal flags at the intersection of Larissas Karditsas highway and the road to Vounena Village. Roadside monuments are common in Greece but mostly as memorials to fatal automobile accidents, with votive offerings for a life miraculously saved in a fatal accident and shrines in an annex of the church.[7] It seems that both monuments of Vounena and Neos Milotopos near the highway reflect the religious roadside monument tradition of the Greeks.

Although Vounena is the village of the Cappodocian Greeks, their monument represents "the fire of Izmir/Smyrna."[8] But the meaning of the monument reveals the message of the villagers in the scope of their self-identification. This monument is not only a sculpture of a saint but also symbolizes the connection of the Cappodocian Greeks with Greek Orthodox and their involvement in "the Asia Minor Catastrophe," a discourse on Greece, and their participation in the pain of Population Exchange. The refugees who originated from Izmir "consider Chrysostomos Kalafatis a saint because purportedly he refused to leave the city the day before when the Greek army left, choosing to remain alongside his flock and becoming a martyr."[9] At the same time "the fire of Izmir/Smyrna" is a part of Greek nationalism, which unites its citizens in a common history. But in an interview about the monument, a participant told us about the connection of the village with the fire. He said that some people from their home village (Sulucaova) were in Izmir at that time and lost their lives during the fire. Therefore, for the refuges, honoring their memory is one of the reasons for building that monument. However, the monument still did not depict the fire; instead, one of the figures of Greek Asia Minor policy and of the church in Izmir was portrayed on the monument.[10] On the other hand, after the loss of the lands of Asia Minor at the end of the Independence War of Turks, the destruction of the *Megali Idea* (Μεγάλη Ιδέα) policy and the Population Exchange enabled Greece to develop political discourses, especially against Turkey. And this feeling of loss and trauma became a central element of Greek nationalism after the settlement of refugees to Greece.[11] In addition, refugees were not embraced by the local Greeks, who sometimes called them "Turks" (τουρκόσποροι).

Greek Orthodoxy is still the strongest common point between the refugees and the locals who survived under the Ottoman *millet* system. During the Ottoman era, the *millet* system was the framework in which the Ottoman state ruled its non-Muslim people. This system was based on membership in a religious and denominational group, not on an ethnic or a linguistic group.[12] *Millet-i Rum* or Greek *millet* contained Serbs, Rumanians, Bulgarians, Vlachs, Orthodox Albanians, and Arabs.[13] Thus, the Greek Orthodoxy continued until the Independence of Greece (1821). After the establishment of the Kingdom of Greece (*Hellas*) in 1830, in order to "protect state sovereignty from foreign intervention," the Church of Greece was established in 1833. Although it was a kind of schism, the autocephaly of the Church of Greece was recognized by the Greek patriarchate in Istanbul.[14] This attempt to establish "a national church" also created a state religion and positioned the Church of Greece as an actor in Greece, making it a critical element in nation building, education, and social relations.[15]

THE MONUMENT OF PAIN: MEMORY AND IDENTITY

Neos Milotopos (Νέος Μυλότοπος) is a village in Giannitsa in Northern Greece. Its population is composed of Cappadocian Greek refugees who migrated from Gürümze, a village located today in Adana, Turkey. When they arrived in their new country, they first settled close to the current village, but later, due to wetlands causing illnesses such as malaria, the Cappadocian Greeks preferred to move to the present village, Neos Milotopos.

Every refugee community has its own unique story about the Population Exchange and its settlement in Greece.[16] According to Neos Milotopos villagers, unlike the other Cappadocian refugees, their ancestors did not peacefully leave their homeland (πατρίδα). In their story, a fatal fire attack against their church while many people were inside was organized by "Kurdish" or "Turkish" gangs. They ran away, taking with them few objects, including clothes, Bibles, icons, and a chalice. This traumatic narrative has a significant place in their collective memory and self-identification; hence, it can also be seen in their monument. The location of the monument reinforces the power of the story; villagers want to make this narrative visible through their monument to all who visit the village.

The monument of Neos Milotopos is on the road to the village at the corner of the Aravissu Explanatu provincial road (figure 11.1). It comprises several components, including a bronze *bas relief* set off on a white marble wall standing on a rectangular surface. The flags of Greece and the patriarchate are on both sides of the monument. The top of the back wall appears broken, like the monument in Vounena. The sculpture in relief illustrates the fire at the church in their home village while they were fleeing. The villagers relate that the text on the lower front side of the monument is quoted from poet George Seferis (1900–1971), also a refugee from Asia Minor.[17] (We could not find the original poem.) Finally, the symbol of the patriarchate, the double-headed eagle, placed next to the quotation, emphasizes their survival in their new lands and confirms their fidelity to their faith.

The monument was built in 2010 by the association of the village with financial support from its members; the purpose was to commemorate their ancestors who experienced the fire attack and the forced migration. Neos Milotopos villagers consider this monument the most symbolic debt of gratitude owed to the memory of their ancestors. The monument was officially opened on September 14, 2011, on "The Day of Remembrance and Commemoration of the Genocide of the Greeks of Asia Minor."[18] By choosing this date, Cappadocian Greeks of Neos Milotopos created a link with other Asia Minor refugees and joined in a common pain. This common pain connects Neos Milotopos villagers with "the Asia Minor Catastrophe" and "the fire of Smyrna/Izmir."

The year 2011 was chosen for the opening ceremony of the monument because of the Gavustima Festival of the Cappadocian Greeks. Gavustima means "come together" in the Greek Misti dialect, which originates from Cappadocia. Since 1997, this traveling festival has been organized every year

Figure 11.1.   Untitled Monument, Giorgos Kikotis, Neos Miletopos Village, Giannitsa, Greece, 2011.
Photograph by Saim Örnek, 2016.

in a different Cappadocian village in Greece, and thousands of Cappadocian refugees from all over the country (and the world) attend the event. This meaningful monument was finished before the Gavustima Festival of Neos Milotopos, according to a leading member of the community, so it could be seen by festival participants.

The monument is not only a message to the visitors of the village but also a marker that helps the villagers remember their past and envision their story. Duffy and Waitt argue that communities utilize the "markers of identity," such as flags, posters, and banners, during the festivals for regulating and reinforcing their notions.[19] In our case, this monument turned into a marker of identity to preserve memory, especially for the young members, by seeing it nearly every day. They see and learn the story of their ancestors and construct their identity upon it.

Since the first generation who experienced this painful event are dead, the story of the fire and migration are now part of collective memory. Today, this story is neither a narrative told only at the village nor belongs only to them. The villagers express explicitly "the pain" their ancestors experienced and unite with others in a refugee identity. And this monument as a marker of identity reveals their story to the travelers passing by on the highway, to the visitors of the village, and to the future generations of the villagers.

THE MONUMENT OF UNITY: DIFFERENT TRADITIONS AND COMMEMORATION

Bafra (Μπάφρα) village is located ten minutes away from the city center of Ioannina in the region of Epirus. Bafra is neighbor to another Cappadocian refugee village called Neokaisareia (Νεοκαισάρεια); unlike this village, the population of Bafra consists of mostly Cappadocians and Pontiacs and also Sarikatsani and Vlach people. The Cappadocians of the village migrated from Çat (Sivas) and Taşlık villages (Kayseri). Pontiac people who first settled in the village migrated from Bafra (Samsun) before the Population Exchange, and they named the village Bafra, the name of their previous village in Turkey. When Pontiac people arrived at Bafra, they faced many diseases because the place was a wetland. Some of them left for a better place and abandoned their houses. For this reason, when Cappadocian people arrived at Ioannina, they found the empty houses in Bafra and temporarily settled there, hoping not to stay long. However, they established their new lives in the village together with Pontiac people. Villagers were from different regions of Asia Minor and had different cultures. Consequently, it was likely that this coexistence would raise some problems.

Coexisting for a very long time, these two refugee groups kept their differences apart until recently. Finally, in 2006 the descendants of the first generation of refugees constructed a monument in the square of the village to commemorate their ancestors and their unity. This monument also indicates the union of the people of different cultures as citizens of Greece. Even though they have different cultures, they found a common ground: they are both refugee communities, which is also a path to unite with other refugees. In their monument, a Pontiac and a Cappadocian man stand side by side on a marble base in their traditional dress. Similar to the other monuments, the flags of Greece and the patriarchate are planted to the sides of the monument. "The monument of the memorable homelands of Pontiacs and Cappadocians" is written on the front side of the base.[20] Under this line, a black rectangle panel pictures a monk holding a cross and many people following him. This example of picturing their migration journey on the leadership of a holy man symbolizes the villagers' fidelity to their religion and to their new country.

However, in this monument, the difference between the two groups was pictured only by traditional dress. In an era of global fashion, traditional "folk" or "national" dress is not only worn for the performances but also function as a way to represent the past and keep it in the collective memory. As Welters revealed in her study, people remember their mothers and grandparents in their traditional dresses.[21] For this reason, we see these dresses in the performances, in the museums, and in the monuments.

CONCLUSION

Nearly one hundred years after the Population Exchange, refugees in Greece (and Turkey) integrated and developed new identities in their new country. Like the three monuments examined in this article, refugees built their own monuments expressing and transmitting their past to new generations. These monuments represent their loyalty to their nation and their state. But they always profess their Christian faith with different symbols. Therefore, the monuments highlighted here represent the various meanings of being a refugee, a Cappadocian and a Greek, with many symbols. In these three cases, Cappadocian Greeks combine the history of their ancestors and their migration and pain in their monument and identity constructions. They picture their will and hope of uniting with other refugees on migration, conflict, pains, and difficulties of establishing a new life in Greece. They combine their stories with other refugees and with the national discourses and symbols, including religious symbols.

All three monuments are centered between the flags of Greece and the patriarchate, which are the symbols of national identity and religion. In this way, the monuments along with the flags, landscape, and the roads constitute monument spaces aiming to help visualize identity and belonging. Opening ceremonies, memorial days, and visits as social activities keep these monuments and their message alive. Although other monuments in the villages commemorating the victims of War World II and the Greek Civil War are not mentioned in this article, they can also be considered symbols of their Greek identity—part of the monument culture of contemporary Greece with its long and layered past.

NOTES

1. For more about the Population Exchange of Turkey and Greece, see Yıldırım, *Diplomacy and Displacement*, and Pentzopoulos, *The Balkan Exchange*.
2. In her study, *Heirs of the Greek Catastrophe*, Hirschon examines the daily life of the Kokkinia people in Greece and the developments in the two sides after the Population Exchange was reviewed in different articles in her editorial book, *Crossing the Aegean*.
3. Even though Greeks are called and considered refugees (πρόσφυγες) in Greece, Muslims who migrated from Greece to Turkey are called immigrants (*göçmen* or *mübadil*) in Turkey.
4. Evangelia Balta's many books and articles are the information source about the Karamanli people. Her new editorial work, *Cries and Whispers in Karamanlidika Books*, contains articles about the Karamanli people in English. In addition, see Balta, *Gerçi Rum İsek de Rumca Bilmez Türkçe Söyleriz*, and Clogg, "A *Millet* within a *Millet*."
5. This paper was based on a research project, named "Identity and Belonging in Karamanli People" (and numbered 5827), and was supported by the Erciyes University Scientific Research Coordination Unit. A part of this fieldwork information was used in this paper.
6. Μνημείο Άγιου Χρυσοστόμου Σμύρνης στα Βούναινα, accessed February 20, 2018, http://www.larissanet.gr/2015/09/14/mnimeio-agiou-chrysostomou-smyrnis-sta-vounaina/.
7. Saccopoulos, "Roadside Monuments in Greece," 144.
8. "The great fire of Smyrna," started on September 13, 1922, is a controversial historical event between Greece and Turkey. According to the Greeks, the Turks are responsible for the fire, but Turkey claims that Greeks burned the city while they were leaving. For an oral history narrative of this issue, see Neyzi, "Remembering Smyrna/Izmir."
9. Kirtsoglou, "Dreaming the Self," 326.
10. Chrysostomos Kalafatis was born in Triglia/Tirilye in Bursa in 1867; he was appointed as metropolitan of Drama in 1902 and became the Archbishop of Smyrna in 1910. For more, see ορθόδοξος συναξαριστής, accessed February 20, 2018, http://www.saint.gr/2408/saint.aspx.
11. Özkırımlı and Sofos, *Tormented by History*, 118.
12. Ortaylı, *Ottoman Studies*, 20.
13. Karpat, "Millets and Nationality," 145; and Clogg, "The Greek Millet in the Ottoman Empire," 185.

14. Grigoriadis, *Instilling Religion in Greek and Turkish Nationalism*, 24–25. For a more detailed example, Roudomet's article, "Greek Orthodoxy, Territoriality, and Globality," begins with a historical review and later analyzes the relations of the Church of Greece and the patriarchate in consideration of social and political changes until 2003.
15. As a recent example, Fokas, in "Greece: Religion, Nation and Membership in the European Union," explains the power of the Church of Greece on public opinion in the case of the European Union.
16. For more about these migration stories, see Pekin, *Yeniden Kurulan Yaşamlar*, and Hirschon, *Crossing the Aegean*.
17. ΚΑΙ ΓΙΝΑΝΕ ΔΕΝΤΡΑ ΜΕΓΑΛΑ / ΞΑΝΑΒΓΑΛΑΝ ΚΛΑΡΙΑ ΚΑΙ ΦΥΛΛΑ / ΤΗΣ ΕΛΠΙΔΑΣ ΠΡΑΣΙΝΑ (and they became big trees / put forth and leafed of hope again).
18. Although it's not accepted as "genocide" in Turkey, September 14 is accepted as "Asia Minor genocide day" in Greece with the decision made by the Greek Parliament on September 13, 1998. For "genocide" allegations, see https://nomoi.info/ ΦΕΚ-Α-234-1998-σελ-1.html.
19. Duffy and Waitt, "Rural Festivals and Processes of Belonging," 47.
20. ΜΝΗΜΕΙΟ ΑΛΗΣΜΟΝΗΤΩΝ ΠΑΤΡΙΔΩΝ ΠΟΝΤΙΩΝ – ΚΑΠΠΑΔΟΚΩΝ.
21. Welters, "The Transition from Folk to Fashionable Dress in Attica, Greece," 48.

BIBLIOGRAPHY

Balta, Evangelia. *Gerçi Rum İsek de Rumca Bilmez Türkçe Söyleriz*. Istanbul: Türkiye İş Bankası Yayınları, 2014.

Balta, Evangelia, and Matthias Kappler, eds. *Cries and Whispers in Karamanlidika Books*. Wiesbaden: Harrassowitz Verlag, 2010.

Clogg, Richard. "The Greek Millet in the Ottoman Empire." In *Christians and Jews in the Ottoman Empire: The Functioning of a Plural Society*. Vol. 1, *The Central Lands*, edited by B. Braude and B. Lewis, 185–207. London: Holmes & Meier Publishers, 1982.

———. "A *Millet* within a *Millet*: The *Karmanlides*." In *Ottoman Greeks in the Age on Nationalism: Politics, Economy and Society in the Nineteenth Century*, edited by Dimitri Gondicas and Charles Issawi, 115–42. Princeton, NJ: Darwin Press, 1999.

Duffy M., and G. Waitt. "Rural Festivals and Processes of Belonging." In *Festival Places: Revitalizing Rural Australia*, edited by Chris Gibson and John Connell, 44–57. Bristol: Channel View Publications, 2011.

Fokas, Effie. "Greece: Religion, Nation and Membership in the European Union." In *Citizenship and Ethnic Conflict: Challenging the Nation-State*, edited by Haldun Gülalp, 39–59. New York: Routledge, 2006.

Grigoriadis, Ioannis N. *Instilling Religion in Greek and Turkish Nationalism: A "Sacred Synthesis."* New York: Palgrave Macmillan, 2013.

Hirschon, Renée, ed. *Crossing the Aegean: An Appraisal of the 1923 Compulsory Population Exchange between Greece and Turkey*. New York: Berghahn Books, 2008.

———. *Heirs of the Greek Catastrophe: The Social Life of Asia Minor Refugees in Piraeus*. New York: Berghahn Books, 1998.

Karpat, Kemal H. "Millets and Nationality: The Roots of the Incongruity of Nation and State in the Post-Ottoman Era." In *Christians and Jews in the Ottoman Empire: The Functioning of a Plural Society*. Vol. 1, *The Central Lands*, edited by B. Braude and B. Lewis, 141–69. London: Holmes & Meier Publishers, 1982.

Kirtsoglou, Elisabeth. "Dreaming the Self: A Unified Approach towards Dreams, Subjectivity and the Radical Imagination." *History and Anthropology* 21, no. 3 (2010): 321–35.

Neyzi, Leyla. "Remembering Smyrna/Izmir: Shared History, Shared Trauma." *History and Memory, Special Issue: Remembering and Forgetting on Europe's Southern Periphery* 20, no. 2 (2008): 106–27.

Ortaylı, İlber. *Ottoman Studies*. Istanbul: Bilgi University Press, 2004.

Özkırımlı, Umut, and Spyros A. Sofos. *Tormented by History: Nationalism in Greece and Turkey*. Columbia: Columbia University Press, 2008.

Pekin, Müfide. *Yeniden Kurulan Yaşamlar: 1923 Türk-Yunan Zorunlu Nüfus Mübadelesi*. Istanbul: Bilgi Üniversitesi Yayınları, 2005.

Pentzopoulos, Dimitri. *The Balkan Exchange of Minorities and Its Impact on Greece*. London: Hurst & Company, 2002.

Roudometof, Victor. "Greek Orthodoxy, Territoriality, and Globality: Religious Responses and Institutional Disputes." *Sociology of Religion* 69, no. 1 (2008): 67–91.

Saccopoulos, Christos A. "Roadside Monuments in Greece." *Ekistics, The Mediterranean—III and IV: Response to Problems within the Local Cultural Contexts* 53, nos. 318/319 (1986): 144–48.

Welters, Linda. "The Transition from Folk to Fashionable Dress in Attica, Greece." *Dress* 11, no. 1 (1985): 57–68.

Yıldırım, Onur. *Diplomacy and Displacement Reconsidering the Turco-Greek Exchange of Populations, 1922–1934*. New York: Routledge, 2006.

CHAPTER 12

Kindertransports in National and Transnational Perspective

AMY WILLIAMS

FROM 1938 TO 1940, AROUND TEN THOUSAND CHILDREN OF JEWISH BACK-
ground, under threat from Nazi anti-Semitism, were rescued to Great Britain.
Despite the importance of this event, which we now know as the Kindertransports, there was a collective amnesia around it for many years after the Second
War World. In later life, many of the former children, or "Kinder," found it difficult to speak about their traumatic experiences of journeying and adapting to
life in strange lands without their families. In the postwar period, Kinder were
still discovering the fates of their loved ones. Therefore, Kinder also may have
been reluctant to discuss their personal stories because of their "feelings of . . .
guilt for having survived while most of their relatives did not."[1] Likewise, many
host nations were not yet ready to listen to them. It took "some sixty years"
before Britain started to rediscover its connections to the transports, probably
as a result of the first reunions in the late 1980s and the early 1990s.[2] Memory
of the Kindertransports today, though, has moved from the fringes of Britain's
national memory of the Second World War and the Holocaust to the center.

Historically, the Kindertransports were transnational in character because
the Kinder embarked upon multiple journeys from their lands of birth
through different countries of transfer and arrived in many different host
countries.[3] For example, some children journeyed from Germany, Austria,
Poland, and Czechoslovakia to Holland, Holland to Britain, and then Britain
to the United States, Canada, or even as far away as Australia. Kinder traveled
to Canada and Australia via Britain not as refugees but as internees. Britain interned one thousand Kinder as type B and C enemy aliens and later deported
these teenagers overseas during the war.[4] Other Kinder started their journeys
in Germany and Austria destined for Belgium or France, and some Kinder
even departed from Czechoslovakia for Sweden. Twenty Kinder also traveled
from Bialystok, Poland, to New Zealand via Britain.

When memory of the Kindertransports did develop in Britain, it focused
on rescue and settlement in Britain, omitting reference to journeys beyond

British shores to other host nations. The typical British narrative therefore ends positively because, although the Kinder suffered hardships along the way, they eventually became valued members of British society. The emphasis is placed on rescue, for it is the journey itself (especially the latter half where the children crossed the border into Holland) and the arrival that are stressed rather than what the Kinder lost. While acts of unity, charity, care, and compassion are stressed, rarely is there reflection on issues of social or political neglect. Britain's national narrative presents the crossing into Holland as a watershed moment because it is in this country that the children started to feel safe again and this sense of jubilation ultimately comes to a climax in Britain as the children find refuge.

Memory of the Kindertransports though are not limited to Britain's national memory because many other host nations as well as the Kinder's former homelands are also remembering these historical events. Over the past twenty years, there has been a growing international awareness of the Kindertransports. Different generations of artists and authors from all over the globe have produced works, which have received worldwide acclaim. Diane Samuels's play *Kindertransport* (1995) is just one example. The upsurge in different cultural representations of the Kindertransports from autobiographies to novels, films, and documentaries highlights the importance of the Kindertransports today. Recently, there have also been parallels drawn between the transports and the current refugee crisis, which further demonstrates the significance of the transports in the present. However, it is memorials that seem to be at the center of this growing awareness, compared to other cultural forms of representation, and in Britain, they have taken on other meanings, questioning Britain's refugee history and its reactions and policies toward refugees today.

When viewed in isolation, Kindertransport memorials, such as Frank Meisler's memorial outside Liverpool Street Station in London, present the British national narrative of the transports, one that is essentially celebratory and emphasizes notions of solidarity. British memorials to the Kindertransports reinforce this positive narrative because they downplay the more negative aspects of the Kindertransports, such as abuse, internment, and the further displacement and disorientation experienced by the Kinder. But Meisler's memorial at Liverpool Street Station is also part of his more critical transnational Kindertransport memorial network (London, Hamburg, Danzig, Berlin, and Hook of Holland), which pinpoints the locations of departure, transfer, and arrival. Like the Meisler network, the Flor Kent transnational network of memorials to the Kindertransports (located in London, Newark, Vienna, and Prague) also presents a critical transnational perspective of the transports. Not only do these transnational networks map the extensive journeys that Kinder embarked upon from their homelands to Britain; they also span different national histories and raise questions about separation, loss, and estrangement. In November 2017, the London Meisler memorial was wrapped up in winter coats to draw attention to the vulnerability of today's refugees and to inspire people to do more to help them. The memorial has also been a site to rally around when debating the British government's approach to helping those who are fleeing crisis today. The future of Kindertransport memorials in Britain is changing as the more negative aspects of the event are brought into focus. This essay will therefore argue that transnational memory and contemporary events can lead to an interpretative reframing of national memorials.

The first section of this essay will reflect upon how national memorials of the Kindertransports present the British perspective of this rescue operation. The Meisler sculpture was the only memorial of its kind in Britain for many years. It depicts a group of children with their suitcases and labels around their necks, images that are now synonymous with the memory of the Kinder-transports in Britain. The second part of this essay will study the transnational network of Kindertransport memorials. It concludes with a discussion about how contemporary events, such as the current refugee crisis and the Center for Political Beauty's recent campaign, titled *Kindertransporthilfe des Bundes* (*Federal Emergency Programme*), are changing our perceptions and thoughts about the memorials to the Kindertransports.

Meisler's London Kindertransport memorial, titled *The Arrival*, was un-veiled in 2006 and reflects the basically positive character of the British national narrative of the transports (figure 12.1). One particular message that this memorial presents is the Kinder's gratitude toward the British public for rescuing them. The statues have cheerful expressions, which suggest a sense of joy as the Kinder arrived safely in Britain. The title of the memorial and the accompanying plaque, titled *Children of the Kindertransport*, also show the British narrative of the transports because the focus is placed overwhelmingly on the rescue and arrival of the Kinder rather than also on the exclusion of their parents and other family members. The only physical reminders of the refugee children's former lives in their native lands is shown by their posses-sions, such as suitcases, and the names of the cities that they departed from, which are displayed around the memorial. The British national narrative is also present because the memorial resides within Hope Square, reinforc-ing the notion of unity. The memorial evokes a sense of how Britons rallied together to help, fund, and care for refugees. It also harks back to Britain's philanthropic history of helping those in need. This memorial encourages the viewer to envisage how the Kinder felt on arrival and how they looked to the future and their new lives in Britain. It is true that the viewer not only gains an insight into the children's sense of adventure but also becomes aware of the children's fears and anxieties about being transplanted to a new land. But these more critical moments are quickly undermined by the memorial's basically positive message about welcome because the memorial "represents a turning point in the children's lives—a new chapter whose pages unfold a history of rescue, gratitude, and hope."[5]

The first memorial to be dedicated outside this station was not Meisler's, but Flor Kent's, unveiled in 2003. Her statue, titled *Für das Kind* (*For the Child*), depicted a single female Kindertransportee standing outside the station next to a large glass suitcase holding artifacts belonging to former Kinder. The memorial however was later replaced by Meisler's sculpture because the artifacts started to decay.[6] These objects included photographs, rucksacks, and books, which drew attention to what the children brought with them on their journeys from Continental Europe. Kent's memorial, it could be argued, also doubled as a small museum because the displayed artifacts testified to the history of the Kinder's journeys and the statue attested to the children's safe arrival.[7] Meisler's memorial also places the Kindertransports in an educational as well as a historical context because it presents five figures of children; a train track; and the children's belongings, such as a teddy bear and a violin. The statues of the children depict varying ages, which is historically accurate, because children ranging from infants to teenagers came to Britain on the Kindertransports. Likewise, the memorial represents the dispersal of the Kinder to different areas of the British Isles as the figures look in different

Figure 12.1 *The Arrival*, Frank Meisler, Liverpool Street Station, London, January 26, 2018.

Photograph courtesy of Hands On London.

directions, signifying how not all journeys ended in London. Rather Kinder would travel from London to places throughout the British Isles, such as Birmingham, Glasgow, and even as far as County Down in Northern Ireland, to find new homes.

When examining the memorial in isolation, the British national narrative of the Kindertransports dominates because the emphasis is placed on the Kinder finding new homes in Britain rather than further movement to other host nations. This exclusive focus on Britain as a haven is problematic: not all Kinder's experiences in Britain were positive because some Kinder would be interned as enemy aliens. Their haven soon became a prison. The memorial to a degree highlights what Tony Kushner calls a "classic" *Kinder* narrative whereby "the notion of escape [is] central to describ[ing] the journeys of the *Kindertransportees*."[8] Kushner indicates that there are three factors that constitute a "classic" Kinder narrative. These are the "parental sacrifice and painful separation" of the saying good-bye; "the journey itself, one of danger, fear, and uncertainty"; and, finally, the "light and hope to counter the darkness of Nazi persecution."[9] In the British national narrative of the Kindertransports, escape, separation, and the journey across Continental Europe are eclipsed by the children's arrival in Britain. Moreover, there are no adults depicted by the memorial. The history of the Kindertransports to Britain has been simplified in the way that we remember it.

Yet while the diasporic character of the Kindertransports (they were movements across and toward different borders) has often been elided in the British national narrative, Meisler's memorial network, seen as a whole, sets this narrative in relation to the transnational narrative and as a result makes us rethink it. Since the memorial network incorporates many different national perspectives and reflects upon the roles of these nations (Britain, Germany, Austria, Czechoslovakia, and Poland) prior to and during the Second World War, it demonstrates a more complex history and memory of the Kindertransports. The Kindertransports are much more than rescue; they are about being stripped of everything, including their rights, home, freedom, family, and identity. As previously discussed, some Kinder who found refuge in Britain were later sent to countries, such as Australia and Canada, as enemy aliens. Their journeys were more far-reaching. The memorial network is part of a wider international rethinking of the Kindertransports, which sets the transports within the context of the Holocaust and the trauma of displacement. The Kindertransports are about exclusion as well as inclusion.

The transnational narrative is not only critical of the British national narrative of rescue because other national narratives are also critiqued. For example, Meisler's sculpture *Trains to Life—Trains to Death*, at Friedrichstrasse in Berlin, is critical of the German national narrative of the Kindertransports because the memorial explores a sense of avoidance in terms of the lack of focus on Jewish exile between 1933 and 1938. The memorial, on the other hand, does make clear that not all children were able to obtain places on Kindertransports. In this sense, the memorial has a "dual function" because it symbolizes "salvation vs. annihilation" and condemns bystanders.[10] Bill Niven has argued that "while the Holocaust over the decades moved to the center of German memory, the mass emigration of German and Austrian Jews which preceded the Holocaust remained a marginal feature of this memory."[11] He also states that "exile tends to disappear behind the larger tragedy of the Shoah."[12] The memorial grapples with this complex history and memory because it indicates that ordinary Germans saw these trains leave. Reflecting upon this further, the memorial network follows the Kinder's journeys from one place to another, which illustrates how they were distanced farther and farther away from their lands of birth. The transnational narrative of the transports demonstrates the Kinder's further displacement and their further separation from their families.

The memorial network incorporates both the perspective of the perpetrator nation and the perspective of the host nation as well as presenting the perspectives of the countries of exit and countries of transit. Therefore, there are many different national memories featured in these memorials. As this essay has previously discussed, the Meisler sculpture in Britain, which is part of this network, seen on its own terms, tends to celebrate the arrival of the Kinder from Continental Europe and thus presents the British national narrative. But it also appears in relation to memorials in mainland Europe. Certainly, this transnational narrative is not always necessarily evident when looking at certain memorials in their isolation because some viewers may not realize that the memorials are in fact part of a wider network. But the network is shown by the memorials themselves because they document the network that they reside within. For example, the suitcases depict how Germany's cultural loss was Britain's gain.[13] The network is also present if we consider various websites and forms of social media, such as Twitter and Instagram, which also showcase these memorial networks and how the various memorials relate to one another. For example, Meisler's website highlights his memorial network by presenting information about when each memorial was dedicated, the titles of each of the memorials, and a brief description about what each memorial represents.

The memorials in Meisler's network were dedicated at different times. The first was dedicated at Liverpool Street and unveiled in 2006. The second memorial, *Trains to Life—Trains to Death*, was inaugurated in Berlin in 2008 (figure 12.2); the third memorial, *The Departure*, was unveiled in Danzig/Gdansk in 2009; *Channel Crossing to Life* in Rotterdam was dedicated in 2011; and the fifth memorial, *The Final Departing*, was unveiled in Hamburg in 2015. The memorial in Berlin further demonstrates loss because it reflects how children made different journeys. The memorial demonstrates how some Kinder journeyed to safety in other nations while other children, such as the Kinder's siblings, were taken to death camps, such as Auschwitz. Britain's national memory has started to incorporate more negative aspects of this historical event because novels such as *Austerlitz* by W. G. Sebald, *The One I Was* by Eliza Graham, and *The English German Girl* by Jake Wallis Simons do discuss notions such as the loss of the self and estrangement. Likewise, museum exhibitions, such as those found at the Imperial War Museums in London and Manchester or at the National Holocaust Centre and Museum in Newark, have reflected upon more negative aspects of the transports. Yet the narratives end triumphantly because the Kinder find homes in Britain. Stories that suggest that some Kinder struggled to adapt to a new way of life are overlooked. Focusing on Meisler's network though, we are rethinking memory of the Kindertransports because the transnational narrative opens up debates about these more negative elements, which challenges the British narrative.

It seems that on a grassroots level, people are reviewing Britain's memory of the transports, thanks to the work, for instance, of charities such as Hands On London. In 2017, the Kindertransport memorials in London and Berlin were sites where memorial activism took place. In London, the memorial was dressed in winter coats by Hands On London with the support of the Association of Jewish Refugees and World Jewish Relief. The charity's Wrap Up London campaign takes place every November and aims to collect as many coats as possible. These coats are then distributed to the homeless, elderly, and refugee charities across London. The modification of the memorial demonstrated how a transnational consciousness for the need to help refugees today is making us reassess Britain's memory of rescue. The process of rethinking the British national narrative starts with bringing Sir Nicholas Winton's story into the frame as he traveled to the Sudetenland in the late 1930s and saw the refugee camps—scenes not unfamiliar when we think of today's refugee crisis.[14] He saw how the children and the elderly needed support. In Britain, we remember Sir Winton greeting the Kinder on their arrival, but his work in the Sudetenland and the parents' anxieties regarding sending their children to Britain with enough clothing to keep them warm are stories that have previously been neglected by the British national narrative of the transports. The campaign also showed how Kinder are helping today's refugees because this group understands what it is like to journey to a new country.

Other groups are also emphasizing the need to help refugees today, and they too have used memory of the Kindertransports to make people more aware of past and present refugee journeys. For example, in Germany, the Center for Political Beauty has used memory of the Kindertransports in its campaigns to draw awareness to the current refugee crisis. The Center is

Figure 12.2. *Trains to Life—Trains to Death*, Frank Meisler, Friedrichstraße, Berlin.
Photograph courtesy of Bill Niven.

suggestively named Federal Emergency Programme campaign, and its critical reanimation of the Berlin memorial to the Kindertransports highlights how the Kindertransport can be "used as a blueprint" for helping refugees today because there are similarities between this historical event and the refugee crisis today.[15] The center argues that "the Kindertransport has retrospectively turned into a choice of life and death."[16] In this instance the center's plea for modern-day Kindertransports to help today's refugees from Syria calls attention to the life or death situation that arises if governments deny entry to refugees. We have not necessarily learned from the Kindertransports because although some refugee families are being reunited and traveling together, there are still many unaccompanied children in Europe. The center's website describes how in a kind of memorial activism the organization designed a memorial to the refugee crisis, which was placed within eyesight of the Kindertransport memorial in Friedrichstrasse. The Kindertransport memorial in Berlin stresses how the Nazis and their supporters did not want to give Jewish children a future and how they had to flee their homelands to find shelter. Germany's national narrative of the Kindertransports is about exclusion, but this new campaign highlights how Germany's relationship to refugees today is about inclusion because this campaign calls for a kind of Kindertransport in reverse: instead of refugee children fleeing Germany, they are instead rescued and helped by the nation.

Britain is still not facing the full history of the Kindertransports when discussing stories about Kinder who were interned or abused. Memorial activism in Germany is more radical compared to the activism in Britain because it has not only criticized Germany's national narrative of the Kindertransports; it has also demonstrated how Germany has also been slow to commemorate the Kindertransports. Britain's national narrative of the transports focuses on rescue, but solely highlighting this point has prevented the public from understanding and remembering the whole story. Monument culture in Britain is changing, yet it is a slow change and could be more inclusive. Meisler's memorials and the memorial activism that has surrounded them have challenged us not only to think about the more negative stories of the Kindertransports but also the conditions refugees are facing today. In doing so, stories that are less positive and that grapple with persecution and destruction have started to now be included in national narratives. The winter coats campaign reminds us that people are still being persecuted today and that they need support because they have left everything behind. There has, then, been progress because Britain and Germany are questioning their memory of the Kindertransports through the practice of memorial activism. Also, memorial activism in Britain and abroad has resulted in a rethinking of national narratives because several campaigns have highlighted government inaction regarding supporting refugees today. Likewise, the transnational narrative of the Kindertransports has also challenged us to reconsider how different nations are remembering this historical event and their lack of interest in more negative stories.

NOTES

1. Pnina Rosenberg, "Footsteps of Memory: Frank Meisler's Kindertransport Memorials," *Prism* 6, no. 5 (2014): 91.
2. Tony Kushner, *Remembering Refugees: Then and Now* (Manchester: Manchester University Press, 2006), 142.
3. For examples of the characteristics of the transnational history of the Kindertransports, see Barry Turner, . . . *And the Policeman Smiled: 10,000 Children Escaped from Nazi Europe* (London: Bloomsbury, 1990); and A. J. Sherman, *Island Refuge: Britain and Refugees from the Third Reich, 1933–1939* (Essex: Frank Cass & Co. Ltd., 1994).
4. For examples of work that explores the internment of refugees by the British government, see Rachel Pistol, *Internment during the Second World War: A Comparative Study of Great Britain and the USA* (London: Bloomsbury, 2019); and John Presland, *A Great Adventure: The Story of the Refugee Children's Movement* (London: Bloomsbury, 1944).
5. Rosenberg, "Footsteps of Memory," 93.

6. Pnina Rosenberg, "When Private Becomes Public: The Für das Kind Memorial Series," 69.
7. Ibid.
8. Tony Kushner, *The Battle of Britishness: Migrant Journeys, 1685 to the Present* (Manchester: Manchester University Press, 2012), 126.
9. Ibid.
10. Rosenberg, "Footsteps of Memory," 94–96.
11. Bill Niven, "Jewish Exile in German Memory," in *Voices from Exile: Essays in Memory of Hamish Ritchie*, ed. Ian Wallace (Boston: Brill Rodopi, 2015), 278.
12. Ibid.
13. Rosenberg, "Footsteps of Memory," 93.
14. Sir Nicholas Winton rescued around 669 refugee children from Czechoslovakia.
15. Center of Political Beauty, "The Federal Emergency Programme," accessed November 28, 2017, http://politicalbeauty.com/kindertransport.html.
16. Ibid.

BIBLIOGRAPHY

Center of Political Beauty. "The Federal Emergency Programme." Accessed November 28, 2017. http://politicalbeauty.com/kindertransport.html.

Kushner, Tony. *The Battle of Britishness: Migrant Journeys, 1685 to the Present.* Manchester University Press: Manchester, 2012.

———. *Remembering Refugees: Then and Now.* Manchester: Manchester University Press, 2006.

Niven, Bill. "Jewish Exile in German Memory." In *Voices from Exile: Essays in Memory of Hamish Ritchie*, edited by Ian Wallace, 276–88. Boston: Brill Rodopi, 2015.

Pistol, Rachel. *Internment during the Second World War: A Comparative Study of Great Britain and the USA.* London: Bloomsbury, 2019.

Presland, John. *A Great Adventure: The Story of the Refugee Children's Movement.* London: Bloomsbury, 1944.

Rosenberg, Pnina. "Footsteps of Memory: Frank Meisler's Kindertransport Memorials." *Prism* 6, no. 5 (2014): 91–96.

———. "When Private Becomes Public: The Für das Kind Memorial Series." *Prism* 6, no. 5 (2014): 68–74.

Sherman, A. J. *Island Refuge: Britain and Refugees from the Third Reich, 1933–1939.* Essex: Frank Cass & Co. Ltd., 1994.

Turner, Barry. *. . . And the Policeman Smiled: 10,000 Children Escaped from Nazi Europe.* London: Bloomsbury, 1990.

CHAPTER 13

A Cubist Portrait of Christopher Columbus

Studying Monuments as Transcultural Works

CHIARA GRILLI

IN AUTUMN 2012, THE JAPANESE ARTIST TATZU NISHI PRESENTED HIS installation *Discovering Columbus*, his first public exhibition in the United States. In his project, the artist encased the statue of Christopher Columbus, which is part of New York's famous Columbus Circle, within the four walls of a contemporary, everyday-like living room. To have access to the exhibition, visitors had to climb a stairway up to the thirteen-foot-high statue of the explorer, situated on top of a seventy-five-foot granite column. Interestingly, his work "prompted reconsiderations of the function of monuments through its historical discontinuities in style and content."[1] The interchangeability of public and private, in other words, leads to a form of cognitive estrangement, forcing the average man or woman to stop in front of the monument and reconsider its meaning and function.

As Nishi metaphorically suggested, it is possible to fully understand the worth of a certain monument only by dislocating it and considering it not as a self-explanatory artifact expressing one single point of view but as an entanglement of different histories and stories, attached by different individuals and groups. In this sense, the figure of Christopher Columbus, caught between history and myth, is emblematic, for it is made of many, sometimes opposing, facets, building an image similar to a decomposed and recomposed cubist portrait. The figure of the Italian explorer is not bidimensional but ought to be analyzed as a concoction of fragments showing the viewer the same story from different points of view. As such, the Columbus Circle's statue, which has recently been the protagonist of an inflamed public debate, is a telling example of the multidimensional and, more specifically, transcultural nature of monuments. Before analyzing the specific case of New York's statue, however, it is essential to define the concepts of collective and transcultural memory.

Following Maurice Halbwachs's groundbreaking work *On Collective Memory*, in which the French philosopher and sociologist demonstrated how autobiographical memories are actually framed and influenced by the sociocultural environment, many scholars have been dealing with the concept of collective memory.[2] In particular, Jan Assmann's work on cultural memory is essential to understanding the role of monuments in the life of groups and communities. When talking about cultural memory, Assmann refers to "a form of collective memory, in the sense that it is shared by a number of people and that it conveys to these people a collective, that is, cultural, identity."[3] Moreover, because groups do not actually possess memories of their own, they "tend to 'make' themselves one by means of things meant as reminders such as monuments, museums, libraries, archives, and other mnemonic institutions."[4] In this sense, monuments are the symbolic representatives of the cultural memory of a certain community and can be thought of as part of a collective repertoire of narratives, values, and mementoes contributing to the definition of the identity of a certain group.

However, while for many years monuments have been considered as totems exclusively belonging to a certain group's culture, many scholars have recently provided a new approach to collective memories and its mementoes. In particular, Astrid Erll has explicitly criticized the notion of a "container culture," binding memory to ethnicity, territory, and nationality.[5] Rather than considering cultures as self-sufficient single units, Erll suggests regarding them as transcultural and dynamic. In her essay "Travelling Memory," the scholar makes explicit reference to the work of the German philosopher Wolfgang Welsch, who suggests that cultures "de facto no longer have the insinuated form of homogeneity and separateness" but they have "assumed a new form, which is to be called *transcultural* insofar that it *passes through* classical cultural boundaries."[6] Accordingly, mnemonic artifacts, such as monuments, ought to be regarded as mediums to define the "routs" of memory across national and cultural confines, rather than as static "sites of memory."[7]

The transcultural nature of monuments, however, does not prevent them from being oversimplified symbols of past events. In fact, their role is not only that of representing certain memories but also of condensing "complex and confusing traces of the past into succinct mnemonic forms."[8] In this sense, mnemonic artifacts might lead to "distortion, even perversion, of memories," in that they "tend to be stripped of their complexity, detached from the details and contextual meanings they originally referred to."[9] The idea of a decontextualization and subjectification of the memories evoked by mnemonic artifacts can be better discussed by considering Alison Landsberg's recent work, *Prosthetic Memory*. In her study, the author explains how, by means of sensuous experience, people who have "no 'natural' claim" to certain memories (because they are not experienced personally) might nonetheless incorporate them into their own archive of memories. According to Landsberg, this connection with the others' past provides the individual with "privately felt public memories," which are supposed to function as medical prostheses.[10]

Landsberg's theory certainly proves to be particularly meaningful in our times of mass consumption and media influence. And yet her emphasis on the importance of experiential and emotional knowledge is arguable. Despite cautiously explaining how she is not undervaluing the significance of historiography by recognizing the large "trend in American mass culture toward the experiential as a mode of knowledge," the author implicitly acknowledges the predominance of emotional experience over historical knowledge in the contemporary relationship between the artifact and the individual.[11] Moreover, even though the author specifically states that prosthetic memories always involve the sensation of "feeling different from the subject of inquiry," she nonetheless explains how these memories are "inflected by our other experiences and place in the world."[12] As a consequence, this theory involves at least two major risks. First, as Richard Crownshaw points out, Landsberg does not take into consideration the "variety of subject positions and how they might speak for such mute objects."[13] Not only is the consumption of those memories affected by the autobiographical experiences of each visitor, but it is informed by mass media as well as by institutions (museums, associations, and organizations). The subjectification, mass consumption, and manipulation of memories are hence considerable risks of an experiential knowledge not supported by historical insights. Second, because artifacts are imbued with personal emotions and memories, the individual might overidentify with them and even turn them and their respective mementoes into fetishes. Remembering might then dangerously regress to a form of "anxious self-reflexiveness."[14]

One of the most important symbols of the Italian American community in the United States has been recently involved in a very similar debate. In September 2017, two major monuments of Christopher Columbus in New York—the first in Central Park, the second in Columbus Circle—were vandalized with red paint and pink nail polish. As many newspapers reported, the paint symbolized the blood of indigenous people staining the explorer's memory. Following the infamous events of Charlottesville, after which many Confederate statues were asked to be removed, the defacement of the Columbus monuments has led to a review of what New York Mayor Bill de Blasio called "symbols of hate."[15] By convening a specific commission, the Italian-American mayor asked for a revision of all the monuments and artifacts dedicated to those historical figures whose past might be considered controversial. Even though none of the Columbus statues was removed, the issue inflamed the public sentiment: Italian Americans celebrated the man as a hero, while many activists described the statue as an inacceptable homage to a violent murderer.

However, as historian David Blight underlined, it is important to avoid a "rush to judgment about what we hate and what we love and what we despise and what we're offended by."[16] Instead, it is essential to interrogate monuments, to ask not only about the history of the man represented but also about the history of the artifact itself: When, where, by whom, and, most of all, why was it built? It is essential, in other words, to examine all the interlacing stories of a monument and to seek support from a comprehensive historical analysis.

As already hinted, the figure of Columbus is fairly complex. The rediscovery of Columbus as an American hero took place during the Revolution, when the explorer started to be celebrated as an icon of the Republic.[17] The iconic role Columbus had within the American cultural memory is perfectly described by Washington Irving in *The Life and Voyages of Christopher Columbus*. In the biography, the Italian explorer was portrayed as the first who, "by his hardy genius, his inflexible constancy, and his heroic courage, brought the ends of the world into communication with each other."[18] Nonetheless, this Eurocentric perspective excluded from the narrative of the American founding myth many other actors, especially from minority groups. Among them, as I shall discuss, Italian Americans, Native Americans, and Hispanic Americans have often chosen to ground their struggles for identity recognition on a passionate reinterpretation of the murky figure of Columbus and the—more or less symbolic—consequences of his enterprise.

Following the American enthusiasm aroused by the Columbus enterprises and eager to be considered part of American history, Italian Americans turned Columbus's discovery of the New World into one of their founding myths. In fact, as Orm Overland points out, in a society that denied the immigrants' memories of their homeland and, at the same time, rejected their role within American society, the only way Italians could define their own identity was to create a new ethnocultural repertoire of memories and symbols.[19] In this sense, by "securing a place of prominence for their group in American history, these immigrants would also secure their position in the nation itself."[20] As an ethnic folk hero, Columbus embodied the struggles of millions of Italians and Italian Americans, who fought to build their lives and to overcome prejudice in their new homeland.

Unlike Italian Americans, of course, many ethnic groups emphasized the traumatic consequences of Columbus's discovery. Native Americans condemn the explorer not only for the dramatic decimation of the indigenous people but also for the establishment of a set of disparaging stereotypes still alive today. The systematic violence brought by Columbus to the New World is often defined as a genocide or a holocaust, for, as the Spanish priest Bartolomé de Las Casas reported in details, Spaniards "slaughtered everyone like sheeps in a corral" and were "extraordinarily cruel so that harsh and bitter treatment would prevent Indians from daring to think of themselves as human beings."[21] Moreover, as Robert Berkhofer discusses, Columbus's actions shaped the perception of Natives henceforth, by introducing and strengthening the stereotypes of the good and the bad Indian, which legitimized the enslavement and exploitation of the native populations.[22] In the twentieth century, and particularly since the sixties, Native Americans have revised the Columbus myth of discovery to affirm their ethnic identity and their sociopolitical role. In this sense, it is revealing to notice that the founding conference of the first national Native American organization, the Society of American Indians, was held in 1911 on Columbus Day.

Hispanics, however, have been profoundly affected by this reassessment of America's discovery myth. In fact, the condemnation of Columbus's colonization turned into a form of anti-Spanish propaganda, known as the Black Legend, reinterpreting the narratives of the discovery myth to depreciate the Hispanic community as a whole.[23] On the one hand, in some major northern cities, such as New York, Hispanic movements reinterpreted Columbus voyages as well as other relevant events of Spanish history, such as the Spanish-American War and the Alamo, in order to underline their contribution to the foundation and progress of the United States.[24] On the other hand, a large number of Mexican American activist groups in the South reread the Columbus myth to sponsor the celebration of a pan-ethnic social movement, known under the name of *La Raza*. Even if, at first, this term referred only to the Chicano culture, during the sixties its meaning became wider and came to represent "the pride of a mixed heritage, that is, a mixture of white heritage with Indian and perhaps black heritage."[25] As in the case of Native Americans, the founding event celebrating *La Raza* as a social movement occurred in El Paso, Texas, on Columbus Day 1967.

Columbus, therefore, ought not to be considered only as a historical figure but as the protagonist/antagonist of many different versions of the same narration, which different cultural communities appropriated to define and affirm their own identity. Of course, Columbus monuments reflect this multifaceted nature which, indeed, is representative of the transculturality of artifacts. Each of them, in this sense, should be considered as the node of different intersecting storylines. In the next part of the essay, I am going to pick one of these storylines and examine its origin to show what an important role historical analysis plays when experiencing and discussing monuments. In particular, the case of the Columbus Circle's statue in New York proves to be emblematic in relation to its Italian American origin. By scratching the surface of myth and emotions, it is possible to unearth the historical reasons behind the construction of the monument, reasons that are less connected to the violence of colonialism than to the struggle of a minority group to find its place in an unwelcoming society. At this point, it should be clear that the Italian American point of view represents just one of the storylines that must be taken into consideration when debating about the role of Columbus monuments and, as a consequence, should be regarded here as an example, one single thread of a much more complex cultural texture.

The Columbus statue was unveiled on the 400th anniversary of Columbus's discovery of the New World, in 1892. Built by an Italian sculptor, Gaetano Russo, the monument was erected at the very geographic center of New York City. The position, of course, symbolically emphasized the centrality of Columbus's figure, an Italian explorer, in American history. Moreover, as General Luigi Palma di Cesnola underlined in his speech during the unveiling ceremony,

> Italians have procured, in contributions great and small, but uniformly large in spirit, the execution of this monument and have erected and presented it in token of their affection and gratitude to this great and beloved country.[26]

Italian residents' participation adds a social value to the monument's historical and artistic meaning. In fact, Russo's work is turned into the statue of all the Italian Americans and into a monument dedicated to the Italian American community at large. The statue, in other words, assumed an essential role within the group's cultural memory.

During the 1892 ceremony, the monument was invested with three major meanings, for it represented a new bond between Italian Americans and the United States, a symbol of the Italian mythic role in the founding of the country, and a metaphor for the experience of Italian immigrants in the New World. First, the statue was the emblem of the long-lasting friendship between the United States and Italy as well as between American society and the Italian American community. This relationship was perfectly embodied by the presence of a young girl, "daughter of Italian-born parents," who unveiled the statue and "sealed a new bond of friendship between the land of her ancestors and the land of her birth."

Second, the monument carved in stone the mythic role played by Italians (and, therefore, by their descendants) in the founding of the United States. According to Carlo Barsotti, at that time president of the Committee of Italian Societies, the statue, "erected by us," evoked "the sacred memory of that great Italian who gave to America the light of civilization, divining and discovering its existence." Barsotti's statement is meaningful, for it establishes a mythic connection between the figure of the explorer and the collective Italian memory, a memory that is "sacred" in that it directly evokes the legendary origins of the United States. Accordingly, Columbus is invested with both mythic and sacred qualities and depicted as a godlike hero. Not too subtly, Barsotti hints that, while modern American society portrays Italian Americans as uncivilized, it was actually an Italian who first brought civilization to the New World.

Finally, the monument vividly celebrates the dramatic and heroic experience of Italian immigrants in the United States. In his address, Di Cesnola makes direct reference to Columbus's troubled life by underlying how "detraction and persecution were in a very large measure the life reward of Columbus, as they are at the present day of men both great and good." Di Cesnola is here creating a metaphoric connection between the explorer's troubled story and the discriminated everyday life of Italian immigrants. In this sense, the monument becomes essential to celebrate Italian bravery and, at the same time, to condemn the unfair prejudice perpetuated by American society against Italian Americans.

However, the connection between Columbus and the Italian experience in the United States is not always accepted. In an interesting article, published on *La Voce di New York* during the 2017 anti-Columbus protests, Stanislao Pugliese and William J. Connell argue that the explorer "hardly is representational of the millions of landless, often poorly educated peasants from Sicily, Calabria or Naples." According to the authors, many other Italian American figures, such as Sacco and Vanzetti or Mother Cabrini, should be celebrated as representatives of the immigrants' experience in the New World. Likewise, other monuments, such as the Our Lady of Loreto church, could be more significant symbols to celebrate the Italian immigrants' hard work and the strong bond between them and their ancestors' country. And yet, Columbus was chosen as a collective folk hero. The reason, as already outlined, lies in the popularity of the explorer's enterprise within the American (and, of course, the Italian) cultural memory. Not only has Columbus been celebrated as an American national hero since the times of the Civil War, but as Barsotti himself remembered, he was the only Italian to be taken into consideration at all:

> Throughout my whole elementary school career, I do not recall one mention of Italy or the Italian language or what famous Italians had done in the world, with the possible exception of Columbus, who was pretty popular in America.[27]

Choosing Columbus as an ethnic folk hero, therefore, was a cultural strategy oriented toward the inclusion of the Italian American community within the American historical and cultural environment as well as a way to dignify the image of the Italian immigrant by creating a transcultural connection between the Italian American and the American cultural repertoire.

During the debate about the "symbols of hate," the importance of Columbus as an icon of the Italian American identity has often been remarked. For instance, in its website, the National Italian American Foundation overtly declared that the Americans of Italian descent still value Columbus's courage and perseverance, qualities that served as inspiration for the early immigrants who faced their journey to the New World. For this reason, when Mayor de Blasio cast doubts on the "morality" of the Columbus Circle's statue, he was accused of being a "fake [Italian] who doesn't know his own values."[28] This and other declarations show how Columbus, as a mythic figure, is still perceived as a core element of Italian American identity, a cornerstone of this mythicized form of Italian-ness.

Giving a solution to this centuries-old question is not only beyond the purpose of this essay but might lead to an oversimplification of the problem. What is really important to emphasize, however, is that to avoid losing oneself among the many narratives and symbolic layers built over the centuries, it is essential to reintegrate historical knowledge into what Landsberg called experiential knowledge. As the case of Columbus Circle's statue demonstrates, the processes of reinterpretation, symbolization, and collectivization of a fact or a figure (be it from the Italian American, the Native American, or the Hispanic point of view), turn history and its mementoes into an intricate concoction of storylines, mixing historical facts, culture, and myth. By actively using history in his or her experience of the monument, the individual is not overwhelmed by his or her own personal story, cultural background, and collective memory. Rather, she or he overcomes the subjective perspective coming from a purely emotional experience of mnemonic artifacts and becomes aware of the many voices intersecting within the monument and of the transcultural and dynamic nature it enshrines. In this sense, history is the fourth dimension making the viewer understand that the cubist portrait she or he is observing is not a flat, one-sided juxtaposition of planes but a round, synchronic, and at the same time, diachronic entanglement of facets, creating a unique story.

NOTES

1. Cher Krause Knight and Harriet F. Senie, "Introduction," in *A Companion to Public Art*, ed. Cher Krause Knight and Harriet F. Senie (Oxford: Wiley Blackwell, 2016), 338.

2. See Maurice Halbwachs, *On Collective Memory* (Chicago: University of Chicago, 1992).

3. Jan Assmann, "Communicative and Cultural Memory," in *Cultural Memory Studies: An International and Interdisciplinary Handbook*, ed. Astrid Erll and Ansgar Nunning (Berlin: Walter de Gruyter, 2008), 110. Besides the cultural concept, Assmann distinguishes two other types of memory: the personal memory, evidently associated with the autobiographical self, and the communicative memory, including all the memories shared by a group of contemporaries. Rather than being based on written history or myths like cultural memory is, collective memory is based on orality and does not need the support of institutions to be preserved. However, according to Assmann, the life of collective memories is short:

after no longer than three generations, they are turned into cultural memories or forgotten forever.

4. Assmann, "Communicative and Cultural Memory," 112.

5. Astrid Erll, "Travelling Memory," *Parallax* 17 (2011): 7.

6. Wolfgang Welsch, "Transculturality—The Puzzling Form of Cultures Today," in *Spaces of Culture: City, Nation, World*, ed. Mike Featherstone and Scott Lash (London: Sage, 1999), 197.

7. Erll, "Travelling Memory," 11. Astrid Erll opposes her concept of "routs of memory" to Pierre Nora's famous notion of *lieux de mémoire*, namely, "sites of memory." Nora's concept strongly informed the field of memory studies on many levels. However, there are two main points that should be discussed here. On the one hand, the French historian considered monuments as symbols of the unstoppable extinction of memory at the hands of our own societies. In this sense, museums, monuments, archives, and celebrations are mere "remains, the ultimate embodiments of a memorial consciousness that has barely survived in a historical age that calls out for memory because it has abandoned it" (12). On the other hand, Nora denounces the emptiness and meaninglessness of these sites of memory, made of pure form without contents, and their essential role in the process of definition of a group's ethnic and national identity. Nora is thus accused of having strengthened the idea of container-cultures. In this regard, see Pierre Nora, "Between Memory and History: Les Lieux de Mémoire, *Representations* 26 (1989): 7–24.

8. Erll, "Travelling Memory," 13.

9. Ibid., 14.

10. Ibid.

11. Ibid., 135.

12. Ibid., 137–38.

13. Richard Crownshaw, "Introduction," in *The Future of Memory*, ed. Richard Crownshaw, Jane Kilby, and Antony Rowland (New York: Berghahn Books, 2010), 6.

14. Richard Crownshaw, Jane Kilby, and Antony Rowland, "Preface," in *The Future of Memory*, ed. Richard Crownshaw, Jane Kilby, and Antony Rowland (New York: Berghahn Books, 2010), x.

15. Edward Helmore, "New York Mayor Considers Christopher Columbus Statue Removal," *The Guardian*, published August 25, 2017, https://www.theguardian.com/us-news/2017/aug/25/new-york-christopher-columbus-statue-de-blasio.

16. Colleen Long, "In Dispute over Statues, Where Do You Draw the Line?" NBC Connecticut, published August 25, 2017, https://www.nbcconnecticut.com/news/politics/In-Dispute-Over-Statues-Where-Do-You-Draw-the-Line-441706443.html.

17. In the following decades, his popularity increased to the extent that, in 1893, during the 400th anniversary of the discovery of America, Chicago hosted the World's Columbian Exposition, celebrating the United States as a new competitive world power. See Laura A. Macaluso, *New Haven's Columbus Day Parade and Monument* (Charleston, SC: Arcadia), 2017.

18. Washington Irving, *The Life and Voyages of Christopher Columbus* (Boston: Twayne, 1981), 10.
19. Orm Overland, *Immigrant Minds, American Identities: Making the United States Home, 1870–1930* (Champaign: University of Illinois, 2000), 48.
20. Overland, *Immigrant Minds, American Identities*, 48.
21. Quoted in David A. Stannard, *American Holocaust: Columbus and the Conquest of the New World* (Oxford: Oxford University, 1992), 70.
22. Robert Berkhofer, *The White Man's Indian: Images of the American Indian from Columbus to the Present* (New York: Vintage Books, 1979), 118–19.
23. Timothy Kubal, *Cultural Movements and Collective Memory: Christopher Columbus and the Rewriting of the National Origin Myth* (New York: Palgrave Macmillan, 2008), 78–79.
24. Kubal, *Cultural Movements and Collective Memory*, 82.
25. Ibid., 83.
26. Anonymous, "Columbus' Monument Is Unveiled by a Little Girl," *New York Herald*, October 13, 1892, 6. The following quotations, if not specified otherwise, are taken from this article.
27. Kubal, *Cultural Movements and Collective Memory*, 110.
28. The statement is reported in Riccardo Chioni, "The Italian Americans Don't Need a Commission to Evaluate Columbus," i-Italy, published November 20, 2017, http://www.iitaly.org/magazine/focus/facts-stories/article/italian-americans-dont-need-commission-evaluate-columbus.

BIBLIOGRAPHY

Anonymous. "Columbus' Monument Is Unveiled by a Little Girl." *New York Herald*, October 13, 1892, 6.

Assmann, Jan. "Communicative and Cultural Memory." In *Cultural Memory Studies: An International and Interdisciplinary Handbook*. Edited by Astrid Erll and Ansgar Nunning, 109–18. Berlin: Walter de Gruyter, 2008.

Berkhofer, Robert. *The White Man's Indian: Images of the American Indian from Columbus to the Present*. New York: Vintage Books, 1979.

Chioni, Riccardo. "The Italian Americans Don't Need a Commission to Evaluate Columbus." i-Italy. Published November 20, 2017. http://www.iitaly.org/magazine/focus/facts-stories/article/italian-americans-dont-need-commission-evaluate-columbus.

Crownshaw, Richard. "Introduction." In *The Future of Memory*. Edited by Richard Crownshaw, Jane Kilby, and Antony Rowland, pp. 3–16. New York: Berghahn Books, 2010.

Crownshaw, Richard, Jane Kilby, and Antony Rowland. "Preface." In *The Future of Memory*. Edited by Richard Crownshaw, Jane Kilby, and Antony Rowland, ix–xiii. New York: Berghahn Books, 2010.

Erll, Astrid. "Travelling Memory." *Parallax* 17 (2011): 4–18.

Halbwachs, Maurice. *On Collective Memory*. Chicago: University of Chicago, 1992.

Helmore, Edward. "New York Mayor Considers Christopher Columbus Statue Removal." *The Guardian*. Published August 25, 2017. https://www.theguardian.com/us-news/2017/aug/25/new-york-christopher-columbus-statue-de-blasio.

Irving, Washington. *The Life and Voyages of Christopher Columbus*. Boston: Twayne, 1981.

Knight, Cher Krause, and Harriet F. Senie. "Introduction." In *A Companion to Public Art*. Edited by Cher Krause Knight and Harriet F. Senie, 337–45. Oxford: Wiley Blackwell, 2016.

Kubal, Timothy. *Cultural Movements and Collective Memory: Christopher Columbus and the Rewriting of the National Origin Myth*. New York: Palgrave Macmillan, 2008.

Landsberg, Alison. *Prosthetic Memory: The Transformation of American Remembrance in the Age of Mass Culture*. New York: Columbia University, 2004.

Long, Colleen. "In Dispute over Statues, Where Do You Draw the Line?" NBC Connecticut. Published August 25, 2017. https://www.nbcconnecticut.com/news/politics/In-Dispute-Over-Statues-Where-Do-You-Draw-the-Line-441706443.html.

Macaluso, Laura A. *New Heaven's Columbus Day Parade and Monument*. Charleston, SC: Arcadia, 2017.

National Italian American Foundation (NIAF). "The National Italian American Foundation Celebrates the Preservation of the Columbus Circle Statue." Accessed February 15, 2017. http://www.niaf.org/niaf_event/national-italian-american-foundation-celebrates-preservation-columbus-circle-statue/.

Nora, Pierre. "Between Memory and History: Les Lieux de Mémoire. *Representations* 26 (1989): 7–24.

Overland, Orm. *Immigrant Minds, American Identities: Making the United States Home, 1870–1930*. Champaign: University of Illinois, 2000.

Pugliese, Stanislao, and William Connell. "Columbus, Our Lady of Loreto and the Ironies of Italian-American History." La Voce di New York. Published October 9, 2017. https://www.lavocedinewyork.com/en/new-york/2017/10/09/columbus-our-lady-of-loreto-and-the-ironies-of-italian-american-history/.

Stannard, David A. *American Holocaust: Columbus and the Conquest of the New World*. Oxford: Oxford University, 1992.

Welsch, Wolfgang. "Transculturality—The Puzzling Form of Cultures Today." In *Spaces of Culture: City, Nation, World*. Edited by Mike Featherstone and Scott Lash, 194–213. London: Sage, 1999.

CHAPTER 14

Visible Differently

Roni Horn's *Vatnasafn/Library of Water* as Memorial

Elliot Krasnopoler

At first glance, it might seem that Roni Horn's project *Vatnasafn/ Library of Water* (2003–2007) is a work of art that is in direct response to global warming.[1] The project, a permanent installation in a stand-alone building located in Stykkishólmur, Iceland, consists of three parts. First, and most conspicuously, a series of vertical glass columns occupy the main room. Collectively titled *Water, Selected*, each column is filled with melted glacial water from twenty-four different Icelandic glaciers (figures 14.1 and 14.2). Another work lies on the floor; this component of the piece, titled *You Are the Weather (Iceland)*, comprises over a hundred Icelandic and English adjectives used to describe weather, each inscribed into a thick rubber substrate (figure 14.3). Finally, the book *Weather Reports You* was published as part of the project, a copy of which can be found in the space. For the book, Horn hired two Icelandic writers to collect stories about local Icelanders' experiences and memories of weather.[2] Their anthropological archive was edited by the artist and published in a collection that Horn describes as a "collective self portrait."[3]

Both melting glaciers and weather are represented in *Library*, two topics often employed by climate change activists to draw attention to their cause. In the documentary *An Inconvenient Truth* (2006), released just one year before Horn's project debuted, Al Gore includes extensive footage of glaciers calving, receding, and disappearing. These images, he says, are evidence the climate is warming. He then points to the weather as further evidence of climate change. Warmer ocean waters intensify weather, causing droughts to worsen, storms to strengthen, and weather-related destruction to increase. In the past decade since the film was released, however, such evidence has largely failed to prompt better governmental policies or ideological changes.

Library's inclusion of both glacial melt and written experiences of weather connects it to environmentalist rhetoric. Yet speaking about the project in a 2009 conversation, Horn plainly states that "I was thinking more about Walter Benjamin than I was about global warming," a shrewd way of denying such

Figure 14.1. Roni Horn, *Vatnasafn/Library of Water*, Iceland, 2007. Courtesy of the artist and Hauser & Wirth.

Photograph by Roni Horn.

Figure 14.2. Roni Horn, *Vatnasafn/Library of Water*, Iceland, 2007. Courtesy of the artist and Hauser & Wirth.

Photograph by Stefan Altenburger.

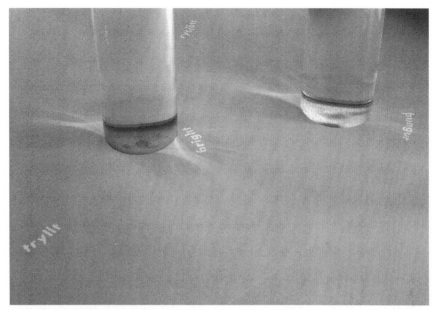

Figure 14.3. Roni Horn, *Vatnasafn/Library of Water*, Iceland, 2007. Courtesy of the artist and Hauser & Wirth.

Photograph by Stefan Altenburger.

an affinity.[4] She goes on to explain that *Library* was "a bid to be more present in local community."[5] Horn elaborates on this idea in a recent interview, explaining that "nature and the actual and experiential are of the utmost importance to me."[6] However, a phenomenological experience of global warming is impossible, a hint at why the artist denies that aspect of the work. Although it really exists, global warming is never experienced directly. Rather, one can only perceive global warming through a series of *effects*, such as intensified weather, melting ice, or extended drought.

I argue that *Library of Water* operates like a pendulum, swinging between what seems to be two irreconcilable attributes: Horn's commitment to local communities and individual experiences and the global urgency of climate change. Through this vacillation between the micro and macro, Horn unites human experience with global change. *Library* emerges as a memorial for the trauma that Earth has been experiencing for years but that humanity (outside of science) is just beginning to notice. The project poses the question: How might we memorialize something so monumental and so vastly inaccessible to human life and experience? *Library* accomplishes this by amassing a series of self-consciously fragmentary interactions with elements of weather, glaciers, and environment. Its human-scaled encounters prompt viewers to recognize their relationship with these elements, as filtered through their own personal experiences. *Library* reveals the importance of experiencing and remembering now, before these earthly artifacts disappear completely.

Horn has been traveling to and producing work about Iceland's remarkable landscapes since the 1970s, but *Library* is her only project sited there. Rather than represent her experiences of the island in transportable works of art, this project beckons travelers to visit the place for themselves. This privileging of travel and place inscribes *Library* into a history of site-specific artworks, such as Robert Smithson's earthworks or a James Turrell *Skyspace* as well as a history of monuments and memorials.[7] However, while the project invites far-reaching visitation, it also serves the town's local population as a community center and gathering place.

Library is housed in the town's original library, a 1950's structure that was overflowing with books when Horn began discussions with the town to use it for this project. Calling it the "Two Libraries Project," Horn suggested that she take over the building after the larger library was built. This began an extended collaboration between Horn and the local Icelandic community. For Horn, the presence and active participation of people forms a critical aspect of the work. Beyond the installation, the space houses many ongoing projects. It currently hosts small concerts of local and international musicians, music lessons taught by the local music school, a women's chess club, and meetings to discuss environmental issues. *Library* also houses an international writer's residency, which prompts participants to integrate into the local community. Anne Carson, for example, read her poetry alongside a group of Icelandic musicians in 2008, and another resident hosted a film series in the space.[8]

Beyond its integration between an artist's project and a community, *Library*'s architecture also encourages visitors to attend to their embodied presence within its space as well as the surrounding environment. For instance, no shoes are allowed. Barefoot, the thick rubber floor compresses and molds beneath the body's weight and movement, asking people to take notice of their physical relationship to their surroundings. Exploring *Library* also involves reading the words inscribed on the floor, a curated collection of adjectives describing the weather. As art historian Briony Fer suggests, many of these words—"calm," "unpredictable," "sultry," "rough," "mild," or "frigid," for instance—could also describe human qualities, foreshadowing the connection Horn elucidates between humanity and weather.[9]

In addition to the flooring, the columns populating the space force careful navigation while simultaneously bending and reshaping the room behind them. The glass columns, at twelve inches in diameter by nine and a half feet tall, are nearly human scale. The pillars of water serve as lenses, refracting and transforming the space as bodies meander within and as weather systems change outside. Horn purposefully renovated the building to enlarge the windows so that views of the sky, water, and mountains surrounding the town would be visible through the glass columns.

Horn also hired teams that collected, transported, and stored the glacial ice for *Water, Selected*. The presence of suspended sediment made the glacial water look slightly different in each column when they were first installed. Years of settling, however, has left the columns completely clear. The once-frozen, suspended glacial dust now forms tiny landscapes at the bottom of each glass container. These small piles of rock and grit encourage close looking and narrate the physical and temporal origins of these waters. Unintended and unforeseen by the artist, it is only in these minute piles that difference can be found, that the glaciers and columns take on an identity relative to their unique locations in Iceland.

The act of removing natural material from an exterior environment and reinstalling it into an interior space recalls the artist Robert Smithson's *Non-Sites*. In these sculptural works, Smithson would collect rocks, sand, or soil from quarries or parks and display the material alongside photographic and textual documentation related to the original site. For Smithson, this displacement was generative, rather than derivative, with the act of collecting bringing new meaning to the selected rocks. *Water, Selected* mirrors this structure, with the published book providing a map of the glaciers from which the ice was sourced as well as several photographs of the act of collection. Unlike *Library*, however, a *Non-Site* is not sited: one created in New Jersey could very well end up in an institution in California. The *Non-Sites* disrupted the urban gallery system, expanding what a work of art could be and what it could reference. Although *Library* builds upon Smithson's earlier artistic practices, Horn's goals are quite different. Sited in a landscape rather than removed from one, *Library* simultaneously references distant landscapes (the glacial sources) and nearby ones (through the windows), prompting a reciprocal rather than exploitative relationship between art and environment. It does not question our conceptions of art or galleries but our conceptions of nature and community.

Scholars Elizabeth Harvey and Mark Cheetham turn to Smithson's writings, rather than his physical works of art, in order to explore the nontraditional qualities of both Horn's work and Carson's poetry. In their essay, "Tongues of Glaciers: Sedimenting Language in Roni Horn's *Vatnasafn/Library of Water* and Anne Carson's 'Wildly Constant,'" they note that *Library* "is a place for engaged reverie."[10] Harvey and Cheetham relate it semantically and metaphorically to Smithson's notion of "glacial reverie," a term he coined in his 1968 essay, "A Sedimentation of the Mind: Earth Works."[11] According to the authors, for Smithson, reverie allows one to create new alliances between mind and matter over an extended geological/glacial time frame in order to consider the poetic nature of disintegration and sedimentation.[12]

Such reverie could turn a *Non-Site*—a mere pile of rocks—into a work of art worthy of value and contemplation.

However, Harvey and Cheetham argue that such reverie can be troubling through its evasion of ecological issues. Horn's collection of water, they claim, is also an elegy for the loss of glaciers. Mining the hidden syntax within the structure of *Library*—the poetics of the columns alongside Carson's word play—the authors suggest that Horn's project "preserves the memory of melting glaciers."[13] They note, for example, that several of the glacial sources in Horn's project have since disappeared, leaving nothing but "liquefied remnants."[14] Through Horn's use of language and the archiving quality of collected ice, they claim that a memory of glaciers is preserved in *Library*.

But what is a memory of a glacier? Can a human body and mind remember or even perceive the monumental and complex structure that is a glacier? I agree with Harvey and Cheetham that *Library* can be elegiac, but it withholds human access to the memories it archives. The infinitesimal fractions of glacial bodies that Horn has collected in this project do not remind one of their ancient icy and geologic sources. Rather than create memories of glaciers, *Library* archives them *as* memories. Because they extend into a temporal and spatial scale impossible to imagine, glaciers cannot be perceived by humans as full entities and are therefore impossible to remember. Glaciers can be measured, mapped, and researched, but these mediated forms enable only an indirect encounter, one that withholds the full ontological weight of these massive objects.

For Timothy Morton, an English scholar who focuses on ecological theory, glaciers, global warming, and weather are all hyperobjects, a term he explains in *Hyperobjects: Philosophy and Ecology after the End of the World*. For Morton, hyperobjects really exist, but humans cannot perceive them. This impossibility has caused humans to often avoid coming to terms, philosophically or ideologically, with such things. He argues that throughout the history of philosophy, humans have subscribed to "correlationism," the idea that the perception of things is what defines them as real.[15] Philosophy, therefore, has been unable to deal with the massive scientific and environmental changes—such as global warming and the nuclear era—that arose during the twentieth century. Morton's theory posits a unique set of relationships between humans and hyperobjects that informs an understanding of Horn's project.

In his book, Morton defines hyperobjects using several terms—viscosity, nonlocality, temporal undulation, and interobjectivity—each of which further reveals the complex relationship *Library* forms between humans and environment. Hyperobjects are viscous because "they 'stick' to beings that are involved with them."[16] This stickiness contributes to all the different effects that hyperobjects cause in the perceptible things around them. As Morton explains, "the shadow of the hyperobject announces the existence of the hyperobject."[17] In other words, like our mediated and partial experience of glaciers and weather in *Library*, we experience all hyperobjects at a remove. The ideal example of this aspect is global warming: we will never observe it directly, but it will overshadow Earth's future for millennia. We are stuck with it and within it.

Hyperobjects are also nonlocal. Rather than being confined to a single place, Morton shows that hyperobjects are "massively distributed in time and space."[18] He uses raindrops as a metaphor for this size discrepancy: "you can feel them on your head—but you can't perceive the actual raindrop in itself."[19] Just as you can't isolate *the* drop that falls on your head, you cannot isolate *the* weather system that is climate. The tiny fractions of glacial ice in *Library* operate similarly. We will never apprehend them fully, but here they can be seen fragmented and shrunken to a local scale.

Weather is also nonlocal, and Horn's understanding and exploration of it in *Library* underscores this idea. In the introduction to *Weather Reports You*, she writes that the weather "may be one of the only things each of us holds in common. And although it varies from here to there, it is, finally, one weather that we share."[20] Weather does not affect only our day-to-day lives; it becomes a connecting force between all of humanity. The titles Horn chose in *Library* further suggest a fluid relationship between humanity and weather. *You Are the Weather (Iceland)*, for instance, proposes that our lived experience is not separate from the weather but integrated with it. Perhaps an unintended resonance, but the line between humanity and climate systems has become further blurred with the increasing presence of global warming and its effects.

Morton's next concept, temporal undulation, corresponds to the vast scales of time that Horn's glaciers and all hyperobjects reside in. He explains that such a large temporal scale creates a "time that is beyond predictability, timing, or any ethical or political calculation. There is an *elsewhere elsewhere*."[21] Invisible aspects of glacial time exist in this "elsewhere elsewhere," points in time that are both distant and unimaginable. Furthermore, temporal undulation reaches into both the unknowable past and the unknowable future. Thus, *Library*'s archive of glacial ice fragments simultaneously references the ancient eroding powers of these icy forms as well as the dismal and destructive future to which they will succumb.

Finally, Morton explains that hyperobjects are interobjective; they exist *only* through their relations to other objects. Hyperobjects change our perceivable world, allowing us to see through time using the changes they enact on the world around them. Consider a dinosaur fossil: according to Morton, even though our relationship to dinosaurs is mediated through time and material—a fossilized bone is not the thing itself—we are still connected to those extinct life forms through the sensuous connection that exists in the fossil.[22] Worldly connections like this, as theorized by interobjectivity, allow us to see and experience the past everywhere. Morton explains this using London as his example: "The streets beneath the streets, the Roman Wall, the boarded-up houses, the unexploded bombs, are records of everything that happened to London. London's history is its form. *Form is memory.*"[23]

Morton's jump from form to memory might seem surprising here, but it is crucial. We might define memory here as the storage and retention within an organism of things learned, evidenced by a modification in the organism's structure.[24] In humans this change in structure occurs at the level of the neuron. However, if we consider a hyperobject as a sort of organism—not quite alive, yet constantly changing and dependent on the world around it—this opens the possibility of nonhuman and nonanimal memory. After all, hyperobjects are complex entities that stretch through time and space. They experience modifications to their structure and form, changes that contain earthly memories. Although these memories might be inaccessible to us, the Earth nonetheless holds a wealth of information and history.

Horn's wordplay in the titles of the works—*Weather Reports You* and *You Are the Weather (Iceland)*—reflects aspects of this dialectic. The titles suggest an active relationship between weather and humanity, one in which the climate has agency and perhaps even memory. Individual memories and experiences of the weather are thus conflated with the hyperobject itself, opening up the possibility that it too might have a memory of its past, present, and future. The columns of water similarly become glacial memories, archiving a history of changing forms within a larger, changing world.

Despite dealing with such massive objects, *Library* operates against the monumental. Occupying a fairly small building, its space is intimate and quiet. In the room, however, it references many of Iceland's monumental features—mountains; glaciers; and harsh, unpredictable weather—through fragmentary and purposefully insufficient means. For instance, the words in the rubber floor might describe many features of the weather, but as a mere collection of words they fail to represent any actual experience of weather systems. Just looking out a window brings one closer to the weather than these adjectives. Similarly, although the columns of glacial ice allow a close encounter with a glacier, each column constitutes such a tiny fraction of the source material that this encounter is necessarily incomplete.

Library enables this intimate encounter between the monumental aspects of the Earth and individual visitors through water. Horn has suggested that water is a highly generative form, one that can create an intimate connection between the displaced objects in *Library* and the hyperobjects it references. She explains, "When I look at water I'm entering into an event of relation.

Rather than an object, water becomes a form—of consciousness, of time, of physicality, of the human condition, of anything I desire to project on it, of anything I want it to be."[25] The water in *Library* not only takes on such an expansive form, but it does so through ancient water, thereby also referencing history, global warming, and climatic systems. Water's physical presence in the space, almost a bodily presence in the vertical columns, calls up the complex and inextricable relationship we have to water, inviting us to, in Horn's words, "consider our existence as part of a universal continuum."[26] While humans need access to water for sustenance, it is also the driving force behind geologic erosion and climate systems. In *Library*, these two radical scales connect, allowing visitors to think about their existence not as individualized and discrete but as part of an interconnected continuum.

However, Horn's project does not just contain water; it is a *Library of Water*, hinting at Horn's act of collection and storage. Libraries have frequently been used in memorials, with the loss of life being equated or analogized through the loss of knowledge. For example, projects such as Rachel Whiteread's *Nameless Library* in Vienna or Micha Ullman's *Memorial for Nazi Book Burning* in Berlin call attention to the loss of knowledge and texts as an allegory for genocide. Like humans, libraries contain a repository of valuable knowledge and narrative. The fact that Horn chose to retain "library" in the project's name makes the aspect of nonhuman memory even more poignant. It suggests that this collection of water also contains knowledge, history, and memory.

Yet amid this collection of water-qua-knowledge, *Library* is also suffused with human language. Between the fragments of descriptions littering the floor and the selections of local memories that populate *Weather Reports You*, words are omnipresent. These words are not meant as interpretations that foreclose meaning; rather they open up new possibilities. Like the windows that overlook the harbor and its landscapes, connecting the interior syntax of *Library* with its outer sources (weather and water, for instance), language connects subjective human experiences to the hyperobjects represented in the small room. Our fragmentary perceptions of hyperobjects are always mediated through language, and *Library* demonstrates this fact. Through its use of language, as well as Horn's careful attentiveness to embodied presence at the site, *Library* encourages a more open relationship to Earth despite its vast inaccessibility.

Throughout, Horn's project reveals its inability to approximate its subjects. Columns of water and a collection of adjectives cannot represent glaciers and weather. Instead, *Library* enables an intimate and slow interaction with fragments of these otherwise distant and unimaginable things. As media theorist Lutz Koepnick proposes, slowness "enables us to explore spatial relationships through physical engagement and mobile interaction. It [allows] us . . . to experience the changing landscapes of the present in all their temporal multiplicity."[27] Visitors meandering through *Library* might notice the tiny landscapes of sediment at the base of the columns, or the feel of the rubber beneath their feet, or even just the weather outside. In this room, the space of *Library* becomes analogous to the space of Iceland and even to the world. Rather than pedantically teaching about the age of glaciers or the dangers of global warming, it invites contemplation.

Although we cannot access the memories present in *Library*, I have tried to show that inaccessibility does not equal absence. Encountering the objects and ideas in *Library* allows one to face both the personal aspects of nature and the global aspects of climate change. Although often spoken about as separate entities, Horn's project disputes that difference. It argues for an interrelation between community and global issues, between human and environment. Just before beginning the *Library of Water* project, Horn wrote: "The blow of the wind across the ocean expanse, through the air, and among the ground cover and wildflowers, makes all things around me visible differently."[28] To see the world differently, all of it, is perhaps all that *Library* asks from us.

NOTES

1. Throughout this paper I use the term "global warming" rather than "climate change." This is partially thanks to Timothy Morton's arguments discussed below. However, global warming is also more precise. As the world warms, the climate will change. Climate change becomes, Morton has argued, a way to anesthetize the seriousness of the problem.

2. Roni Horn, *Weather Reports You* (Göttingen: Artangel/Steidl, 2007).

3. Roni Horn, "Introduction to *Weather Reports You*," in *Vatnasafn/Library of Water* (Göttingen: Steidl, 2009), 107.

4. Tate Modern, "Roni Horn in Conversation," published February 25, 2009, accessed December 20, 2017, http://www.tate.org.uk/context-comment/video/roni-horn-conversation.

5. Ibid.

6. "Moving Water: The Flow of Roni Horn. Julie Ault in Conversation with Roni Horn," in *Roni Horn: Everything Was Sleeping as If the Universe Were a Mistake* (Barcelona: Foundacío Joan Miró, 2014), 119.

7. For more on the history of land-based art, a practice that both Smithson and Turrell are known for, see the catalog for the exhibition *Ends of the Earth: Land Art to 1974*. In it, the curators argue that land art "must be considered in relation to rather than in opposition to the urban," suggesting that a vacillation between society and environment has always been part of this type of practice. Philipp Kaiser and Miwon Kwon, "Ends of the Earth and Back," in *Ends of the Earth: Land Art to 1974* (Munich: Prestel, 2012), 21.

8. I took particular note when I learned of the film series. During my two weeks traveling through Iceland, I did not encounter a single movie theater in any of the towns I visited. A film group, I imagine, would be a unique and special occurrence.

9. Briony Fer, "Storm of the Eye," in *Vatnasafn/Library of Water*, 23.

10. Elizabeth D. Harvey and Mark A. Cheetham, "Tongues of Glaciers: Sedimenting Language in Roni Horn's *Vatnasafn/Library of Water* and Anne Carson's 'Wildly Constant,'" *Word & Image* 31, no. 1 (2015), 20.

11. Smithson's practice was frequently infused with language. His *Non-Sites*, for example, always contained a short description of the site where the material was collected. This essay can be found in *Robert Smithson: The Collected Writings*, ed. Jack Flam (Berkeley: University of California Press, 1996), 100–113.

12. Harvey and Cheetham, "Tongues of Glaciers," 21.

13. Ibid., 26.

14. Ibid., 20.

15. Timothy Morton, *Hyperobjects: Philosophy and Ecology after the End of the World* (Minneapolis: University of Minnesota Press: 2013), 9.

16. Morton, *Hyperobjects*, 1.

17. Ibid., 32.

18. Ibid., 48.

19. Ibid., 11–12.

20. Horn, "Introduction to *Weather Reports You*," 107.

21. Morton, *Hyperobjects*, 67.

22. Ibid.

23. Ibid., 91, my emphasis.

24. The full definition, adopted from *Merriam-Webster*, reads "The store of things learned and retained from an organism's activity or experience as evidenced by modification of structure." Merriam-Webster, s.v., "memory," accessed December 20, 2017, https://www.merriam-webster.com/dictionary/memory.

25. Roni Horn quoted in Kathleen Merrill Campagnolo, "Notes from a Conversation," in *Roni Horn: Still Water* (Santa Fe: SITE Santa Fe, 2000).

26. Campagnolo, "Notes from a Conversation."

27. Lutz Koepnick, *On Slowness: Toward an Aesthetic of the Contemporary* (New York: Columbia University Press), 9.

28. Roni Horn, "September 14th, 2002," Iceland's Difference, accessed December 20, 2017, https://web.archive.org/web/20160105212348/http://libraryofwater.is/icelands_difference_16.html.

CHAPTER 15

Monuments and Other Things That Change

Several Attempts at Titling a Photograph

Masha Vlasova

Several years ago, I was walking the streets of Bishkek with a camera in hand. I had come to the Kyrgyz Republic to make a film about monuments in the city. Framing monuments, public spaces, and parks through my viewfinder, I felt at once welcomed and estranged, returned and displaced. The urban plan of Bishkek strongly resembled the town in which I spent my childhood. I imagined that I could navigate the city equipped with the memory of my hometown. But I could not. I was an outsider: a speaker of Russian and English but not Kyrgyz and a former citizen of the Soviet Union but not a local of Bishkek.

Out of this disorientation, a project emerged. It encompassed two sculptures, a film, a sixteen millimeter film installation, a film screening featuring experimental videos and documentaries from around the globe that take up monuments as their subject, and a series of talks given at visual ethnography and anthropology conferences. Evolving over several years, between the United States, Kyrgyz Republic, Kazakhstan, and Russia, the project became shaped by events as diverse as the annexation of Crimea and a failing relationship. With the recent controversy over the dismantling of monuments to the Confederacy in the United States, my questions and desires for the project, originally crystalized within the context of Bishkek, seem to have come full circle. The conversation, which previously seemed foreign, pertaining to shifting regimes and politics of far away, came home. This encircling urges me to return to the project today.

In 2012 in the National Archives in Bishkek, I found an image that captivated me. It didn't have a title, an author, or a definitive date. The catalog card was remarkably terse: "Bishkek, ca. 1970." The picture depicted a monument during a celebration after it had rained. In the picture, a man was standing by a puddle looking and smiling in the direction of the camera or perhaps a person holding the camera. The frame cropped the monument above the pedestal, but the puddle catches V. I. Lenin in reflection. Because the photographer had

165

pushed Lenin out of the frame, the image seemed to unwittingly foreshadow other images and events: the collapse of the Soviet Union and dismantling of Lenin from his pedestals all over the former Soviet Bloc.

I originally went to the National Archives looking for images of the removal of another Lenin monument from the main square in the city. I was researching what I came to call "monument rotations" in Bishkek and was particularly interested in a pedestal on the main square that has borne three different monuments in the mere two decades since Independence. My arrival to Bishkek came shortly after a revolution (the second one since Independence) in Bishkek, the northern capital, and a civil war in the south. Each shift in state authority put a new face on the main square of the country: from a Lenin to an allegorical image of Liberty, *Erkendik*, represented by a woman holding a symbol of the Kyrgyz home, to the current statue of Manas, the Kyrgyz epic hero and the mythological founder of the Kyrgyz nation.

In combing through the archives, I had an idea of what I was looking for—something resembling a scene from Wolfgang Becker's film *Good Bye Lenin* (2003),[1] where a shot follows a statue of Lenin flying through midair. In the film the protagonist's mother falls into a coma and sleeps through the fall of the Berlin Wall, unwittingly waking to a changed Berlin. The protagonist and the viewer both know that Lenin is being taken down from his plinth, but what the unknowing mother sees is Lenin on his way to a pedestal. Moved by the image from the film—an overwhelmingly literal illustration of the ambiguous state of transition and the fall of the Eastern Bloc—I wanted to seek out other such symbolizations. I found this image instead (figure 15.1). This image doesn't depict the monument in a state of transition. In this image the monument exists and does not exist simultaneously.

This image is symmetrical, split by a reflection, as if a metaphor for the photographic medium itself—the medium of reflections. In this image there is a mystery—no title, no author, no definitive date. The limited entry on the catalog card seemed to invite a wide variety of interpretations. I accept the invitation, and I give this image four different titles, four stories, four possible readings, hoping to find various ways of looking at the monument from the outside and within.

TITLE ONE: "A DISMANTLING OF THE MONUMENT TO V. I. LENIN ON DERZHINSKIY STREET (FUTURE ERKENDIK BOULEVARD), CA. 1970, BISHKEK, KYRGYZSTAN."

On Chuy Street, two kilometers from two Manas monuments. One is from the early 1970s; the other was put up after the 2010 revolution. This doubling echoes the two Lenin monuments that stood two blocks apart in Bishkek, ca. 1970. One stood in the spot of the new Manas until 2003. The other was cap-

Figure 15.1. The Photograph: Anonymous, Untitled, ca. 1970, Bishkek, Kyrgyz Republic. Archived at Kyrgyz National Archives, Bishkek, Kyrgyz Republic.

tured reflected in the puddle of rainwater by the anonymous photographer. Why isn't Lenin in the frame here? Did the anonymous photographer think, what's the harm in one less Lenin?

In the picture, Lenin is cropped out of the frame, cut off his pedestal, dismantled, twenty years before countries all over the former Soviet Bloc—in Europe and Central Asia—began taking Lenins down from their pedestals and replacing them with celebrated poets, national leaders, and mythic heroes.

Whereas many post-Soviet cities have erased artifacts of state socialism, in Bishkek, Soviet-era and postindependence monuments often share the same block. Similarly, postriot ruins and racist graffiti in Osh, the so-called Southern capital, share walls with a very different kind of graffiti—tags and declarations of love layered over the city's faded wall texts. These bittersweet markers create a complex image of a country in transition. Like the image of the monument edited out of the frame, they propose a view of history that is not vertical—in strata—but a horizontal web of interconnected events, a space in which Lenin can be both on and off the pedestal at the same time, a palimpsest.

Mentally holding the image from the archives, I navigated the palimpsest of the city on foot. And I carried my camera everywhere, filming without a tripod, and letting it be at once an entry point into a space and a mediator between my body and the space. The relationship between a body and an unfamiliar space, as mediated by the camera, is common within the tourist's experience. The camera serves at once as a mediator between the tourist and place: it frames the place for the vulnerable outsider and, at the same time shuts the tourist out of the place, creating a barrier or a veil between his or her body and the place.

Yet I was not quite a tourist. In many ways, I experienced Bishkek as a familiar post-Soviet urban space. Russophone, many of the streets bearing the same names as in my hometown in Russia, the town I left over a decade ago for New York City. Monuments, the layout of the city, trademarks of Soviet urban planning, made this unfamiliar place recognizable to me. At the same time I was very much outside of it—a cultural, historical, and even a linguistic foreigner.

In a story I once read as child, a woman could never get lost in an unfamiliar setting, guided by a mind map of the house in which she grew up. She ultimately finds herself in a foreign country, where she happens upon a house that is a mirror image of her childhood home.[2] Bewildered by this coincidence, she wonders if the memory has ever truly been hers to begin with. This existential crisis is interrupted when she finds a flaw in the reflected home, cracks the code of the faulty mirror, and forgets her childhood home completely. Without this mental guide, she becomes a true foreigner in a foreign land, finally able to be lost at last. If I am lost, do I see the city better?

My favorite graffiti in Bishkek: someone had scratched, "I'm a monument" into a city wall. Did the author of this anonymous gesture suggest that graffiti is a form of commemoration and remembrance? Was she, more radically, claiming monument status for herself? "I'm a monument" questions the function of a monument in the city. We think of monuments as erected by the government as a form of communication with the people, not the other way around. Perhaps this is what allows one pedestal to accommodate different messages, depending on the regime. This artist reverses the communication by claiming her graffiti to be a monument. I've turned to various wall texts and graffiti to seek out captions or possible titles for my photograph. I'd like to think that, much like the author of "I'm a monument," the city's anonymous graffiti artists, vandals, and subversives were writing on the sides of walls and buildings with the purpose of titling my found photograph, as though through some great unconscious collective effort.

Possible titles of the untitled photograph of the monument to V. I. Lenin, Bishkek, ca. 1970:

"We're with the Nation"
"So What?"
"I [heart] You"
"Bishkek I Love You"
"He Is We"
"Video Surveillance"
"November 9th, 2013"
"I Went Out to Get Bread to Tashkent"
"Tsoi is Alive"
"Victor Tsoi is Alive, 2012"

TITLE TWO: "LENIN IS FLOATING IN A PUDDLE OF RAINWATER, KNOCKED OFF HIS PEDESTAL BY AN ANONYMOUS SUBVERSIVE CAMERA, CA. 1970"

I am turning the photograph around in my hands. The photograph is turning Lenin on his head. The specific gesture of the photographer to leave Lenin in the puddle reveals the unique meaning of a subversive action during the period often identified as Late Socialism (dated roughly from the mid-1950s to the late 1980s). The anthropologist Alexei Yurchak examines Late Socialism in his influential work *Everything Was Forever Until It Was No More*. In it, he rejects the Cold War binary that an individual must choose to either actively embrace or subvert sociopolitical life, insisting that many Late Soviet citizens actually opted to do neither. Instead, they remained outside the state, even while their citizenship and geographic embedment positioned them very firmly *within* it. He turns to the Russian term *vnye*, to define this experience further.

> To be *vnye* usually translates at "outside." However, the meaning of this term, at least in many cases, is closer to a condition of being simultaneously inside and outside of some context—such as, being within a context while remaining oblivious of it, imagining yourself elsewhere, or being inside your own mind. It may also mean being simultaneously a part of the system and yet not following certain of its parameters.[3]

With the concept of *vnye*, defined as a unique state of being simultaneously inside and outside a state-assigned social setting or ritual, Yurchak proposes a radical refiguration of Late Socialist historiography, dismantling the common Cold War–born assumption that the Soviet experience was inherently polarized. Taken in Soviet Bishkek, probably in the 1970s, my found image exemplifies the monument to Lenin in the state of *vnye*, as both depicted and excised, both present and absent. Furthermore it reveals *vnye* as a possible motivation behind the image.

In Soviet Kyrgyzstan, the period of Late Socialism is linked with a revival of Kyrgyz cinema, the so-called Kyrgyz New Wave, known as "The Kyrgyz Miracle." It was a movement in the arts that challenged the accepted narrative of history through visual narration in film. Films such as *The White Mountains* (1964)[4] and *The Sky of Our Childhood* (1966), among others, veiled their often-controversial ideas in visual metaphor and cultural references obscure to the censors in Moscow. In *The White Mountains*, a young man stumbles upon a burned down encampment where only one yurt has survived. There he falls in love with a girl, who is soon to be married off to a rich *bai* (herdsman). Maybe the love story helped the film escape censorship. In small moments of dialogue, imagery, and music, the film illuminates a moment in Kyrgyz history that came to be known as the Kyrgyz genocide and the exodus of 1916.

After Kyrgyzstan became part of the Russian Empire at the end of the nineteenth century, Russian settlers moved into fertile lands, pushing the Kyrgyz out and sparking an uprising that the empire violently put down. Until the Bolshevik Revolution ended the genocide, thousands of Kyrgyz died or fled to China. In the film, there is no one left to bury the dead. There aren't even any yurts left to perform the burial ritual. Only the yurt's skeletal frames remain, as if the whole country has become a cemetery. Although obscure outside of Kyrgyzstan, the film has a second title, *Difficult Crossing*. It alludes to the girl's perilous escape to the other side of the river, which her lover does not survive. And it suggests another painful transition—a difficult parting with the past.

By the 1970s, photographers all over the Soviet Bloc were shooting Lenins in puddles, in pieces, and off pedestals. Was the author of the image an artist of the "Kyrgyz Miracle"? Did he try to get rid of it, afraid of the anti-authoritative connotations it might carry but couldn't bring himself to destroy it? Did he hide it in the safest place of all—the dusty archives—certain that no one would face digging in the bins, wrangling with grumpy archivists, and deciphering cryptic handwriting on a catalog card, just to find her small picture? Not to mention the dangers of actually finding the photograph, looking at it, or possessing it, even if only in memory? Did this image and others like it cause the collage and the ultimate dismantling? How dangerous was it to break with the past in the 1960s? In the 1970s? In the 1980s? In 2012? In 2017?

On a pedestal outside of Bishkek, Lenin's dates of birth and death are engraved. Was it a fluke, an anomaly, a Freudian slip, or another subversive act that slipped by the authorities: to bring Lenin's mortality into focus and to turn a pedestal into a gravestone?

TITLE THREE: "THE HAUNTED PEDESTAL: GHOST OF LENIN APPEARING IN A PUDDLE OF RAINWATER. INDEFINITE DATE"

What if the monument to Lenin was already removed at the time this photograph was taken and his captured reflection is simply a trick of photo processing? What if the monument to Lenin was already removed at the time this photograph was taken and the reflection is a ghostly apparition of Lenin, peeking through the veil of history?

In Bishkek of 2012, when the memories of both revolutions and the civil war in the south were still fresh, one couldn't ignore the ghosts. One such ghost is the monument to Liberty, *Erkendik*. It was a gold-plated statue of a winged woman, reaching up to the sky, holding a *tyunduk*, an element of the traditional Kyrgyz home, the yurt, and symbol of the Kyrgyz nation, which also appears on the Kyrgyz flag. In 1999, *Erkendik* stood in the place of Lenin in the photograph from the archives, before being moved to the main square. After the second revolution of 2010, the monument to Manas replaced *Erkendik*. Since then, she has been a phantom that appears on outdated postcards and in documentaries—all monuments in their own right.

In Dalmira Telepbergenova's documentary film, *Crash Down from the Seventh Floor* (2005),[5] the author tries to make sense of the violence of 2005, outraged by the brutality of the revolution that overthrew Kyrgyzstan's first president, Askar Akaev, in what is known in the West as the Tulip Revolution. One thing about this therapeutic exercise in filmmaking that interests me is what the camera framed by accident. Here the *Erkendik* monument is cropped out of the frame, leaving an empty pedestal, already a ghost (figure 15.2).

Kyrgyzstan was again the scene of unrest and riots in 2010, when ethnic clashes between the Kyrgyz and the Uzbek population in the south of the country led to a full-blown civil war in Osh. The ghostly remnants of that violence—the ruined bazaar, the graffiti, the rubble—are impossible to ignore. Some graffiti, demarcating ethnic neighborhoods, has been painted over, but it still peeks through, like a ghost appearing through a layer of time. When I went to the bazaar to film the ruins, it happened to be the first day that the city started cleaning up the ruins in two years.

Also, in Osh, I saw another strange relic: a one-handed Lenin who was once pointing into the bright socialist future. Unlike the "main" Lenin monument that towers over Lenin square, down Lenin Street on an enormous pedestal and with plenty of space for a viewer to contemplate his magnitude, my one-handed Lenin floats over a sea of greenery in a small park near a hospital. The park is overgrown, unkept. The only sign of someone paying attention

Figure 15.2. Monument to *Erkendik* (Liberty) cut out of the frame; film still from *Crash Down from the Seventh Floor* (*Vniz s Sed'mogo Etazha*). Dalmira Telepbergenova, dir., 2006, Kyrgyz Republic.

Courtesy of the author.

to this abandoned park are shiny *tyundyuks* welded onto the rusting gate—a reminder of the 2010 events and a territorial marking of the space of Kyrgyz.

My one-handed Lenin is almost to scale, life sized. He stands on a humble pedestal but remains the tallest construction in the park. What remains of other monuments and skeletons of once-benches is covered in graffiti. Lenin is also signed in the front and back.

Perhaps removing Lenin's hand is an artistic act, and the auteurs signed their names on Lenin's pedestal and body after finishing the job. Perhaps they are the same artists who took my picture. Perhaps undermining Lenin through the photographic medium was not enough for them, and they needed to physically disarm him. Like the author of "I'm a monument," the graffiti artists level the field with Lenin.

TITLE FOUR: "PORTRAIT OF AN UNKNOWN MAN BY AN UNKNOWN PHOTOGRAPHER BY THE STATUE OF VLADIMIR ILYICH LENIN ON THE DAY OF HIS BIRTHDAY FLOATING IN THE PUDDLE OF RAINWATER"

The found photograph is a personal picture like so many in Soviet families, including my own: beside monuments, against the backdrop of history. I look at the photograph through a veil of shared history and see faces of my mother and her sisters, young, dressed up, posing in front of a monument to Lenin in their hometown in Russia. Taken in the 1970s, those snapshots embrace and inhabit the liminal space of *vnye*.

In this image, the man is standing by the puddle, looking straight into the camera, smiling. He is the only one in this scenario facing away from Lenin and remains anonymous like the photographer. At the same time he is extremely familiar, posing in front of the monument for the camera. Did he come to the monument with the photographer to get his picture taken next to Lenin? Could he be a foreigner like me? Is he a friend, a sibling, a lover of the photographer? These possibilities form an entryway into the image. A personal story and a mystery emerges from this photograph, one that exists in sync with revolutions and riots; regime shifts; and political, social, and cultural histories yet remains outside of the subversive act read into the image earlier.

Maybe the photographer came to the celebration as others lay flowers at Lenin's pedestal. Maybe it's Lenin's birthday in April, Bishkek's rainiest month. He or she comes there and chooses to cut out the hero of the occasion. It is an accidental transgression, perhaps, to leave Lenin lying in the cold puddle. But more so, it's a personal decision, to put this smiling man literally before the state.

POSTSCRIPT

Lenins started falling all over Ukraine during the Euromaidan protests in late 2013, like they did in the 1990s. At the same time in Russia, renovated Lenins—once dismantled or vandalized in the late 1980s and early 1990s—were erected back onto their pedestals. As through the window of the found Bishkek photograph, I was seeing Lenin on his way to and off the pedestal once again. Have I been looking at the Bishkek photograph upside down all along, mistakenly taking the reflection for the original? By reading the present into this image of the past, might we begin to see the future in the images of the present?

Through the many windows of my screen, I followed video reportages of Michael Khodorkovsky and members of the Russian activist art group Pussy Riot as they were released from prison, in the ominous gesture of the state's generosity before the upcoming Olympic Games in Sochi. My thoughts returned to the 1980 Summer Olympics in the Soviet Union, when twenty-four countries led by the United States boycotted the Games, a mere decade before its dissolution. My thoughts returned to a mural I saw when I was traveling in Osh, with the Olympic Bear and the date "1980" depicted on it in commemoration of the event, intact, sharing the street with a mosque, a bank, and the burned down remnants of the 2010 ethnic riots.

In 2014, when it came time to record the voiceover for the film, the Russian Federation annexed Crimea. In the middle of the recording, my voiceover actress, Yelena S., who it turned out was originally from Crimea, went off script. She spoke of the intensity she experienced seeing her hometown on the front

Figure 15.3. Empty pedestal that once supported a double equestrian statue to Stonewall Jackson and Robert E. Lee and graffiti: "HONOR" and "HISTORY," Baltimore, Maryland, 2017.
Courtesy of A.K. Gatewood.

page of the *New York Times*; of the helplessness she felt being *here*, in America, while things are happening *there*; of not being able to let go and not knowing how to locate her responsibility from the liminal space of *vnye*, of being in between languages, countries, nationalities.

Today, I'm captivated by a different image, of a different pedestal. The image has an author and a definitive date. The picture is of an empty pedestal that once supported a double equestrian statue to Stonewall Jackson and Robert E. Lee in Baltimore, Maryland. In the early morning of August 16, 2017, the statue was removed. A few weeks later, my friend A. K. Gatewood took a picture of the empty pedestal on her morning jog and emailed it to me (figure 15.3).

I'm drawn to the graffiti: two words are painted on the bench, in the foreground of the image. "HONOR" is in pale yellow with a black outline. "HISTORY," perhaps painted by the same hand, and now erased by a different hand, is barely legible.

NOTES

1. Wolfgang Becker, dir., *Good Bye Lenin!* (Los Angeles, CA: Sony Pictures Classics, Hollywood Classic Entertainment, 2003), DVD.
2. Milorad Pavic, "The Warsaw Corner" ("Varshavskij Ugol"), collection *Russian Hound (Russkaya Borzaya)*, 1979 (Amfora, Russia, 2000).
3. Alexei Yuchak, *Everything Was Forever Until It Was No More: The Last Soviet Generation* (Princeton: Princeton University Press, 2005), 129.
4. Melis Ubukeev, dir., *The White Mountains/Difficult Crossing (Belye Gory/Trudnaya Pereprava)* (USSR, 1964), published in *Two Epochs of National Self-Determination in Central Asian*.
5. Dalmira Telepbergenova, dir., *Crash Down from the Seventh Floor (Vniz s Sed'mogo Etazha)* (Kyrgyz Republic, 2005), published in *Two Epochs of National Identity Formation: Documentary Films of Central Asia* (Budapest: The Open Society Institute, 2008), DVD.

CHAPTER 16

Illegal Monuments

Memorials between Crime and State Endorsement

Nausikaä El-Mecky

A BRONZE SCULPTURE OF A GIRL COULD HAVE IMPLICATIONS FOR THE NORTH Korean missile crisis. An artistic installation in a small German village is called a terrorist act. In New York City, a monument that was visible for only a few hours prompts the New York City Police Department to conduct DNA tests. These are just a few examples from the extreme world of illegal monuments.

The creators of these monuments do not wait for permission to commemorate certain persons and occurrences. Instead, they present a version of events that runs counter to the established political or historical narrative: suddenly, enemies of the state are recast as heroes; forgotten victims are remembered and vindicated. One might assume that most of these illegal monuments are short lived and fleeting. But the various international examples in this essay show that illegal monuments can have tremendous influence on a national or even global scale. In addition, they do not exist only in the unlawful realm. Practically overnight, they can become state sanctioned or transform from activist objects into works of art, showcased in galleries and museums. Illegal monuments are slippery and often harbor many contradictions, merging humor with trauma or the virtual with the real. Thus, they may be impossible to define. And yet—at the same time—it is precisely their shifting nature that allows us to reconsider what a monument, be it legal or illegal, actually *is*.

VIDEO GAME MONUMENT

The easiest way to create an illegal monument may be to transform an existing one: smear it with red paint so that it appears to be dripping with blood, change the inscription or—as happened to a Christopher Columbus monument in Detroit in 2015—tape a hatchet to its forehead.[1] If you search online for "illegal" and "monument," the vast majority of news reports will show similar incidents where existing monuments are modified, defaced, or outright destroyed. This can create the impression that there are only two options: either accept the monument that the authorities have created or attack it. And yet far less attention has been given to a third option: to create an entirely new monument from scratch, bypassing the official channels entirely. This "third way" can be expensive and dangerous, but sometimes the payoff surpasses the activists' wildest expectations.

This happened, for instance, in 2016, the year Pokémon Go, an augmented reality video game, became a global craze. In August of that year, an anonymous artist installed a five-foot statue of Pikachu, the game's most recognizable character in a switched-off fountain in New Orleans's Lower Garden District. They called it #Pokemonument. The sculpture combined two seemingly mutually exclusive things: it was unlawful and playful but also used the visual language of traditional state-sanctioned monuments. Although Pikachu was made of fiberglass, it had a coating that made it look like bronze.

Perhaps it was exactly this combination of the irreverent and the traditional that made the action so successful: blogs, newspapers, and social media all over the world talked about it. Yet only two weeks later, before the local government had even decided what to do about the unauthorized monument, #Pokemonument disappeared. A YouTube video was published in which the anonymous artist(s) explained their decision to auction off the sculpture while interest was high. They stated: "Public sculpture, *whether sanctioned or not*, has the potential to transform and energize community spaces [italics added]."[2]

Ultimately, the proceeds would be donated to benefit the neighborhood parks.[3] But despite its online fame, #Pokemonument ultimately fetched the relatively modest sum of $2,000 at auction.[4] What happened with another illegal monument in South Korea in 2011 had much more dramatic consequences. And unlike #Pokemonument, which may have lingered in the public's minds for a few months, its impact has only increased since it was first installed seven years ago.

CLENCHED FISTS AND HAND-KNITTED BOOTIES

In 2011, an unauthorized monument appeared in front of the Japanese Embassy in Seoul, South Korea. It consisted of two bronze chairs: one empty and the other one occupied by a life-sized young woman, also made of bronze and dressed in traditional Korean *Hanbok* dress. Her fists were clenched, and her face wore a puzzling expression that looked neutral from afar but could be interpreted as melancholy or even anger from up close. Called the "Statue of Peace,"[5] it was installed to commemorate a historical trauma, which has been little acknowledged. During the Second World War, the Japanese Army set up stations for so-called comfort women. This soothing term is deeply misleading: an estimated two hundred thousand women and young girls, mostly Koreans, were forcibly taken to brothels servicing Japanese soldiers under horrific conditions.[6] After the war, many survivors faced rejection and shame.[7] Only in the 1990s did these women start speaking out about the ordeal they had faced. Soon after, in 1992, demonstrations began in front of the Japanese Embassy in Seoul, campaigning for reparations. Nearly twenty years later, the activists wanted to create something to commemorate the 1,000th demonstration. "If the Japanese government didn't react so excessively, it would probably have just been a small memorial stone," activist and sculptor Kim Seo-kyung told CNN.[8] Angered, she and her husband designed the much larger memorial of the young girl instead.

The effects were dramatic: even though they had never given their permission for its installation, the South Korean government refused to remove the memorial. This resulted in a diplomatic row between Japan and South Korea, which finally appeared to be resolved with an agreement after several years, in December 2015. Japan apologized, and a fund of $8.7 million was set up to financially support the surviving comfort women.[9] But the matter was far from over—and would take on global proportions.

Despite apologizing, Japan had not accepted legal responsibility. The official agreement treated the past as a closed chapter: Japan and South Korea would no longer bring up the matter in international forums. In addition, the sculpture in front of the embassy was supposed to be removed.[10] Activists accused the government of accepting a deal that found little support among either the survivors or the South Korean population.[11] And so the illegal monument became not only a symbol of this activist movement but also a treasured site. People were willing to face extreme discomfort: traveling for hours to Seoul, even temporarily dropping out of university to guard the Statue of Peace, in freezing conditions as well as in extreme heat.[12]

The bronze girl was not only shielded from the authorities but also from the elements: she was dressed in different hats and scarves and even customized knitted booties. Though activists had to contend with some friction with local police, the statue with the clenched fists was not only left in place; it multiplied.

On December 28, 2016, exactly a year after the agreement between the two nations,[13] a nearly identical Peace Statue appeared in front of the Japanese consulate, this time in the South Korean town of Busan. Unlike with the Seoul statue, the local police intervened swiftly and confiscated the monument. Yet within hours, massive protests broke out. Social media was filled with angry comments and videos; the local website of the Busan ward office received so many complaints that it shut down.[14] Quickly, the local mayor apologized and returned the statue: "This is an issue between the two nations, and I realize it's too much for a local office like mine to handle."[15] An international matter it was indeed. Japan withdrew its ambassador in protest for the duration of several months and accused South Korea of breaching the 1961 Vienna Convention, which guarantees the peace and safety of diplomatic missions.

This was a problem of global proportions because it was not only a disagreement between two neighboring nations but also between two key American allies against North Korea. Reports all over the world, from the *New York Times* to the *Japan Times*, mentioned the statues in one breath with the North Korean missile crisis and how the monuments posed a real threat to the stability in the region. Undeterred, South Korea passed new legislation that transformed the illegal monument in Seoul into an official one under government protection.[16] Nearly forty memorials to comfort women appeared all over South Korea. At the Japanese consulate in Busan, staff was even confronted with *two* memorials: the permanent bronze one and a traveling version, which sat on the bus line that stopped right in front of the consulate.[17]

What began with a few illegal memorials in South Korea has now strained diplomatic relations between Japan and numerous other nations: authorized and unauthorized comfort women memorials have sprung up from China to Europe and the United States, with dramatic or surprising consequences: president of the Philippines, Rodrigo Duterte, had no qualms about breaking national and international laws by supporting the unlawful killing of thousands in his war on drugs,[18] but when it came to an unauthorized Peace Memorial in Manilla, he said: "That is a constitutional right which I cannot stop. It's prohibitive for me to do that."[19] Meanwhile, an authorized comfort women monument in San Francisco has led to the severing of ties with its Japanese partner city of six decades, Osaka.[20]

Twenty-five years ago, protests began, calling for the suffering of the comfort women to be acknowledged. But it was an illegal monument of a girl with clenched fists that transformed a small activist movement into an international political and diplomatic phenomenon.

UNTIL HE KNEELS AND BEGS FOR FORGIVENESS

The Peace Statues are only one example of the fluidity of a monument's legal status. In Iraq, for instance, it was an offense to damage any of the hundreds of monuments glorifying Saddam Hussein. But after the US invasion of 2003, the opposite was enforced: holding on to sculptures of the fallen dictator was akin to harboring a criminal. A director of the fire department in Nineveh (Iraq) was arrested for hiding a large Saddam sculpture in the department's basement.[21] A monument can also be unintentionally illegal: Din Kossova, an Albanian immigrant living in the United States, wanted to create a monument dedicated to President Woodrow Wilson, who had supported Albanian independence and is a revered figure in his home country. Little did Kossova know that what he assumed to be "No Man's Land"[22] was in fact just inside the unmarked perimeter of Joshua Tree National Park. Kossova was subjected to a trial and received a $9,000 fine, and his monument will, in all likelihood, be destroyed using explosives.[23]

Then, there are the unauthorized protest monuments with all the trappings of illegality: intentionally created to shock, not approved in any way by authorities or politicians—and yet they are not *actually* illegal. The monument created by the artistic activists of the German Center for Political Beauty[24] (CPB) had to achieve two things: cause a scandal and not land its creators in jail. And so, months before the unveiling, the CPB activists did everything to cover themselves legally.

Their action was triggered in January 2017, when Björn Höcke, a local leader of the far-right Alternative for Germany (AfD) Party,[25] said in a speech that "Germans are the only people in the world who plant a monument of shame in the heart of the capital."[26] He was referring to the Memorial to the Murdered Jews of Europe, an immersive installation of more than two thousand concrete slabs of varying height in central Berlin.

The outraged CPB activists began investigating how to retaliate and discovered that the garden adjacent to Höcke's house in Bornhagen, a small German village, was available for rent. They spent the next ten months preparing in secret, working with a stage designer, architects, and several lawyers.[27] Their large following crowdfunded the project, even though the CPB activists did not disclose to anyone what they were planning. Then, on a November morning, Höcke woke up to his own private Holocaust memorial—right next to his house. The CPB activists had reconstructed a part of the Berlin monument in true size. Twenty-four hollow pieces of hardboard, covered with concrete and made to resemble the original memorial's uneven texture, were placed in full view of the politician's house (figure 16.1). Its name, *Monument der Schande* (*Monument of Shame*), was taken directly from Höcke's incendiary speech.

"We had only one shot at getting it right,"[28] says Cesy Leonard, one of the CPB's leaders. The disassembled slabs were brought in three days prior; a crew of twenty people worked through the night to put them up. How was it possible that such a large group could work day and night without anyone noticing? "We told the neighbors that we were celebrating an engagement,"[29] Leonard says, "and that, since it was a surprise for the fiancé, who would arrive in a few days, everything had to be kept under wraps. The neighbors were quite moved by that. Nobody else seemed to care what we were doing."[30]

Working nervously under tarps, using low-volume drills, the CPB activists managed to finish their monument and achieve the wow effect they had been hoping for. "We are existing in an economy of attention,"[31] says Leonard, and so, the action could be called a success only if journalists picked up on it. Fortunately for the CPB, it caused a sensation, with national and international outlets reporting. The landlord was less than pleased when he found out and

Figure 16.1. *Monument of Shame* (with politician Björn Höcke's house in Bornhagen, Germany in the background), Center for Political Beauty, 2017.
Courtesy of Patryk Witt / Center for Political Beauty.

took the CPB to court. But the activists had gone over all eventualities with their lawyers months prior and had even contacted the local building authority. Anyone was permitted to construct a work of art in their garden, as long as it was lower than three meters.[32] Their preparations had paid off: the landlord lost,[33] and there are sufficient funds for the monument to stay up for another seven years, guarded by security cameras and volunteers.

But this does not mean that the CPB is out of the woods yet, legally speaking. There is another—invisible—part of the action that might be illegal, after all, and for which the activists are being investigated by the police.[34] The CPB activists have been following Höcke and collecting details about his private life, and they will not stop until he kneels in front of the monument and asks for forgiveness.[35] Therefore, the monument itself may not be illegal, but its *function* is in a gray area. The surveillance of Höcke and the monument are one and the same project. The monument is a ritual site: the ritual of Höcke's apology, that is, if the pressure of being followed gets the better of him.

WHISTLEBLOWERS AND HOLOGRAMS

The success of unauthorized monuments today may stand and fall with their impact online. The confiscated Statue of Peace in Busan was swiftly returned after outrage exploded on social media. The CPB has more than two hundred thousand followers on Facebook and over three thousand people funding their latest project through their crowdfunding website. But the virtual realm not only plays a key role in an unauthorized monument's creation and preservation but also—if it is removed—in its afterlife.

In April 2015, a four-foot-high bronze bust of whistleblower Edward Snowden was placed on an existing pedestal in Fort Greene Park, New York, by artists disguised as construction workers. It was an illegal monument within a legal monument, placed inside a memorial landscape that was also a burial ground for over eleven thousand people who died in British captivity during the American Revolutionary War. As with the German CPB's *Monument of Shame*, the Snowden monument engages in a dialogue with the older monument. "It would be a dishonour to those memorialized here to not laud those who protect the ideals they fought for, as Edward Snowden has by bringing the National Security Agency's 4th-Amendment-violating surveillance programs to light," the artists said in a statement. "All too often, figures who strive to uphold these ideals have been cast as criminals rather than in bronze."[36] The response was rapid: within a few hours, the bust had been hidden by the authorities under blue tarpaulin while the police department took DNA samples to trace the culprits.[37]

The monument may have been taken into custody, but it was still reaching people. In spite of its classical appearance, the monument was very much part of the digital era. Even its title, *Prison Ship Martyrs 2.0*, sounds like the updated version of a software program. The artists initially remained anonymous and released their statement and video of the installation online.[38] After news of the monument broke, the Illuminator Art Collective, a separate group of artists, arrived at the site. They threw ashes into the air, and onto these loose particles they projected, with blue light, a hologram of Snowden's face.[39] That the effect lasted for only about ten minutes did not matter, as long as other artists would be inspired to pursue similar actions or as collective member Grayson Earle said: "the idea and the conversation can still take place, even though that material structure is gone."[40] Since not that many people saw the actual hologram, the artists probably expected to reach audiences online with images of their stunt. The creators of the Snowden monument's plan B also relied on the internet. They shared a file that allowed people from all over the world to reproduce the bust themselves using a 3-D printer.[41]

In the end, the creators of the Snowden monument were a lot luckier than Din Kossova of the Joshua Tree monument: they were spared the costs for towing and storage of their bust and only had to pay $50 for trespassing.[42] In addition, the bust has been shown in various museums and exhibitions. "I've never had anything in any museum," one of the artists said.[43] And so, an illegal monument that was visible for only a few hours had a much longer virtual afterlife and, in the process, became a legitimate work of art.

MINIATURE MONUMENTS

Berlin-based artist Evol also moves between the illegal sphere and the established art world. He has been a part of exhibitions from Finland to China, but for the past fifteen years, he has also left over five hundred illegal "miniature monuments" in cities all over the world.

Monuments commemorating the everyday are rare, yet Evol creates just that: tributes to the dreariness of people's daily existence under socialism. His inspirations are the crumbling socialist-era estates he saw all over Berlin. Across the Soviet Union and its satellite states, including East Berlin, these estates were built to house the workers. Cheaply built, they were often damp and dark, decay setting in as soon as the building was completed. For Evol, these buildings symbolize the stark contrast between the Socialist ideal of an equal, classless society and the actual reality, where "individuality was erased by the state. In these buildings, an anonymous mass was put to bed, just so it could go back to work the next day."[44] Evol wanted to show "how this utopian dream turned into a distopian reality. This past still affects relationships between people today. The inequalities of socialism endure in today's capitalism."[45]

It turns out that most cities already provided the raw materials for his monuments: electricity enclosures, those white or gray cabinets that can be

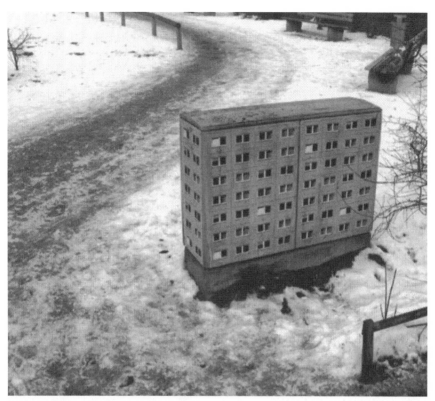

Figure 16.2. *Nuremberg Interventions,* Evol, spray paint on transparent paper, wheatpaste, Nuremberg, Germany, 2005.
Courtesy of the Artist.

found on most streets. Using stencils and several layers of spray paint, he creates doors, windows, and sometimes a few balconies, turning dull, everyday objects into eye-catching illusions of socialist buildings—the dirt and banality of the architecture made strangely beautiful by the artist's skill (figure 16.2).

As with the unauthorized monuments created in South Korea and Bornhagen, his work invites public participation. People have put cutout photos in the tiny windows, and graffiti artists add miniature versions of their tags. But Evol also has to accept that by putting his work out on the street, the majority of his pieces are papered over by posters or covered with graffiti. He has much more control over his legal artistic practice. In his studio, he also creates miniature buildings, but they are mostly inspired by older architecture. They are made on cardboard, using a similar technique, but with a lot more stencil layers and details. As with the CPB, the line between his legal and illegal work is unclear. He has shown gallerists his unauthorized monuments as well as his legal studio work, and he is regularly invited to create his monuments for street art festivals that are supported by city councils. He earns his living with his legal studio works about architecture, but he continues to create their illegal twins "whenever the mood strikes me."[46]

UNAUTHORIZED. UNDEFINABLE.

Unauthorized monuments appear to exist in many different spheres all at once: they can be illegal but become treasured by the state; they are physical objects, which may still unfold their greatest impact online; they can look innocent or playful but harbor a much darker message; they can use the traditional visual language of state-sanctioned monuments but express a strong anti-establishment message. Perhaps it is their self-contradictory nature that makes unauthorized monuments so fascinating. In addition, they suggest that anyone can erect a memorial, at any time—not just the state. These memorials can transform a forgotten fountain or a sidewalk into a dramatic site for community bonding, diplomatic conflict, or ritual. Unauthorized monuments challenge who and what we commemorate and say as much about the past as about the future.

NOTES

1. Sarah Cascone, "Detroit Statue Vandalized as Anti-Columbus Day Sentiment Grows," Artnet News, published October 13, 2015, accessed February 18, 2018, https://news.artnet.com/art-world/detroit-columbus-statue-vandalized-339696.
2. "Artist Statement," video, 0:49, posted by Pika Pika, August 14, 2016, https://www.youtube.com/watch?v=6p6cjT3LPXw&ab_channel=PikaPika.
3. Della Hasselle, "Coliseum Square's Pokemon Statue to be Auctioned; Proceeds to Benefit Neighborhood Parks," *The New Orleans Advocate*, published August 14, 2016, accessed February 18, 2018, http://www.theadvocate.com/new_orleans/entertainment_life/arts/article_5555af14-624c-11e6-b866-db952531d7fc.html?utm_medium=social&utm_source=email&utm_campaign=user-share.
4. New Orleans Advocate Staff, "Mysterious Pokemonument Statue Sells for $2,000 at Auction Sunday," *The New Orleans Advocate*, September 25, 2016, accessed February 18, 2018, http://www.theadvocate.com/new_orleans/news/article_1b280f10-8341-11e6-b643-4fba7c7f2de3.html?utm_medium=social&utm_source=email&utm_campaign=user-share.
5. The statue is also known as the "Peace Statue" or "Peace Monument."
6. See, for example, Carmen Argibay, "Sexual Slavery and the Comfort Women of World War II," *Berkeley Journal of International Law* 21, no. 2 (2003): 375–89, accessed February 6, 2018, https://doi.org/10.15779/Z38VW7D.
7. See, for example, Pyong Gap Min, "Korean 'Comfort Women': The Intersection of Colonial Power, Gender, and Class," *Gender and Society* 17, no. 6 (2003): 938–57, accessed February 18, 2018, http://journals.sagepub.com/doi/abs/10.1177/0891243203257584.

8. Sol Han and James Griffiths, "Why This Statue of a Young Girl Caused a Diplomatic Incident," CNN, modified February 10, 2017, accessed February 18, 2018, https://www.cnn.com/2017/02/05/asia/south-korea-comfort-women-statue/index.html.

9. See, for example, Justin McCurry, "Japan and South Korea Agree to Settle Wartime Sex Slaves Row," *The Guardian*, published December 28, 2015, accessed February 18, 2018, https://www.theguardian.com/world/2015/dec/28/japan-to-say-sorry-to-south-korea-in-deal-to-end-dispute-over-wartime-sex-slaves.

10. Justin McCurry, "Buses in Seoul Install 'Comfort Women' Statues to Honour Former Sex Slaves," *The Guardian*, published August 16, 2017, accessed February 18, 2018, http://www.theguardian.com/cities/2017/aug/16/buses-seoul-comfort-women-statues-korea-japan.

11. See, for example, Joseph Yi, "Confronting Korea's Censored Discourse on Comfort Women," *The Diplomat*, published January 31, 2018, accessed February 18, 2018, https://thediplomat.com/2018/01/confronting-koreas-censored-discourse-on-comfort-women/.

12. Yaerin Ku, "Young Women in South Korea Fight to Gain Justice for the 'Comfort Women' of WWII," International Press Foundation, published January 3, 2017, accessed February 18, 2018, http://the-ipf.com/2017/01/03/south-korea-comfort-women/.

13. "Japan Recalls Korean Envoy over 'Comfort Women' Statue," BBC News, published January 6, 2017, accessed February 18, 2018, http://www.bbc.com/news/world-asia-38526914.

14. Hyon-hee Shin, "Seoul Faces Dilemma over 'Comfort Women' Statue in Busan," *The Korea Herald*, published January 3, 2017, accessed February 18, 2018, http://www.koreaherald.com/view.php?ud=20170103000764.

15. See, for example, Choe Sang-Hun, "'Comfort Woman' Statue Reinstated Near Japan Consulate in South Korea," *New York Times*, published December 30, 2016, accessed February 18, 2018, https://www.nytimes.com/2016/12/30/world/asia/south-korea-comfort-women-wwii-japan.html.

16. Bo-eun Kim, "Local Gov't to Be in Charge of Comfort Woman Statue," *Korea Times*, published February 28, 2017, accessed February 18, 2018, http://koreatimes.co.kr/www/news/nation/2017/02/113_224830.html.

17. McCurry, "Buses in Seoul."

18. As has been signaled by, for example, Human Rights Watch, see "Philippines: Duterte's 'Drug War' Claims 12,000+ Lives," Human Rights Watch, published January 18, 2018, accessed February 7, 2018, https://www.hrw.org/news/2018/01/18/philippines-dutertes-drug-war-claims-12000-lives.

19. "Duterte Says 'Comfort Woman' Statue a 'Constitutional Right,'" ABS-CBN News, published January 18, 2018, accessed February 18, 2018, http://news.abs-cbn.com/news/01/18/18/duterte-says-comfort-woman-statue-a-constitutional-right.

20. Eric Johnston, "Osaka Mayor to Terminate Six-Decade Ties as San Francisco Designates 'Comfort Women' Memorial City Property," *Japan Times*, published November 23, 2017, accessed February 18, 2018, https://www.japantimes.co.jp/

news/2017/11/23/national/politics-diplomacy/osaka-mayor-terminate-six-decade
-ties-san-francisco-designates-comfort-women-memorial-city-property/#.WpV
hbWbGyRs.

21. Nausikaä El-Mecky, "Recycling Saddam: The Pragmatic and Esoteric Transforma-
    tion of a Dictator's Monument," in *Bildergewalt*, ed. Birgit Ulrike Münch, Andreas
    Tacke, Markwart Herzog, and Sylvia Heudecker (Petersberg: Michael Imhof Ver-
    lag, 2018), 154–60.

22. Brett Kelman, "He Built a Monument to His Favorite President: The Feds Fined
    Him $9,000 and Plan to Blow It Up," *Desert Sun*, published October 13, 2016,
    accessed February 18, 2018, https://www.desertsun.com/story/news/crime_
    courts/2016/10/13/joshua-tree-illegal-monument/91609716/.

23. Kelman, "He Built a Monument."

24. Also known as Zentrum für Politische Schönheit under their German name.

25. Short for Alternative für Deutschland [Alternative for Germany].

26. See, for example, Lizzie Dearden, "German AfD Politician 'Attacks Holocaust
    Memorial' and Says Germans Should Be More Positive about Nazi Past," *Inde-
    pendent*, published January 19, 2017, accessed February 18, 2018, http://www.
    independent.co.uk/news/world/europe/germany-afd-bjoern-hoecke-berlin-holo
    caust-memorial-shame-history-positive-nazi-180-turnaround-a7535306.html.

27. Interview with Cesy Leonard, February 21, 2018.

28. Ibid.

29. Ibid.

30. Ibid.

31. Ibid.

32. Ibid.

33. Sebastian Leber, "Björn Höcke bekommt keine Ruhe," *Der Tagesspiegel*,
    published February 14, 2018, accessed February 18, 2018, https://www.tages-
    spiegel.de/themen/reportage/stelenfeld-in-bornhagen-bjoern-hoecke-bekommt-
    keine-ruhe/20958826.html.

34. See, for example, Michael Bartsch, "Wohnen mit Aussicht," *Die Tageszeitung
    (TAZ)*, published November 26, 2017, accessed February 18, 2018, http://www.
    taz.de/!5462693/.

35. Ibid.

36. Jon Azpiri, "Artists Create Edward Snowden Hologram after Statue Removed
    from Brooklyn Park," *Global News*, published April 8, 2015, accessed February 6,
    2018, https://globalnews.ca/news/1926679/artists-create-edward-snowden-holo-
    gram-after-statue-removed-from-brooklyn-park/.

37. See, for example, "Giant Edward Snowden Sculpture Appears on War Monument
    in Brooklyn Park," NBC New York, published April 6, 2015, accessed February 8,
    2018, https://www.nbcnewyork.com/news/local/Edward-Snowden-Statue-Bust-
    New-York-NY-Brooklyn-War-Monument-298782461.html.

38. Via the AnimalNewYork.com website, which was canceled and taken offline by
    its creators in 2015.

39. Sam Sanders, "An Edward Snowden Statue Was Replaced by a Hovering Snowden
    Image Last Night," NPR, published April 7, 2015, accessed February 10, 2018,

https://www.npr.org/sections/thetwo-way/2015/04/07/398119206/an-edward-snowden-statue-was-replaced-by-another-snowden-image-last-night.

40. Sanders, "An Edward Snowden Statue."

41. Andy Greenberg, "Now You Can 3-D Print Your Own Copy of NYC's Illegal Snowden Bust," Wired, published May 8, 2015, accessed February 18, 2018, https://www.wired.com/2015/05/now-can-3-d-print-copy-nycs-illegal-snowden-bust/.

42. Colin Mixson, "Rogues Gallery! Confiscated Snowden Bust Headed for Brooklyn Museum," Brooklyn Paper, published January 12, 2016, accessed February 18, 2018, https://www.brooklynpaper.com/stories/39/3/dtg-brooklyn-museum-snowden-bust-2016-01-15-bk.html.

43. Mixson, "Rogues Gallery!"

44. Interview with Evol, February 21, 2018.

45. Ibid.

46. Ibid.

CHAPTER 17

Transnational Social Media Monuments, Counter-Monuments, and the Future of the Nation-State

JOHNNY ALAM

SHORTLY AFTER THE NOVEMBER 2015 TERRORIST ATTACKS IN PARIS, Facebook introduced a filter that allowed subscribers to overlay the French flag over their profile pictures by clicking a button that was dovetailed with the message: "Change your profile picture to support France and the people of Paris." In a matter of days, millions of individuals around the globe chose to overlay the *Tricolour*—an ultimate national symbol—on top of their Facebook profile picture—an image of the self (figure 17.1). In a parallel offline phenomenon, public monuments around the globe were also draped with the French Tricolour (figure 17.2). By wearing a symbol of another nation, these national symbols were transformed into palimpsestic transnational monuments that were also featured in global mass media newscasts and social media outlets. This chapter delves into the underpinnings of such oxymoronic transnational-patriotic commemorative gestures, which bind culturally diverse individuals through mass and social media. It inquires into the forces that drive people to mourn, protest, and commemorate persons they never knew and probably never will in public squares and cyberspaces. What is the role of mass media in general and its interactions with social media in particular in promoting, controlling, and possibly short-circuiting individual and collective mourning? Can we, for instance, consider Facebook's French flag filter a social media monument? Do such mediated transnational monuments jeopardize the already challenged model of the nation-state? What is the life cycle of media monuments? Do they outlive their concrete counterparts?

We tend to think of monuments as relatively enduring sculptures or architectural structures, yet the word "monument," according to the *Merriam-Webster Dictionary*, may also refer to a written legal document, a distinguished person, or an identifying mark. A monument, therefore, regardless of its material or immaterial form, can be defined as that which is meant to embody, mark, carry, preserve, or protect the memory of something else against forgetting. In this respect, the Facebook profile pictures draped with

Figure 17.1. Representation of the Facebook French flag filter by the author.

the French flag may be considered monuments because they have mainly been perceived as a gesture for commemorating the victims of the Paris attacks on the one hand and a token of support for the principles of Western democracy and human rights on the other. These may be two separate intentions, but they have been increasingly intertwined and politicized through recent discourses on memory and trauma, which have taken a global dimension that challenges the current model of the nation-state.

Feeling compelled to react to the mass murdering of civilians in Paris may well be a natural impulse, but the global adoption of the Facebook French flag monument was arguably grounded in a culture of remembrance conditioned by mass and social media interactions. The stark majority of individuals who chose to apply the Facebook French flag option experienced the Paris massacres as "distant suffering,"[1] that is, indirectly through media outlets (tele-

Figure 17.2. The Sydney Opera House lit in the colors of the French flag as a tribute to Paris during the November 2015 Paris attacks. Photo: Clint Budd 16 November 2015. Courtesy of Wikimedia Commons.

vision, radio, newspapers, websites, social media apps, etc.), which relayed the event with a sense of urgency and crisis that demands/impels a moral reaction. Over the past three decades, such moral reactions have increasingly taken the form of public acts of remembrance performed as a civic obligation. According to Sébastian Ledoux, distant suffering and mediated crises are two major factors behind the development of this sociopolitical and legal culture of remembrance in France that is distilled in the speech-act term *"devoir de mémoire,"* which literally translates to "duty of memory." He explains that in an "era of testimonies" reflected in projects, such as Claude Lanzmann's film *Shoah* and the television series *Holocaust,* the term "duty of memory" does not only respond to a desire to pay tribute to victims, but it carries an injunction to treatment.[2] The author uses the French public's revision of the role played by the Vichy regime in the Holocaust as an example of such restoration of social order and treatment of past suffering by explaining that "the forgetting of this event is increasingly presented as a moral and political fault which hinders the future of [the French] society."[3] Forgetting the traumas of the past, he opines, has become criminal because it is "fueled by the legal concept of the imprescriptibility of past crimes."[4] Remembering becomes a national obligation. In this respect, the 2015 Paris attacks presented yet another instance where "mourning becomes the law."[5]

This sort of obligation to remember past collective traumas is by no means limited to France. It has been sweeping nations for the past three decades. Much ink has been spilled in explaining the proliferation of the culture of trauma and the notion of remembering as an act against past injustices since the 1990s, particularly in the West. At large, the battles for memory have resulted in several official public apologies for past injustices in many nations. Related efforts toward reconciliation have included creating monuments in the form of artworks, landmarks, museums, official laws, trials, public truth-seeking commissions, days of remembrance, and legal settlements to commemorate the tragic events. In opposite scenarios, calls for reconciliation have resulted in vandalizing or removing controversial monuments from the public sphere. Recent examples include the rowdy toppling of the statue of the *Confederate Soldiers Monument* in Durham, North Carolina, United States (2017), the vandalism of several Sir John A. Macdonald monuments in Canadian cities (2013–2018), and the measured removal of the statue of Edward Cornwallis in Halifax, Canada (2018). The common bedrock and fuel for the majority of grievances against past injustices has been the discourse of human rights. Yet it is precisely this discourse that grants trauma culture a transnational dimension and puts the future of the current nation-state model at risk as Daniel Levy and Natan Sznaider have suggested in their writings about the "global memory imperative."

Levy and Sznaider define the global memory imperative as a decontextualized universal code for addressing human rights abuses and past injustices "both legally as well as in commemorative terms."[6] They contend that "the language of human rights provides us with a framework to begin to understand why pictures of strangers being beaten and tortured [in the case of the Paris attacks, massacred] by other strangers concern us."[7] The authors believe that the human rights discourse has resulted in transnational solidarities where individuals identify with strangers, foreigners, and "others" to form a new global citizenry that transcends kinship, race, religion, and nationhood.

Resonant articulations of alternative global citizenries forged through the circulation of media featuring abuses of human rights have been brought forth by scholars such as Alison Landsberg in *Prosthetic Memory* (2004), Ariella Azoulay in *The Civil Contract of Photography* (2012), Sharon Sliwinski in *Human Rights in Camera* (2011), and Dora Apel in *War Culture and the Contest of Images* (2012). This genre of studies has been inspired by Benedict Anderson's seminal work *Imagined Communities* (1983), in which the author argues that mediated representations help strangers bond together to form imagined collective wholes. For the better part of the past century, these collective wholes have been perceived as the nation-state;[8] however, the work of scholars, such as Arjun Appadurai, shifted this discourse toward transnational identifications.

Hence, once perceived to be bound to the nation, collective memory is nowadays seen as transnational and multidirectional.[9] In this respect, transnational humanitarian solidarities—perceived in gestures such as the Facebook French flag—posit a fundamental challenge to the current model of the nation-state because they solicit a belonging to an "imagined community" (a political entity) that is larger than our existing nation-states. Levy and Sznaider remind those who are doubtful of such globalist visions that the concept of the nation-state was also dismissed for being too broad of a unit to conceive at one point in time:

> The claim that the nation-state is an unproblematic container for solidarity is profoundly ahistorical. Ironically, when national cultures were invented, they were open to the same criticisms as those directed at global culture today. They were dismissed as superficial and inauthentic substitutes for local cultures that were once rich in tradition, and they were taken to task for being much too large and alienating. Surely, it was argued, nobody would ever identify with the impersonal image of the nation. As history has shown, this prediction was wrong.[10]

The second and more immediate challenge to the current model of the nation-state posited by the politicized discourse of human rights is, according to Levy and Sznaider, the weakening of the constitutive sovereignty of nations:

> The principle of "noninterference" in so-called internal affairs is exactly the opposite of the human rights regime, which claims that there is no such thing as "internal affairs." When it comes to certain types of abuses, human rights are about humans and not about members of specific states.[11]

In other words, foreign powers can use (and have used) human rights claims as an excuse to invade or intervene in the affairs of other states without permission. This has been one of the key concerns with the Facebook French flag phenomenon, seen by a number of critics as a public mobilization campaign aiming to garner support for a disproportionate French and/or Western countermilitary retaliation in Syria.[12]

A second major concern with this social media campaign revolved around the irony and dark symbolism of the French flag, which—in contrast to its standard association with liberty, equality, and fraternity—was historically used to spearhead colonial missions in the guise of humanitarian interventions in countries, including Syria, eventually giving rise to terrorist groups such as ISIS, which claimed responsibility for the Paris attacks.[13] A third common criticism against Facebook's French flag campaign—one that paradoxically undermines while being inspired by the discourse of human rights—was the selectivity of mourning perceived through the fact that Facebook exclusively created a flag filter for France and not for other countries that were also victims of ISIS attacks in the preceding days, such as Lebanon and Kenya. Dubbed as Eurocentric and white supremacist, Facebook's move gave the impression that when it comes to supporting human rights, "some [humans] are more equal than others."[14]

Together with the aforementioned three common critiques of the Facebook French flag campaign, the fourth—which relates to the futility of this commemorative effort—reminds us that memory attached to online and offline monuments is, sooner or later, contested. This condemnation suggests that Facebook's French flag feature was a corporate branding initiative in the guise of human kindness that provided an easy form of public mourning that neither helps the victims of the attacks nor generates a substantial contribution to their cause.[15] This view chimes with the results of an academic study that suggests that people who endorse a cause through social media are less likely to contribute any financial or in-kind support to that cause later on.[16] The phenomenon is called "slacktivism," and its researchers believe that it occurs because public endorsement satisfies the desire to look good to others, thereby reducing the chances to commit resources to the cause in the future. This kind of "easy" or "lazy" delegation of commemorative effort, however, applies to all monuments. In his 1992 essay on Holocaust monuments in Germany, James Young explains that "the more memory comes to rest in its exteriorized forms, the less it is experienced internally."[17] He further adds:

> Rather than embodying memory, the monument displaces it altogether, supplanting a community's memory-work with its own material form . . . once we assign monumental form to memory, we have to some degree divested ourselves of the obligation to remember.[18]

Akin to physical monuments, social media monuments could also be seen as displacements of memory-work that offer easy commemoration and satisfy the desires to both remember and forget near and distant atrocities. The fact that several Facebook users complained that they were unable to remove the French flag from their profile pictures shortly after embracing it—and that only a small fraction of individuals (if any) are still intentionally displaying a commemorative French flag on top of their profile pictures today—reveals that social media monuments, like their concrete counterparts, are ultimately ephemeral. For if a monument should manage to stand tall against the passage of time, the collective meaning it conveys will constantly change as new generations lose track of its memorial legacy and project new meanings and remembrances onto it.

The material of a conventional monument is normally chosen to withstand the physical ravages of time, the assumption being that its memory will remain as everlasting as its form. But . . . the actual consequence of a memorial's unyielding fixedness in space is also its death over time: a fixed image created in one time and carried over into a new time suddenly appears archaic, strange, or irrelevant altogether. For in its linear progression, time drags old meaning into new contexts, estranging a monument's memory from both past and present, holding past truths up to ridicule in present moments. Time mocks the rigidity of monuments.[19]

Young wrote these words in an article describing the work of artists who were deconstructing the common assumptions about monuments and highlighting the transitory nature of collective memories attached to them. Creating counter-monuments to represent the legacy of the Holocaust in Germany during the 1980s and 1990s, these artists were clearly aware that people may completely ignore monuments in their own neighborhoods and that monuments "built with much care and purpose by political authorities and tourist promoters can seemingly disappear or be forgotten when they are encountered and experienced as elements of a lived-in, everyday local landscape."[20] As a result, the artists Jochen and Esther Gerz created a self-destructing monument made of a twelve-meter-high aluminum structure, which invited locals and visitors to inscribe their names on its surface while it incrementally plunged into the ground, completely disappearing in a few years. According to Young, this counter-monument—installed in a busy Hamburg neighborhood—challenged cherished memorial conventions because its aim was:

Not to console but to provoke; not to remain fixed but to change; not to be everlasting but to disappear; not to be ignored by its passersby but to demand interaction; not to remain pristine but to invite its own violation and desecration; not to accept graciously the burden of memory but to throw it back at the town's feet.[21]

In the same counter-monument spirit, the artist Horst Hoheisel created a negative-form monument in the late 1980s, which may well be the source of inspiration for the US *National September 11 Memorial*. To commemorate the destruction of the Aschrott-Brunnen fountain—a historical monument destroyed by the Nazis for its Jewish affiliation—Hoheisel built a replica of the original, only to invert it and bury it in the ground, creating an aquatic abyss. For him, the absence of the original fountain would be preserved in its subversive negative-form duplicate. Describing the inverted fountain, Young—who served on the *National September 11 Memorial* design selection committee—writes:

On our approach, we detect the sound of water rushing into a great underground hollow, which grows louder and louder until we finally stand over the Aschrott-Brunnen. Only this sound suggests the depth of an otherwise invisible memorial, an inverted palimpsest that demands the visitor's reflection.[22]

From internal reflection to external projection, Young's third case study of Holocaust counter-monuments in Germany was that of Norbert Radermacher, installed on the site of a former forced-labor Nazi camp in the Neukölln district of Berlin. Radermacher designed a pedestrian-activated slide projection that overlays historical narratives describing the site's dark past upon its seemingly innocent present space. The slides would appear for only a short while before disappearing, and their content would constantly change as schoolchildren would sequentially add their own narratives to the slide presentation. In this, Radermacher's design succeeded in literally highlighting the transience of collective memories projected by viewers upon memorial sites.

Beyond Germany, in a country whose intergenerational war trauma continuously burns under the ashes of peacetime, flaring up whenever international winds of political change re-incinerate another local civil strife, Lebanon has an abundance of monuments from conquering civilizations[23] but very few of its own since independence. None of these monuments commemorate the victims of the 1975–1990 "uncivil" wars, which have not really ended. In the face of this drought in national memorials—partially caused by the contested nature of collective memory in this country—the commemoration of the war victims (deemed martyrs) is projected upon a statue in downtown Beirut, which initially commemorated the martyrs of independence from the Ottoman Empire following the First World War. Beyond this constantly recycled *lieu de mémoire*,[24] photographic posters from different political parties fill in the gap left by the lack of official acts of remembrance. Akin to the aforementioned German artists, a group of transnational artists who grew up in Lebanon during the "uncivil" wars have been creating counter-monuments that highlight the abuse of the memory of the war victims through contemporary art practices that seem iconoclastic. Their artworks reveal the ephemerality of the partisan memorial posters by documenting the physical and mnemonic deterioration of these mass-produced "icons of modernity" over time, thereby desecrating these public memorials.[25]

Another informative example of counter-monuments comes from Ukraine, whose government issued a series of decommunization laws in 2015 that called for the removal of communist monuments. Believing that scrapping existing monuments, regardless of their historical connotation, constitutes a kind of vandalism, the Ukranian artist Alexander Milov came up with a whimsical workaround. Instead of uprooting a statue of Vladimir Lenin, which stood in a commercial courtyard in the city of Odessa, he embalmed it in titanium enclosures, a helmet, and a light saber, which effectively transformed the sculpture into a monument for Darth Vader, fully equipped with a Wi-Fi access point. While this was not the first instance where the Dark Lord of the Sith appeared in recent Ukranian politics, the transformation of this monument has been commonly seen as an anti-Russian, pro-Western signalization.[26] Of course, the makeover is not short of postmodern irony or dark humor, for one is compelled to wonder whether the artist was actually trying to mask or unmask the true face of Lenin.

In a reminiscent artistic gesture meant to raise debate about the removal of monuments from public spaces, the artists Bartosz Szydlowski and Malgorzata Szydlowska installed a temporary fluorescent green statue of Lenin, taking a leak, in the public square of Nowa Huta, Poland. A former bronze statue of Lenin stood in the same location for years before it was removed in postcommunist Poland in 1989, when the plaza was also renamed the *Ronald Reagan Square*.[27] The artists called their green statue *The Fountain of the Future*.

Poland is also the homeland of Krzysztof Wodiczko, who is considered a pioneer in the art of critical engagement with public monuments. Convinced that official memorials are meant to "kill memory" through their "obscene necro-ideology,"[28] Wodiczko created close to eighty memorial projections over a period of three decades, each uncovering memories suppressed by public monuments in more than fourteen countries. The artist states:

> The aim of the memorial projection is not to "bring life to" or "enliven" the memorial nor to support the happy, uncritical, bureaucratic "socialization" of its site, but to reveal and expose to the public the contemporary deadly life of the memorial. The strategy of the memorial projection is to attack the memorial by surprise, using slide warfare, or to take part in and infiltrate the official cultural programs taking place on its site.[29]

Wodiczko's relatively recent memorial projections include a twenty-three-minute video featuring fourteen US veterans from Vietnam, Iraq, and Afghanistan projected upon the statue of Abraham Lincoln in New York City's Union Square. The projection perfectly superimposed the hands and faces of these veterans on those of Lincoln's sculpture, yielding a jarring effect that motivates the passersby to listen to the veterans speak from a position of power. The artist wished to "draw parallels between the experiences of often estranged, neglected and traumatized US war veterans today and of those who survived the carnage of the Civil War," through the figure of Lincoln, "who, as president, presided over the nation's bloodiest conflict."[30] Wodiczko's work shows us how communities can interact with and project their own memories upon the monuments that surround—and supposedly represent—them.

The memorial projections of Wodiczko on statues and public monuments bring us full circle back to the French flag projections on worldwide national monuments and on Facebook profile pictures following the November 2015 terrorist attacks in Paris. In the various instances of virtual and physical monuments and counter-monuments presented here, we have seen a common pattern wherein collective memory is consistently transforming. In turn, this movement of memory causes a relentless change in the ways we imagine ourselves as groups and nations that project interpretations of who we are upon memorials from which we simultaneously derive a sense of identity. Monuments, memorials, and nations are, therefore, ephemeral and contested because memory is not a fixed object but a dynamic, interactive process. And if the "global memory imperative" suggests that the future of the nation-state is larger than the current ones, the relatively recent cases of Brexit and Catalonia prove that imagined communities can also shift toward the opposite direction, partially depending on the way in which social media algorithms learn how to direct and/or reinforce our existing biases. Indeed, the malleability of nation-states may sound like a crazy idea, but I often return to a quotation from Nietzsche, who reminds us that "insanity in individuals is something rare—but in groups, parties, nations and epochs, it is the rule."[31]

NOTES

1. Luc Boltanski, *Distant Suffering: Morality, Media and Politics* (Cambridge, UK: Cambridge University Press, 1999).
2. Sébastien Ledoux, "Pour une généalogie du « devoir de mémoire » en France," trans. Sébastien Ledoux (Paris: Centre Alberto-Benveniste, EPHE-Sorbonne, 2009), 7.
3. Ledoux, "Pour une généalogie," 5.
4. Ibid.
5. Judith Butler, *Mourning Becomes the Law: Judith Butler from Paris* (Versobooks.com, 2015), accessed November 14, 2015, https://instituto25m.info/mourning - becomes-the-law-judith-butler-from-paris/
6. Daniel Levy and Natan Sznaider, *Human Rights and Memory* (University Park, PA: Penn State University Press, 2010), 4.
7. Levy and Sznaider, *Human Rights and Memory*, 2.
8. Ann Rigney and Chiara De Cesari, *Transnational Memory* (Boston: De Gruyter, 2014).
9. Michael Rothberg, *Multidirectional Memory: Remembering the Holocaust in the Age of Decolonization* (Redwood City, CA: Stanford University Press, 2009).
10. Daniel Levy and Natan Sznaider, "Memory and Human Rights," in *Handbook of Human Rights*, ed. Thomas Cushman (New York: Routledge, 2012), 491–99, 494.
11. Levy and Sznaider, *Human Rights and Memory*, 2.
12. Judith Butler, Lulu Nunn, Sam Sanders, and Jackie Salo have outlined the outcries against the Facebook French flag phenomenon in their respective articles.

13. Lulu Nunn, "Got a French Flag on Your Facebook Profile Picture? Congratulations on Your Corporate White Supremacy," *Independent*, published November 16, 2015. http://www.independent.co.uk/voices/got-a-french-flag-on-your-facebook-profile-picture-congratulations-on-your-corporate-white-supremacy-a6736526.html.

14. George Orwell, *Animal Farm: A Fairy Story* (New York: Houghton Mifflin Harcourt, 2009 [1945]), 192.

15. Jackie Salo, "Facebook French Flag: Why You Shouldn't Change Your Profile Picture to Support the Paris Attacks," *International Business Times*, published November 17, 2015, http://www.ibtimes.com/facebook-french-flag-why-you-shouldnt-change-your-profile-picture-support-paris-2187416.

16. Kirk Kristofferson, Katherine White, and John Peloza, "The Nature of Slacktivism: How the Social Observability of an Initial Act of Token Support Affects Subsequent Prosocial Action," *Journal of Consumer Research* 40, no. 6 (April 2014): 1149–66.

17. James E. Young, "The Counter-Monument: Memory against Itself in Germany Today," *Critical Inquiry* 18, no. 2 (1992): 267–96, 294.

18. Young, "The Counter-Monument," 267–96, 294.

19. Ibid.

20. James Opp and John C. Walsh, *Placing Memory and Remembering Place in Canada* (Vancouver, BC: UBC Press, 2010), 15.

21. Young, "The Counter-Monument," 277.

22. Ibid., 293–94.

23. Among the hundreds of such monuments, the Nahr El Kalb Memory of the World UNESCO site is particularly interesting. This rocky cliff overlooking the Mediterranean Sea holds twenty stelae chiseled over a period of three millennia by fourteen civilizations. Each of these monuments boasts the successful invasion of this location in a language inspired from the preceding memorials created on this historical ridge. See Lucia Volk, "When Memory Repeats Itself: The Politics of Heritage in Post Civil War Lebanon," *International Journal of Middle East Studies* 40, no. 2 (2008): 291–314.

24. Pierre Nora, "Between Memory and History: Les Lieux de Mémoire," *Representations*, Vol. 26 (Spring 1989): 7–24.

25. Johnny Alam, "Undead Martyrs and Decay: When Photography Fails Its Promise of Eternal Memory," *Contemporary French and Francophone Studies* 18, no. 5 (October 20, 2014): 577–86.

26. Henri Neuendorf, "Ukrainian Artist Turns Lenin Statue into Darth Vader," *Artnet News*, published October 27, 2015, https://news.artnet.com/art-world/statue-ukraine-lenin-darth-vader-347880.

27. Mark Cheetham and Linda Hutcheon, *Remembering Postmodernism: Trends in Recent Canadian Art* (Oxford, UK: Oxford University Press, 1991), 89.

28. Krzysztof Wodiczko quoted in Cheetham and Hutcheon, *Remembering Postmodernism*, 88.

29. Micaela Martegani quoted in Lelong, "Krzysztof Wodiczko: Abraham Lincoln: War Veteran Projection," *Artmap*, published November 18, 2012, https://artmap.

com/lelongnewyork/exhibition/krzysztof-wodiczko-abraham-lincoln-war-veteran-projection-2012.

30. Krzysztof Wodiczko quoted in Cheetham and Hutcheon, *Remembering Postmodernism*, 88.

31. Friedrich Nietzsche, *Beyond Good and Evil*, 1886. Translated by Helen Z, Project Gutenburg, February 4, 2013.

BIBLIOGRAPHY

Alam, Johnny. "Undead Martyrs and Decay: When Photography Fails Its Promise of Eternal Memory." *Contemporary French and Francophone Studies* 18, no. 5 (October 20, 2014): 577–86.

Anderson, Benedict. *Imagined Communities: Reflections on the Origin and Spread of Nationalism.* New York: Verso, 2006.

Apel, Dora. *War Culture and the Contest of Images.* New Brunswick, NJ: Rutgers University Press, 2012.

Appadurai, Arjun. *Modernity at Large: Cultural Dimensions of Globalization.* Minneapolis: University of Minnesota Press, 1996.

Azoulay, Ariella. *The Civil Contract of Photography.* Cambridge, MA: Zone Books, 2008.

Bennett, Jill. *Empathic Vision: Affect, Trauma, and Contemporary Art.* Redwood City, CA: Stanford University Press, 2005.

Boltanski, Luc. *Distant Suffering: Morality, Media and Politics.* Cambridge, UK: Cambridge University Press, 1999.

Butler, Judith. *Mourning Becomes the Law: Judith Butler from Paris.* Versobooks.com, 2015. Accessed November 14, 2015. https://instituto25m.info/mourning-becomes-the-law-judith-butler-from-paris/

Cheetham, Mark, and Linda Hutcheon. *Remembering Postmodernism: Trends in Recent Canadian Art.* Oxford, UK: Oxford University Press, 1991.

Gayle, Damien. "Polish Town Erects Fluorescent Yellow Statue of Lenin Taking a Leak." *Daily Mail Online*, June 13, 2014. http://www.dailymail.co.uk/news/article-2657458/From-Poland-love-Polish-town-erects-fluorescent-yellow-statue-Lenin-urinating-called-Fountain-Future.html.

Hodgins, Peter. "Our Haunted Present: Cultural Memory in Question." *Topia* 12 (Fall 2012): 99–108.

Johnston, Russell, and Michael Ripmeester. "That Big Statue of Whoever." In *Placing Memory and Remembering Place in Canada*, edited by James Opp and John C. Walsh, 130–56. Vancouver, BC: UBC Press, 2010.

Kristofferson, Kirk, Katherine White, and John Peloza. "The Nature of Slacktivism: How the Social Observability of an Initial Act of Token Support Affects Subsequent Prosocial Action." *Journal of Consumer Research* 40, no. 6 (April 2014): 1149–66.

Landsberg, Alison. *Prosthetic Memory: The Transformation of American Remembrance in the Age of Mass Culture.* New York: Columbia University Press, 2004.

Ledoux, Sébastien. "Pour une généalogie du « devoir de mémoire » en France." Translated by Johnny Alam. Paris: Centre Alberto-Benveniste, EPHE-Sorbonne, 2009.

Lelong. "Krzysztof Wodiczko: Abraham Lincoln: War Veteran Projection." Artmap. Published November 18, 2012. https://artmap.com/lelongnewyork/exhibition/krzysztof-wodiczko-abraham-lincoln-war-veteran-projection-2012.

Levy, Daniel, and Natan Sznaider. *Human Rights and Memory*. University Park, PA: Penn State University Press, 2010.

———. "Memory and Human Rights." In *Handbook of Human Rights*, edited by Thomas Cushman, 491–99. New York: Routledge, 2012.

McHugh, Molly. "Facebook's Tragedy Features and the Outrage They Inspired." Wired. Published November 16, 2015. https://www.wired.com/2015/11/facebook-safety-check-french-flag-filter-tragedy-features-and-the-outrage-they-inspired/.

Micale, Mark S., and Paul Lerner. *Traumatic Pasts: History, Psychiatry, and Trauma in the Modern Age, 1870–1930*. Cambridge, UK: Cambridge University Press, 2001.

Nietzsche, Friedrich. *Beyond Good and Evil*. 1886. Translated by Helen Zimmern. Project Gutenburg. February 4, 2013.

Neuendorf, Henri. "Ukrainian Artist Turns Lenin Statue into Darth Vader." Artnet News. Published October 27, 2015. https://news.artnet.com/art-world/statue-ukraine-lenin-darth-vader-347880.

Nora, Pierre. "Between Memory and History: Les Lieux de Mémoire." *Representations*, Vol. 26 (Spring 1989): 7–24. doi:10.2307/2928520.

Nunn, Lulu. "Got a French Flag on Your Facebook Profile Picture? Congratulations on Your Corporate White Supremacy." *Independent*. Published November 16, 2015. http://www.independent.co.uk/voices/got-a-french-flag-on-your-facebook-profile-picture-congratulations-on-your-corporate-white-supremacy-a6736526.html.

Opp, James, and John C. Walsh, eds. *Placing Memory and Remembering Place in Canada*. Vancouver, BC: UBC Press, 2010.

Orwell, George. *Animal Farm: A Fairy Story*. New York: Houghton Mifflin Harcourt, 2009.

Rigney, Ann, and Chiara De Cesari. *Transnational Memory*. Boston: De Gruyter, 2014.

Rothberg, Michael. *Multidirectional Memory: Remembering the Holocaust in the Age of Decolonization*. University Park, CA: Stanford University Press, 2009.

Salo, Jackie. "Facebook French Flag: Why You Shouldn't Change Your Profile Picture to Support the Paris Attacks." *International Business Times*. Published November 17, 2015. http://www.ibtimes.com/facebook-french-flag-why-you-shouldnt-change-your-profile-picture-support-paris-2187416.

Sanders, Sam. "#MemeOfTheWeek: French Flags on Facebook." NPR. Published November 21, 2015. http://www.npr.org/2015/11/21/456820583/-memeoftheweek-french-flags-on-facebook.

Sliwinski, Sharon. *Human Rights in Camera*. Chicago: University of Chicago Press, 2011.

Volk, Lucia. "When Memory Repeats Itself: The Politics of Heritage in Post Civil War Lebanon." *International Journal of Middle East Studies* 40, no. 2 (2008): 291–314.

Weilnböck, Harald. "The Trauma Must Remain Inaccessible to Memory: Trauma Melancholia and Other (Ab-)Uses of Trauma Concepts in Literary Theory." *Eurozine*, March 19, 2008.

Young, James E. "The Counter-Monument: Memory against Itself in Germany Today." *Critical Inquiry* 18, no. 2 (1992): 267–96.

CHAPTER 18

Citizens as Walking Memorials

Rethinking the Monument Genre in the Twenty-First Century

Tanja Schult

DESPITE BEING PROCLAIMED OUTDATED, EVEN DEAD MANY TIMES, MONUMENTS still fulfill important functions: as reminders of historical events and as sites where values and norms are publicly renegotiated. Increasingly, more and more monument makers in Western democracies also use the genre to nurture democratic ideas. My interest is in works that produce new forms of commemoration and display an altered understanding of the role citizens are supposed to have in democratic societies, namely, to be active agents who take part in shaping cultural memory. The new designs generate new performative relationships (not least in their use of new technologies), which often depart from common notions of what a monument is and looks like. To extend the common notion of what a monument is, I will use *The Invisible Camp—Audio Walk Gusen* as an example. The walk leads visitors through the grounds of former concentration camps in Upper Austria, now residential areas. While the walk remains basically invisible, the users are temporarily turned into walking memorials. I will argue that the walk qualifies as a democratic monument par excellence due to its content and design but also by its coming into being and the impact it has on audiences.

DEMOCRATIC MONUMENTS—AN ANACHRONISM?

Before I take you to Gusen, let me clarify a few aspects. Democracy and monuments (as art and politics) are widely perceived as anachronistic antipodes. This has a number of reasons: the genre's misuse by twentieth-century dictatorships; modern art's self-perception that resists functional use; and the genre's persistent dependence for realization on ruling powers, even in democracies. Despite all skepticism of the genre, monuments still exist, and new ones are constantly raised—even in democracies—indeed, to a degree that has been described as "memorial mania,"[1] reminiscent of the *Denkmalflut* of the 1880s. Old and new democracies not only have to live with the memorial markers of previous regimes or yesterday's great men; they also produce new ones.

Let's recall how monuments are commonly defined: as visible (artistic or architectonic) markers in public space, made of durable material (such as marble or bronze), that are supposed to fulfill an educational function, namely, to commemorate a historic event or person considered worth remembering by contemporary and future generations. Who and what is commemorated in a democracy necessarily differs from what is found memory worthy in a dictatorship. Current norms and tastes as well as technological possibilities also inevitably influence the designs. So while a democratic monument commemorates past events or people, it does so for different reasons and in different ways. In a digital age, this may lead to new expressions that depart radically from established understandings of the genre.

Albeit significantly different from most monument tasks of previous times, monuments in democracies also continue to have didactic missions: they encourage citizens to reflect critically and act as responsible citizens to strengthen democratic values.[2] Instead of postulating positive affirmations of past events and people, democratic monuments display a variety of subjects. They often commemorate formerly marginalized groups or victims and confront rather shameful national pasts; instead of placing the subjects of admiration on high pedestals, often fenced off, with limited ways to interact, reducing the viewer's experience mainly to the role of a passive recipient of visual information, monuments in democracies provide—but also demand—a greater degree of agency from the participant.[3] So what might such a democratic monument look like?

THE AUDIO WALK GUSEN AND AUSTRIAN CULTURAL MEMORY

Let us turn to Upper Austria. It is here, in the market towns Langenstein, Gusen, and St. Georgen, fifteen kilometers from Linz, where *The Invisible Camp—Audio Walk Gusen* (2007) takes place. The ninety-six-minute walk was created by Austrian-born, Berlin-based artist Christoph Mayer, who grew up in the region. The walk enables the user to navigate through the places where one-third of the 120,000 concentration camp victims died in Austria during World War II, including the majority of the Jews incarcerated in the country. In contrast to nearby Mauthausen, which became Austria's most prominent site commemorating the history of World War II, Gusen was turned into a residential neighborhood a decade after the war. It has never been the focus of international or national attention, although it was in fact Gusen, not Mauthausen, that had the higher death rate and was described by survivors, who had been transported there from Auschwitz, as the hell of hells.[4] Consequently, Gusen remains widely unknown (figure 18.1).

For decades, Austria nourished the myth of having been Hitler's first victim.[5] But during the past thirty years, Austrians have increasingly confronted this past and their own role during the war, including being collaborators in the Holocaust. Subsequently, places other than Mauthausen have become the focus of attention. In fact, there has been much work done to remember the past in the wider region.⁶ Mayer's audio walk testifies to this development. It actively strives to confront and integrate this past into people's consciousness. The walk locates the atrocities committed in the same place as the everyday occurrences that dominate the scene today. It seeks to bridge the growing distance in time to the historical events by making visible that which has long been hushed up.

Only occasionally did survivor committees cause ruptures in the daily routine of forgetting. One visible marker was, however, preserved right in the middle of the living area of Langenstein: the crematorium and the memorial that was built around it. This concrete cube contrasts sharply with the environment in which it is embedded with its family homes. It is here, at the Memorial Gusen, that one collects the MP3 player with the audio walk. This building was erected by Italian and French survivors in 1965 when the locals, as most Austrians, were not interested in remembering what happened here between 1938 and 1945. Thanks to the survivors, the crematorium was not, as planned, relocated to Mauthausen. The survivors bought the land, and the Italian architect group B.B.P.R. built the memorial. For decades, this concrete building remained a "foreign matter" in the neighborhood.⁷ The Austrian state took over responsibility for the memorial only in 1997,⁸ and in 2004, a visitors center was built next to it, this time with official support. Since 2005, it has housed an exhibition on the history of the camp, and since 2007, it has provided the audio walk *The Invisible Camp Gusen.*

Figure 18.1.   Site of *The Invisible Camp—Audio Walk Gusen*, Austria.
Photograph by author.

Interestingly, it is the memorial—the monument in the established sense of the meaning—that provides the new genre monument, the audio walk. But it is the walk that ensures that the camp is no longer invisible. And by picking up the MP3 player at this site, one realizes that this painful past was never concealed completely.

THE INVISIBLE MONUMENT

Presenting Mayer's audio walk is a challenge given that it is based on sound and should be experienced in situ. However, I use the opportunity to introduce this exceptional artwork to a wider audience unable to travel to Upper Austria and to discuss what a democratic monument in the digital age may look like. I do not provide an in-depth analysis of the work's performative nature and its artistic quality here; I carve out only some of the work's most important characteristics. Among them is "the voice," delicate and soft, which leads one through these unfamiliar streets. The voice is the walk's fundamental element. It makes one comfortable enough to walk, pause, look, and move around in what is other people's daily life.[9] Falling into the rhythm of its footsteps, this gentle voice becomes a kind companion, a reliable support when listening to the accounts of survivors, perpetrators, bystanders, and residents of the housing area built on the grounds of the Gusen concentration camps—a camp complex I had not heard of earlier but which I now encountered by crisscrossing the space it formerly occupied. I visualized the camp and its atrocities, pictured it in the here and now of the cozy living area, by listening to traits of narratives interwoven with each other into a well-thought-out collage, which let me envision the historical complexity in its many nuances and reflect over its meaning today.

It is this voice that sets the tone—literally, thematically, and in what the walk demands from the participant: a willingness to listen, picture history, and brainstorm its consequences with empathy. The walk uses its surroundings, both its history and its presence, to create a soundscape that depends on bodily engagement. It is me listening, walking, imagining—to different voices that I cannot easily keep apart[10] and whose dialects sometimes are difficult for me to follow. The walk demands my full attention.

Despite not physically being present, the voice guides me safely through this unknown territory. The careful composition and choreography of the walk is impressive. When the voice wonders if I see the house that once was the camp brothel, I only have to look slightly over the fence to what is now a family home. I nod, but it is a survivor's voice answering: "Yes, this is the brothel." This example shows the technical brilliance of timing and dramaturgy, both characteristic qualities of the work. These elements in turn testify to the long and careful production process, which involved many engaged collaborators and adept partners.

Mayer and his team have arranged a multidimensional memory patchwork, a poetic collage of a number of voices—of citizens of the region then and now, of survivors and perpetrators.[11] This impression is even stronger in the English and Italian versions, which allow the original voices with their different dialects and vocal qualities to be heard before the translation kicks in. The traits of the narratives are interwoven with each other, covering a wide range of topics, such as guilt, the scope of action, and what it means to live in this contaminated place. Together, the traits act as a string that pulls the listener forth, through imagined and real space. Its fragmentary character shows itself already in the uttered sentences, often not completed, and in the questions that remain unanswered.

Mayer's memory cluster succeeds in locating history by creating spatial and temporal simultaneities and through the immersive reprojection of the past into the present.[12] Although no memorial, the work enables the walker to grasp the dimensions of the former camps, Gusen I and II, and gives an idea of the scale of *Bergkristall*, where during World War II tens of thousands of slave workers were forced to work under inhumane conditions. Many of them lost their lives constructing the giant underground factory producing *Messerschmitt* jet planes. The "act of experiencing [the walk] is simultaneously an act of witnessing which provokes an intellectual process of coming to terms with a site, its history, and its imaginary visuals," as Wegner writes accurately.[13] While walking, one also realizes that the former camp has not completely vanished, is not entirely invisible. Mayer succeeds in unearthing what was covered or overlooked for many decades. There are still relicts left; some concrete fence pillars; even entire buildings adapted to a new use, often functioning as private residences.

All elements combined—sound, spoken words, site specificity—are crucial to the work's character. History urges itself on us. We listen to the conflicting narratives of the survivors and perpetrators while facing the inhabitants' privacy, passing by their houses, realizing the burden of living here day to day. When houses or swimming pools are built in the area, one still finds human remains in the soil, as the audio walk conveys.

Most Holocaust museums concentrate on survivor stories in order to give back to the victims the identities the Nazis bereft them of and to offer the visitor a person to identify with (as, for example, in the United States Holocaust Memorial Museum, which provides identity cards upon entry). Mayer's walk, by contrast, allows for a multitude of perspectives, but it provides no chance to identify with someone. This is of utmost importance. The collage of voices forces us to take in different points of view, standpoints that are constantly shifting from one sentence to the next. Nonidentification forces us to really take in what is said—no matter how uncomfortable or difficult. This ensures that we really listen to uncomfortable statements, as when the perpetrators are saying that they initially had no idea of what awaited them or that what they were confronted with was completely shocking for them too. Moreover, the quick change of viewpoints forces us to refrain from easy judgments. Thrown from one statement to another, it is only after the walk has ended, after one-and-a-half hours, that the visitor has time for reflection. You stand at the entrance to *Bergkristall* but need to return the MP3 player at the memorial, a twenty-five-minute walk. The return walk is important and actually part of the work because you need time to digest; reflect quietly or discuss with others; reenvision scenes called forth during the walk; and recall the narratives told, trying to understand what all this means for the people who live here now and for yourself as a visitor.

WALKING MEMORIALS PERFORMING COLLECTIVE MEMORY

Although Christoph Mayer has created his work carefully, each person experiences the walk differently. The walk depends on who you are, how you are met by those you encounter during the walk, and whether you walk alone or as part of a group. There will be encounters only *you* will have, details only *you* will see, and moods only *you* will feel on *your* tour. And if you do the tour again, it would not be the same because you may freeze in the rain or find it hard to concentrate on a hot summer's day or may walk past a garden party or meet no one at all on a gray afternoon. This walk needs a receptive participant. And what the work calls forth in you depends solely on your image repertoire—consisting of images mediated by history lessons, popular culture, family history, books, documentaries—an individual image and knowledge repertoire you and I might, or might not, share. So while the work remains the same, the experience depends on other factors out of the control of the artist.

Despite the bodily engagement and individual experience, Mayer's walk is far from being a product of the experience economy, a "been there done that" to be posted on social media. Listening with headsets is an inverted process, intimate and lonely, but here, this process is displayed in public. Mayer describes his work fittingly as "sculpture of memory"[14] but also as a "walkable sculpture"[15] that has a physical component: the user moving through space. Indeed, the user becomes a walking monument, reminding the residents once again of the past, reminding them to remember (figure 18.2). Not everyone feels comfortable being a mobile monument. Some feel like intruders into the privacy of the family homes. The layers of memory, the multitude of thought-provoking insights, the realization of the past's outreach into the present, and the different responses to the past overwhelm and disturb many listeners. I was relieved to be able to escape this place the following day. However, by doing the walk, I had made a statement: I wanted to remember—and this statement was visible to others as inspiration, confirmation, or affront.

Figure 18.2.   Mayer's audio walk turns users into walking monuments.
Photograph by the author.

COMING TO TERMS WITH THE PAST AS DEMOCRATIC TEAMWORK

A work such as Mayer's could not come about out of the blue. It is a response to more than thirty years of engagement by many enthusiasts and volunteers who since the 1980s have researched; cooperated with survivors; urged local authorities to pay attention to the camp's history; organized public lectures with eye-witnesses, historians, and writers; published memoirs; contributed to radio documentaries; and organized historical walks. Together with survivor committees, they have held the annual *Gedenk-und Befreiungsfeiern* (Commemoration and Liberation Ceremony) since 1995 and started several associations, such as the *Gedenkdienstkomittee* (Commemoration Service Committee) *Gusen*, which was and remains active on a local as well as an international level. Over the decades, they also succeeded in getting municipal support and public funding. Their engagement inspired others, who in 2011, set up the *BürgerInnenbeteiligungsprojekt Bewusstseinsregion* (Citizens Involvement Project for Awareness of the Region) *Mauthausen—Gusen—St. Georgen*.[16] Thanks to these individuals and associations, Gusen's history during 1938–1945 has not been forgotten. And it was their work that made the audio walk possible. Local enthusiast Rudolf Haunschmied, from the Gusen Memorial Committee, introduced Mayer to the hidden history, which Mayer, fifteen years later, made accessible in his audio walk.[17] Engaged citizens actively contributed to setting up the walk, Haunschmied, above all, with his historical expertise but also by measuring, in freezing midwinter, the steps it takes to get from one place to another so that the user is directed toward the right spot, the house to look at, the bench to sit down on.

Mayer wanted to make sure that the work works not only time wise but that it was also comprehensible to a wide range of people. Therefore, he involved his father and his colleagues, all craftsmen, to test out the walk and then to answer a comprehensive survey. Mayer always works as part of a team. In Gusen, this team included a number of committed specialists and acclaimed artists and even an honorary board, to which the eminent scholars Aleida Assmann and Harald Welzer belonged.[18] During the process of producing the audio walk, Mayer and his collaborators arranged public hearings with citizens to gain acceptance and find participating witnesses. A wide range of voices are integrated into the actual project, but they also, from early on, influenced the working process and its outcome.

Thus, this walk's very existence is the product of cooperation. It builds on interviews with witnesses and results from a close dialogue with the region's inhabitants and engaged citizens, educators, local and regional authorities, and other artists, making it a unique artistic creation. It is this working method that I regard as truly democratic. However, Mayer's success in involving the local population in his art project was prepared by years of nonconfrontational engagement by the local committees. What now is the work's characteristic—that it is a gentle but forceful instrument of commemoration that treats the local population sensitively and with respect[19]—could be accomplished only by the foregone years of working through and with the local population.

DOING DEMOCRATIC RESEARCH

Studies of audience reception are essential in evaluating whether democratic art functions as intended. Therefore, the analysis of Mayer's walk draws not only on my own experiences but also on an evaluation of the 111 surveys filled out by other users after taking the walk between the autumns of 2016 and 2017.[20] This rich material assured me that my understanding of the project was not just the result of being a trained art historian and a scholar of Holocaust memory. From the surveys, I know that most of the participants were not trained academics. They did however share my understanding and appreciation of the work, despite the fact that they, as I, experienced the walk at times as unbearable. Many participants therefore valued the work no less but rather on the contrary. Although the effect of being exposed to this multitude of conflicting emotions as well as unresolved questions was disturbing, the absolute majority described their experience in positive terms and as profoundly thought provoking. While I had assumed that the walk might overburden the user and would be appreciated by only people who already knew a lot about the subject, I was proven wrong. The majority of participants welcomed the chance to use their imagination and were impressed by the walk's capacity to visualize the past in the present and to experience several layers of history at the same time. Two-thirds of the participants would want to do the time-consuming walk again.

Many praised the walk for mediating historical knowledge in a new, innovative, and unique way. This is remarkable given that Mayer's work is far from inventive when it comes to the technical solutions the digital age offers some ten years after the project came into existence. It is still described by most people as novel, authentic, and innovative (or at least as different to established Holocaust education, which already, given a growing Holocaust fatigue, seems positive). The individual experience provided was widely appreciated and seems crucial given that we live in highly individualized societies.

Harald Welzer considers it the work's strength that Mayer does not shy away from integrating uncomfortable statements by perpetrators.[21] The surveys confirmed this: participants felt that they were taken seriously, and they valued being exposed to this past's difficult complexities. During the walk, existential questions were raised and made immediate by walking through this topography of terror. The walker senses that much more lurks beneath the surface. Mayer has the courage to confront the uncomfortable and to leave it unresolved, without making moralistic judgments,[22] trusting the user to further contemplate the questions raised. Although this is not a historical audio guide as known from museums, the absolute majority answered that they had gained substantial knowledge about a camp they had not known of or had known very little about. Furthermore, they felt inspired to develop their knowledge and to talk to others about the subject and the experience made.

DEMOCRATIC MONUMENTS AS COLLECTIVE RESPONSIBILITY

Mayer's audio walk is located in a living environment. That demands maintenance, for example, to ensure that views to certain spots pointed out in the walk are not overgrown. However, newly built homes are a different matter. In 2017, when I returned to Gusen, it was no longer possible to follow the path leading to the walk's last stop. Two huge apartment houses and a building fence hindered me from following the prescribed route. This could be seen as a blatant disregard of the attempts to commemorate the past and proof of once again sweeping this history under the carpet. However, such conclusions may be overhasty.[23] I encountered a thriving memorial landscape in this region. That Mayer's walk is an invisible monument—which according to common understanding might not even qualify as a representative of the genre—makes it vulnerable. The walk is not a suitable showcase for politicians, and it cannot be integrated into ritualized memorial practices, such as the laying of wreaths or making commemorative speeches. Thus, its design may act to its disadvantage because it risks being forgotten. However, the local authorities are apparently willing to support the changes necessary to adjust the walk's route and to rerecord the last section, despite its being complicated and costly.[24] I argue that a work such as Mayer's would profit from an extended understanding of the monument genre. The question of maintenance makes clear that dealing with this history is not a responsibility of a few people but demands the long-term engagement of society as a whole.

AUDIOWEG GUSEN—A DEMOCRATIC MONUMENT PAR EXCELLENCE

From James E. Young's scholarship on Holocaust memorials erected in Germany since the 1980s, we know that the confrontation with this difficult past led to radical questionings of the genre. It also led to the refusal of the genre's claim to permanence and to an urgency to find more timely designs that then produced entirely new iconographies on loss and trauma. Mayer's walk reflects these developments that made it impossible for many artists to simply carry on using just the established formal repertoire. Still, expectations on the genre are often much more bound to convention than the works actually produced by contemporary artists, who in their turn utter their skepticism of the genre by refraining from labeling their works as monuments.[25]

In this essay, I have used Mayer's walk to rethink and expand our understanding of the genre. Without doubt, Mayer's work clearly acts as a monument: it publicly commemorates past events widely considered worthy of remembrance. And following the German term *Denkmal*, it clearly has the capacity to make you think. In its design, it departs from common notions of what a monument is. But in today's digital world, we should allow monuments to take different shapes. Mayer's work is unique. Given its site specificity, it cannot simply be copied elsewhere. But by studying it at close range, its coming into being, its layered being, and the effects it holds on its users and beyond, we can detect a method: a form of working through, of taking in, of retrieving and processing that can inspire the production of other art works.

Due to the way Mayer's work came into being, how it is constructed, and the way it engages with participants, it has a high potential to reach out and render the Holocaust imperatives of "never forget" and "never again" significant, the imperatives that guided the local initiatives in Upper Austria during the decades[26] and are relevant in many Western societies. It is the way of engagement that can give orientation and inspiration to how democratic commemoration can be created elsewhere as well, in different creative structures but guided by the same impetus, namely, to provide knowledge and raise critical awareness and empathy among citizens.

The work's outreach capacity relates foremost to the effect it has on single users, but it also acts as a multiplier. This way of working through the past has set balls rolling. It has produced a number of spin-offs and caused aftereffects, which in their turn, call for renewed attention—thus, acting not only as a *Denkmal* but also as performative: demanding a doing.[27] Thus, Mayer's walk truly acts as a democratic monument in the way it commemorates this painful history with the aim of turning users into active agents of commemoration who take moral responsibility for the present.

ACKNOWLEDGMENT

This text results from the research project *Public Perceptions of Performative Holocaust Commemoration since the Year 2000*, financed by the Swedish Research Council (Vetenskapsrådet) [421-2014-1289].

NOTES

1. Erika Doss, *Memorial Mania: Public Feeling in America* (Chicago and London: University of Chicago Press, 2010).
2. Tanja Schult, *A Hero's Many Faces: Raoul Wallenberg in Contemporary Monuments* (Basingstoke/New York: Palgrave Macmillan, 2009/2012), here 292; and Erika Doss, "Monument med mänskliga proportioner," *Svenska Dagbladet* (January 27, 2010).

3. Schult, *A Hero's Many Faces*, 289–92; Quentin Stevens and Karen A. Franck, *Memorials as Spaces of Engagement: Design, Use and Meaning* (New York/ London: Routledge, 2016), 28–32.

4. For the history of the Gusen camps, see Rudolf Haunschmied, "NS-Geschichte 1938/1945," in *300 Jahre erweitertes Marktrecht St. Georgen an der Gusen* (St. Georgen an der Gusen: Marktgemeinde St. Georgen an der Gusen, 1989), 74–112; Rudolf Haunschmied, "Die Bevölkerung von St. Georgen/Gusen und Langenstein," in *Gedenkstätten für die Opfer des Nationalsozialismus in Polen und Österreich. Bestandsaufnahme und Entwicklungsperspektiven*, ed. Bogusław Dybaś, Tomasz Kranz, Irmgard Nöbauer, and Heidemarie (Frankfurt am Main: Peter Lang, 2013), 135–69; Rudolf Haunschmied, "Zur Bedeutung des Pfarrgebiets von St. Georgen/Gusen als Schlüsselregion zur Ausbeutung von KZ-Häftlingen durch die Schutzstaffel," *Denk.Statt* 2014, 26–38; Christian Dürr, "Von Mauthausen nach Gusen und zurück. Verlassene Konzentrationslager—Gedenkstätten—traumatische Orte," in *Erinnerungsorte in Bewegung. Zur Neugestaltung des Gedenkens an Orten nationalsozialistischer Verbrechen*, ed. Daniela Allmeier, Peter Mörtenböck, and Rudolf Scheuvens (Bielefeld, 2016), transcript, 145–65.

5. Dürr, "Von Mauthausen nach Gusen und zurück," 151, 155.

6. Heidemarie Uhl, "Gedenken 'vor Ort.' Das Denkmalprojekt in St. Georgen im Kontext der neuen Erinnerungskultur," in *Denk.Statt, Neue Wege der Erinnerungskultur*, ed. Plattform Johann Gruber (Linz/Donau: Wagner Verlag, 2014), 58–63.

7. Haunschmied, "Die Bevölkerung von St. Georgen/Gusen und Langenstein," 151–52.

8. Dürr, "Von Mauthausen nach Gusen und zurück," 160.

9. The majority of the survey participants (see note 20) do not mention the voice. I regard the narrator's voice and its timbre as essential. So does Wegner, who in her master's thesis, investigates the narrator's fundamental significance at close range: Susanne Elisabeth Wegner, "Erinnerungsort Stimme: der AUDIOWEG GUSEN" (Unpublished master's thesis, Kunstuniversität Linz. Institut für Medien, Medienkultur- und Kunsttheorien); see in particular 35, 38–47.

10. Cp. Wegner, "Erinnerungsort Stimme," 63.

11. Cp. Peter Larndorfer, "Unsichtbares hören. Der 'Audioweg Gusen,'" *Zeithistorische Forschungen/Studies of Contemporary History* 8 (2011), 315–21.

12. Cp. die jungs kommunikation, *Das Unsichtbare Lager AUDIOWEG GUSEN*. With contributions by Christoph Mayer, Aleida Assmann, Harald Welzer, and Rudolf Haunschmied. Broschure. (Vienna: die jungskommunikation, 2007); and Wegner, "Erinnerungsort Stimme," 38–40.

13. Wegner, "Erinnerungsort Stimme," ii.

14. Ola Larsmo, "Rösterna från Gusen," *Dagens Nyheter*, December 20, 2007.

15. audioweg.gusen.org

16. Cp. Haunschmied, "Die Bevölkerung von St. Georgen/Gusen und Langenstein"; Martha Gammer, "Vom 'Unbekannten Gusen' zum Bewusstsein Historischer Verantwortung," *Denk.Statt*, 2014: 64–67; Brigitte Halbmayer and Alfred Zauner,

"Mit dem Wissen um die Vergangenheit die Zukunft gestalten," *Denk.Statt*, 2014: 68–71; gusen.org.

17. die jungs kommunikation; Gammer, "Vom 'Unbekannten Gusen' zum Bewusstsein Historischer Verantwortung."

18. Mayer is completely unpretentious. It is always the work that is the focus. This might explain why each work has its own home page, while the artist himself has none.

19. Cp. Larsmo, "Rösterna från Gusen"; die jungs kommunikation; and Larndorfer, "Unsichtbares hören," 317.

20. The surveys, composed after I took the walk in July 2016, were handed out by Bernhard Mühleder, educator at the Memorial Mauthausen and contact person for the Memorial Gusen, who provides those interested with the MP3 players and headsets and sometimes accompanies smaller groups on their tour or awaits participants on their return, offering them the opportunity to talk about their experiences. According to Mühleder, around five hundred people take the walk each year. More than one out of five took a copy of the survey, and almost all of them answered it. The majority of people take the tour in German during April and July; approximately 10 percent of the users are locals (email from Mühleder to the author, October 18, 2017). The survey participants were between fifteen and seventy-four years old, with a slight preponderance of women; more than half of them were pupils or students, and most were Austrians.

21. die jungs kommunikation.

22. Wegner is of a different opinion ("Erinnerungsort Stimme," 77). According to her, the walk is rather manipulative, and the narrator's voice is used as an instrument of power (41–42). By contrast, Larndorfer regards Mayer's walk as nonmoralistic ("Unsichtbares hören," 318–19).

23. See Wegner, "Erinnerungsort Stimme," 79–80. This contrasts with Uhl ("Gedenken 'vor Ort,'" 62), who describes this region as a pioneer when it comes to raising awareness about the Nazi past.

24. According to a conversation with Bernhard Mühleder during my visit in September 2017.

25. Schult, *A Hero's Many Faces*, 284–89, 26; and "Monument med mänskliga proportioner," Svenska Dagbladet (27 januari 2010), http://www.svd.se/kultur/under strecket/monument-med-manskliga-proportioner_4157797.svd

26. Cp. Wegner, "Erinnerungsort Stimme," 16.

27. Here are only three examples: Renate Herter's artwork *Passage against Forgetting* (2014) in St. Georgen; Johannes Epple's novel *Gesternstadt* (Wien: Labor, 2012); and the decision of the Bundesdenkmalamt from 2014 that the relicts and remaining buildings of the former camp Gusen are worthy of protection.

CHAPTER 19

Exhibiting Spectacle and Recasting Memory

Commemorating the First World War in New Zealand

Kingsley Baird

Monuments have long sought to provide a naturalizing locus for memory, in which a state's triumphs and martyrs, its ideals and founding myths, are cast as naturally true.[1]

Recently, monuments—often perceived as minor forms of cultural expression[2]—have found themselves at the center of civil discord in diverse locations throughout the world.[3] In New Zealand, the authority of Pākehā narratives has been challenged and disrupted by acts of dissent,[4] including vandalism perpetrated against memorials to political, military, and exploration heroes of the colonial period. In contrast to these sites of contested memory, monuments promulgating national identity narratives associated with New Zealand's participation in both world wars—particularly in relation to the ANZAC story[5]—are generally received with widespread support. Significantly, on commemorative occasions concerning these external conflicts, the collective memories of Pākehā and indigenous Māori are largely aligned.

Despite the First World War occurring a century ago and our homeland being physically far removed from the war's main theaters, for many twenty-first-century New Zealanders, it remains the defining moment in the creation of the country's national identity.[6]

Over the period of the World War I centenary (2014–2018), thus far there has been little dissent to official measures commemorating the anniversary.[7] This harmony contrasts to attitudes in the 1960s when remembrance practices and memorials—perhaps inevitably associated with New Zealand's military involvement in the Vietnam War—became occasions for and sites of protest.[8]

Following a "period of apathy and neglect" in the 1970s, 1980s, and early 1990s, interest in the world wars began to develop again.[9] Jock Phillips speculates on a number of reasons for the renewed interest in the First World War, including that of historians, beginning with Christopher Pugsley's 1984 pioneering book,[10] *Gallipoli: The New Zealand Story*, and a related TV documentary. A younger generation intrigued by their grandfathers' and great-grandfathers' martial experiences, greater availability of first-person accounts of the war, the approaching First World War centenary, and increasing public funds supporting local commemorative initiatives all contributed to the growing interest, according to Phillips.[11] Additionally, following a period of decline, growing numbers of people were attending Anzac Day commemoration services, seemingly to remember the fallen of earlier wars.[12]

From the late 1990s—coinciding with a new government, a political agenda concerned with promoting national identity, the imminent First World War centenary, and a prime minister with strong familial ties to that war[13]—New Zealand saw a succession of new national memorials—in Canberra (2001), Wellington (2004), and London (2006)—and the creation of a new memorial park (2015) at the National War Memorial in Wellington.

These developments, while signaling a changing attitude in the country to war commemoration, fall within conventionally understood notions of memorialization. Paul Williams defines "memorial" as "an umbrella term for anything that serves in remembrance of a person or event," including non-material forms such as a holiday or song.[14] Applying his broad definition, this chapter discusses an exhibition held at the Museum of New Zealand Te Papa Tongarewa (Te Papa) in Wellington from April 2015 to April 2019. *Gallipoli: The Scale of Our War* tells the story of New Zealand's involvement in the 1915 Gallipoli campaign in Turkey. The chapter argues that *Gallipoli* serves a commemorative as well as a conventional scientific function because of the objectives of Te Papa and the exhibition development team, including its creative director, Sir Richard Taylor of Weta Workshop, and its public reception, thus becoming a memorial exhibition.

In attempting to assume this dual role of museum exhibition and memorial, is *Gallipoli*'s objective scientific credibility ultimately compromised? The chapter explores how the use of the theatrical trope of spectacle in the *Gallipoli* exhibition—including hyperrealism and the monumental scale of figures representing real people—contributes to one of New Zealand's key foundational myths. Using one of my own small-scale bronze sculptures—a point of difference to the colossi in *Gallipoli*—it is argued that contemporary memorial forms can encompass the recognition of sacrifice and duty while critiquing the use of the past in the present.

> Roll up! Roll up! Ladies and gentlemen, boys and girls, to the greatest show in our history . . . the memory industry invites all of us into a narcissistic world, one in which the pleasures of loss or nostalgia are part and parcel of the bittersweet and profitable business of remembering.[15]

The multimillion-dollar *Gallipoli* exhibition has proven to be very popular, with an excess of seven hundred thousand visitors in its first year, making it the most visited exhibition in the museum's history.[16] Jay Winter observes that museums dealing with contemporary history have succeeded in attracting very sizeable visitor numbers in recent years, arguing the reason for their attendance is that they are sites where "family history and world history come together."[17] This melding of histories is true of the *Gallipoli* exhibition; many New Zealand visitors would certainly have ancestral connections to, if not the Gallipoli campaign, then certainly the First World War (this author included).

Gallipoli's theatrical tone is established at the dramatic—and paradoxical—entrance. The bold coloring of the large-scale lettering of the exhibition's title and (lower key) figurative imagery—both more reminiscent of the Ringling Bros. and Barnum & Bailey Circus or the cover of a war comic than an exhibition concerned with a military failure and associated casualties—is undeniably captivating from across the expansive floor space in front of the entrance. Following a short briefing by a museum attendant, visitors enter the exhibition through a gap between the first two letters of the three-dimensional word, "WAR," as a flattened, cutout World War I New Zealand soldier in an action pose towers above them.

Being "the hybrid offspring of the movie and museum worlds," the stylistic approach to the exhibition should not be a surprise.[18] Departing from Te Papa's usual practice, the museum "wanted to engage with the spirit and culture of film-making" and, "capitalising on Wellywood's brand recognition and audience 'pulling power,'" chose to "co-create" the exhibition with "an external creative partner,"[19] Weta Workshop, an award-winning film and television special effects and prop company based in Wellington. Employing Weta's "emotive storytelling and compelling characters" would "allow Te Papa's commemorative efforts to be heard above the din" of the World War I centenary in New Zealand and contribute to the museum's "long-term objective of animating and expanding Te Papa's approach to exhibition-making."[20]

Though more subdued, the entrance's stagey treatment is maintained inside the narrow, exhibition space with the somber, mood-setting music of the specially composed soundtrack, the cries of soldiers engaged in combat, spotlights illuminating the exhibits in the dark, and voices-overs personifying some of the characters represented. In the incommodious spaces, visitors are sometimes required to wait, give way, and move in single file. Spatial intimacy with the exhibits and each other has the effect of contributing to a shared experience among visitors. The materiel of war is on display along with life-sized sets, dioramas, and models; 3-D digital maps; photographs; and original film footage as well as modern reenactments and letter and diary extracts. Some of the exhibition enables direct engagement: visitors can peer through a trench periscope or try on soldiers' hats.

Williams contends that "Memorial museums . . . are acutely aware of the role of primary artifacts, not only because they give displays a powerful appeal, but also because in many cases they exist as tangible proof in the face of debate about, and even denial of, what transpired."[21] Te Papa employs this "rhetorical strategy."[22] An original soldier's kit and memorial stones from the sea at Anzac Cove in Gallipoli (the latter gifted by the Republic of Turkey) add a compelling authenticity as possible witnesses to the events and the genius loci of 1915. Information panels describe soldiers' experiences in persuasively colloquial and vernacular language, "written" according to Te Papa, "as if from the soldier's perspective."[23] As one of the exhibition's "many movie-inspired elements,"[24] this text is treated "more like a film script" in order to locate the "audience within the action, and to reduce visitors' emotional distance."[25]

The small, dark exhibition chambers are divided thematically by titles such as "The great adventure," "Order from chaos," and "Stalemate." Progress through the exhibition is chronological; *Gallipoli*'s April to December 1915 time frame is marked by a red line on the floor along with small red crosses marking each New Zealand death. The latter, according to exhibition lead curator, Kirstie Ross "enabled us to acknowledge the cumulative loss of life on the Turkish peninsula without recreating a full-blown war memorial."[26]

The exhibition's subtitle apparently refers to more than the size of the nation's commitment to the First World War. The heroes of *Gallipoli* are the eight, 2.4 times life-sized human figures created by Weta Workshop, which represent real people who served at Gallipoli. Ross describes the giant figures as forming "the scaffolding for the exhibition's narrative framework," while Taylor asserts they possess the "X factor" that would "capture" audiences. "The emotional state of the giants provides the exhibition's affective arc," maintains Ross.[27]

When confronted with the sculptures and *mise en scène* located in the center of the exhibition chambers, visitors tend to automatically encircle them as if drawn by a gravitational pull into the orbits of the tableaux, enabling "an emotional connection."[28]

The relationship between enlarged scale and *Gallipoli*'s emotional reception is a fundamental strategy employed by the exhibition makers: "The resizing of figures . . . magnifies the main characters' emotions," argues Ross.[29] Scale also enables the use of filmmaking devices, such as "movie close ups, when the thoughts and feelings of an individual fill the screen."[30] Focusing on real-life individuals "humanizes and personalizes" the New Zealanders involved in the campaign and, according to Ross, "helps to dislodge Gallipoli from the received wisdom that the campaign forged New Zealand's collective national identity."[31]

Te Papa "employed diversifying criteria" in their selection of the giant figures who represent a "broad cross section of human experiences" as well as the original cast at Gallipoli, including officers and ranks, an army doctor and nurse, Pākehā and Māori, young and mature.[32] Crucially, individuals were selected "who could act as emotional gateways to the 'action-packed' thematic episodes."[33] Poses vary from a tearful nurse, perching on a wooden chest reading of her brother's death at Gallipoli to two soldiers positioned behind their machine gun in the heat of battle. Intentional or not, these larger-than-life figures appear to reference stone and bronze statues in a museum of antiquity: *Boxer at Rest*, *The Dying Gaul*, or *Poseidon Launching His Trident*. Their realism—lifelikeness—is impressive. So too is fidelity and attention to detail, such as sweat on brows or dripping from the end of a nose or giant flies in wounds and corned beef. I was privileged to visit Weta before the exhibition opened and watched as individual stubble hair was painstakingly stitched by hand through a giant soldier's rubbery skin. Perhaps it is only the effects of the air-conditioning, but Nurse Lottie Le Gallais's long, blond locks really do sway gently in a breeze. Visitors stand in wonderment at the scale and verisimilitude of these giants from a bygone era, take discreet photographs, whisper to each other, or sit and reflect before the spectacle. "The statues are absolutely outstanding, so life-like and will stay with me forever. Amazing[,] so moving."[34]

Near the end of the exhibition, visitors are invited to text a message to Te Papa's website. For some of these visitors, their emotional response to the exhibition is directly linked to the seductive impact of the Weta figures—particularly their size and authenticity—but also their identification with the sculpted, real-life characters, what Williams calls "an empathetic projection of one's self onto the object of contemplation."[35] Others directly address the long-dead soldiers with a message of appreciation, whereas a small number bemoan the waste of lives or express an anti-war sentiment. Meanwhile, as expressed by Te Papa's former chief executive, Rick Ellis's emotive description of the "astonishing" response of the public reinforces the affective nature of the exhibition:

Beyond the sheer numbers, we have been humbled by the depth of feeling we see in our visitors. . . . They are coming in family groups, they are immersing themselves in the information and the emotion, and they are leaving with a new understanding, and often, with tears in their eyes.[36]

We are prepared before we enter the exhibition space: "we come in respect, bringing with us a sense of history, often loaded with familial significance."[37] Gallipoli is apparently central to our identity as New Zealanders, a belief that the exhibition confirms. The public's online messages indicate the success of what I speculate to be key objectives of the exhibition, to *inform* and to *move* the audience as well as have them identify with those whose stories are told as true or fictive kin.

Before visitors leave the exhibition, they pass the final figure, Sergeant Cecil Malthus, a Gallipoli veteran now depicted serving on the Western Front (figure 19.1). Portrayed standing in a shell crater; around him—instead of muddy water—is a pool of paper poppies supplied by the museum for visitors to cast into the crater.[38] In what Williams describes as "social *practices* of visitation,"[39] tributary offerings are made around this survivor of the Gallipoli campaign, who stands in for the sacrifice of his less fortunate comrades. According to Te Papa, "over half a million poppies have been left by visitors to date."[40] Although presumably not an intended outcome, one of the consequences of the exhibition's eliciting a heightened emotional response is the "romanticization of war"[41]; we, the visitors, leave with "two motifs—war as *both* noble and uplifting *and* tragic and unendurably sad."[42]

THE GREAT WAR EXHIBITION

In addition to Te Papa's *Gallipoli*, another significant First World War exhibition in Wellington has received multimillion-dollar support from the government: *The Great War Exhibition* (April 2015–November 11, 2018), whose creator is filmmaker, Sir Peter Jackson, who also employs filmmaking

Figure 19.1. *Sergeant Cecil Malthus (the Somme) in Gallipoli: The Scale of Our War*, **Weta Workshop, mixed media, Museum of New Zealand Te Papa Tongarewa, 2015.**
Courtesy of the Museum of New Zealand Te Papa Tongarewa.

techniques in its storytelling as a "stunning array of movie-like sets depict the war; scene by scene; year by year."[43] While, in contrast to Te Papa's giants, the very realistic Weta Workshop figures in this exhibition are life-sized, the nationalistic rhetoric is not scaled down:

> The lives and experiences of New Zealanders who served and lived during that time highlight the bravery and enduring spirit which helped shape who we are as a people and what it means to be a New Zealander.[44]

A significant part of the exhibition is dedicated to New Zealand's Gallipoli story, including a very large diorama of Chunuk Bair summit containing five thousand hand-painted miniature figurines who "reenact" the battle and a new display, the Quinn's Post Trench Experience, which "recreates the sights, sounds and smells experienced by soldiers at Quinn's Post on the Gallipoli Peninsula in 1915."[45] The Victorian theatrical technique of "Pepper's ghost" is used to create "ghostly images of real-life soldiers" who guide exhibition visitors through the trench.[46] According to Jackson, the thirty-minute experience is "designed to take you as far out of today's world as you possibly can, and put you back into something approximating what it was like back then."[47]

"CHUNUK BAIR: A NEW ZEALAND EPIC" AND THE *GALLIPOLI* SCULPTURE[48]

One of the key themes in both exhibitions concerns Chunuk Bair, a summit on the Gallipoli peninsula captured by New Zealand troops on August 8, 1915. Briefly, the Allies held the position until it was overrun by a massive Turkish counterattack. This is a real story of heroism and sacrifice on both sides of the encounter, of a very high price paid to secure an objective that—it was mistakenly thought—could have wrenched the initiative from the seemingly intractable Turks. If only the heights—so bravely and costly won—had been retained it was thought, the course of the campaign might well have been different. However, the position did not have the strategic value attributed to it at the time, and the valiant action was an exercise in futility. No matter, Chunuk Bair became central to New Zealand's Gallipoli mythmaking.

The genesis of New Zealand (and Australian) Anzac mythology can be traced along a well-worn trail to the Gallipoli campaign in the Dardanelles in 1915. The failure of the expedition to establish a second front seemed to count for little, and New Zealanders at home, according to Ian McGibbon, were "thrilled to learn that their men were taking part in the top league."[49] Former New Zealand Chief of the Defence Staff, Lieutenant General Sir Leonard Thornton, maintained the Dardanelles "débâcle" "came to be seen as giving tentative expression to a new national consciousness, setting us apart as New Zealanders, not merely British, and more than the affiliates of Australia."[50]

The centenary of the First World War, and in particular, the Gallipoli campaign, provides an opportunity to reassess the role that this conflict played in contributing to New Zealanders' sense of national identity. Exhibitions and memorial forms and rituals can play a vital role in assisting the public to acquire a better understanding of their history and how it shaped the past and shapes the present. Some historians and institutions continue to promulgate the formative influence of an event that both New Zealand and Australia have so enthusiastically invested in for the last century, rising to, in commemorative practices, a "civil religion."[51] Others—controversially, in some cases—critique this national obsession and its role in shaping history and values.[52]

Interrogating the Anzac legend and its perpetuation in memorial building, remembrance rituals, exhibitions, and written histories is a principal role of the *Gallipoli* sculpture (figure 19.2). The sculpture, comprising a bronze lemon squeezer hat (with which New Zealand soldiers have become associated) and a Lego Trojan horse, conflates Ancient Greek and New Zealand martial mythology located in the Aegean. The hat might be interpreted as being physically representative of the Gallipoli peninsula of flat plains and razor-sharp hills. Its extended, pinched peak also references exaggeration, tales of heroism and superhuman feats. Lieutenant Colonel William Malone, commander of the Wellington Infantry at Gallipoli and the troops who took Chunuk Bair, is said to have adopted the lemon squeezer for his soldiers because its outline re-

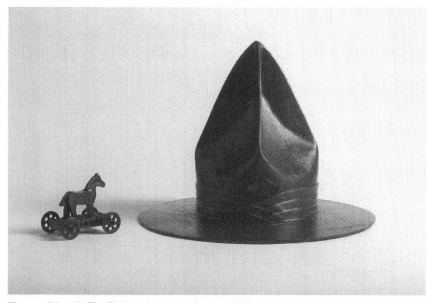

Figure 19.2. *Gallipoli*, **Kingsley Baird, bronze, 50 cm x 35 cm x 23 cm, 2015.**
Artist's collection, photo courtesy of Jane Wilcox.

minded him of the mountain near where he lived, Taranaki-Egmont, and for practical reasons, aiding rain runoff.[53] The badge of the Taranaki Rifles (which was under Malone's command) depicts the mountain. The Lego Trojan horse alludes to childhood war toys and games and connects Anzac mythology with a much earlier tale from Homer's times, set across the Dardanelles at Ilium.

The role of a memorial artist immediately after the First World War, according to Jay Winter, was to make sense of the conflict's devastating destruction and assuage the loss of the bereaved.[54] While temporal distance does not absolve us from an obligation to recognize the sacrifice of *Our Glorious Dead*, the act of contemporary witnessing by artists—*and* historians—includes the moral necessity to critique the use of the past to justify action in the present. The *Gallipoli* sculpture is intended to expose, challenge, and problematize foundational myths and national identity narratives, warning that pride in sacrifice and heroism of the past should not be used to encourage nationalist tendencies or unjustified contemporary or future overseas martial escapades. It is intended to do the *work* of art by negotiating between the acknowledgment of sacrifice in the past and our obligation as citizens as we send others to fight and possibly die in our name.[55]

AN "UNEASY CONCEPTUAL COEXISTENCE"

Winter cautions against constructing an authentic experience in war museums or exhibitions: "The most serious pitfall in this cultural domain is what might be termed *pseudo-realism*, the false claim of those who write about war or design museums about it that they can bring the visitor into something approximating the experience of combat."[56] Rather than attempting the impossibility of inserting us back into history with artful devices, there are alternatives to the clamor of the spectacle. Winter describes the approach taken by those—including himself—who established the tone of the Historial de la Grande Guerre museum in Péronne, France: "No pseudo-realism here; no sounds, no voices, no mimetic recreation, no appeals to the familiar and the comforting. Instead we have a museum which enables people quietly to contemplate the past—a cruel and violent moment in the past—without being told that they can share the 'experience.'"[57]

The visitors' experience at the Historial that Winter described above is far removed from that of the *Gallipoli* exhibition. Certainly, Te Papa has achieved its goal of presenting an "immersive and affective exhibition,"[58] and the overwhelming popularity (in terms of record numbers of visitors and very favorable online responses) combined with the lack of negative critique evidently attests to the success of the exhibition. Indeed, these outcomes suggest to Ross that "*Gallipoli* is delivering Te Papa's vision—to change hearts, minds and lives."[59]

However, is "scaling up emotion" the museum's role?[60] The local audience, at least, is receptive: the legend of Anzac and Gallipoli is ostensibly inherent and ubiquitous, from the school curriculum to attendance at Anzac Day ceremonies. New Zealanders are apparently willingly co-opted into this national identity and foundational narrative, seemingly electing "a sentimental substitute for a complex engagement with the past,"[61] one that unifies rather than divides as confronting historical conflict close to home might do. Ross denies that this is Te Papa's intention, claiming: "Rather than unifying visitors under a banner of mindless patriotism, the extraordinary size of these ordinary individuals has the power to unsettle standard readings of the war."[62] And it seems the public has not seen the end of such cocreated exhibitions, which will "serve to shape our exhibition-making concepts and practice in the future."[63]

The visionary concept development and rigorous research that underpins much of Te Papa's exhibition and the oversized characters at its center are truly impressive. However, does *Gallipoli* represent what Williams describes as an "uneasy conceptual coexistence of reverent remembrance and critical interpretation."[64] He argues that while a history museum "is presumed to be concerned with interpretation, contextualisation, and critique," "traditional formal distinctions" between museums and monuments and memorials are often ill defined.[65] Williams attributes this lack of differentiation to "an increasing desire to add both a moral framework to the narration of terrible historical events and more in-depth contextual explanations to commemorative acts."[66] The mission of memorial museums—and, by extension, memorial exhibitions—according to Williams is clear: "to illuminate, commemorate, and educate about a particular bounded and vivid historical event."[67] We trust the authority of the historians and curators and consume their offerings as those of experts operating within the ideological context of the present.

However, is the *Gallipoli* exhibition an example of "memory as re-enchantment" versus "the coldness of historical analysis"?[68] The scale of the figures and the cinematic and theatrical support cast, including mood music, atmospheric lighting, and rhetorical voice-overs, are summoned to produce the effect of what Winter describes as "re-sacralization of the past."[69] Seduced by the spectacle, are the viewers' emotions conscripted into the exhibition's sensory and emotional narrative? Despite many admirable elements in the exhibition and very favorable public feedback, the overwhelming impression for this visitor was one of emotional manipulation. Instead of being guided to reach my own conclusions about this historical event solely from insightful scholarship and dispassionate communication, in the exhibition's narrow passages, I was channeled toward an effective response by some remarkable puppetry.

NOTES

1. James E. Young, "Memory and Counter-Memory: The End of the Monument in Germany," *Harvard Design Magazine* 9 (Fall 1999): 6.

2. Jock Phillips, *The Sorrow & the Pride: New Zealand War Memorials* (Wellington: Department of Internal Affairs, 1990), 10.

3. For example, monuments to Cecil Rhodes in Cape Town and Oxford and the Confederacy in the United States.

4. Pākehā (or Pakeha) originally referred to fair-skinned people of European descent. Recently, the definition has broadened to also include any non–Māori New Zealander.

5. The Australian and New Zealand Army Corps (ANZAC) made its operational debut at Gallipoli on April 25, 1915, and Anzac Day commemorates this landing. "Anzac" soon described all Australian and New Zealand soldiers who fought on the peninsula and eventually any soldier from these nations. "Anzac continues to denote . . . a distinctive nationalistic spirit of sacrifice and courage" in Australia and New Zealand: Ian McGibbon, "ANZAC," in *The Oxford Companion to New Zealand Military History*, ed. Ian McGibbon (Auckland: Oxford University Press, 2000), 27. The 1915 Gallipoli campaign was an Allied expedition aimed at gaining control of the Dardanelles and Bosporus straits, capturing Constantinople, and opening a Black Sea supply route to Russia.

6. This is perhaps not surprising given the significant losses suffered and the size of the force enlisted in relation to the country's population. Just under 10 percent of the population of 1.1 million served overseas, of which more than 18,000 died. "History Guide," New Zealand WW100, accessed February 28, 2018, https://ww100.govt.nz/history-guide.

7. On Anzac Day 2016, Peace Action Wellington installed three "guerilla" sculptures in Wellington commemorating New Zealand's First World War conscientious objectors.

8. Jock Phillips, *To the Memory: New Zealand's War Memorials* (Nelson: Potton & Burton, 2016), 199.

9. Phillips, *To the Memory*, 204.

10. Ibid., 207.

11. Ibid.

12. Ibid.

13. Prime Minister Helen Clark's great-uncle, Frank Clark, died at Gallipoli in August 1915. David McMurray, Clark's maternal grandfather, fought in the Battle of the Somme on the Western Front along with his five brothers. Clark knows of ten great uncles who served in the Great War and of four who died in military service to the British Empire. Graham Hucker, "A Determination to Remember: Helen Clark and New Zealand's Military Heritage," *The Journal of Arts Management, Law, and Society* 40: 106, https://www.tandfonline.com/doi/abs/10.1080/106329 21.2010.485088.

14. Paul Williams, *Memorial Museums: The Global Rush to Commemorate Atrocities* (Oxford and New York: Berg, 2007), 7.

15. Jay Winter paraphrasing Charles Maier in Jay Winter, *Remembering War: The Great War between Memory and History in the Twentieth Century* (New Haven: Yale University Press, 2006), 286.

16. "Te Papa Marks a Record Year for *Gallipoli: The Scale of Our War*," Museum of New Zealand Te Papa Tongarewa, modified April 25, 2016, accessed July 3, 2017, https://www.tepapa.govt.nz/about/press-and-media/press-releases/2016-news-and-media-releases/te-papa-marks-record-year-for. Three years on from the opening of *Gallipoli*, the exhibition continues to attract large numbers of visitors.

17. Winter, *Remembering War*, 222.

18. Kirstie Ross, "Conceiving and Calibrating *Gallipoli: The Scale of Our War*," *Museums Australia Magazine* 24, no. 1 (Spring 2015): 29.

19. Ross, "Conceiving and Calibrating Gallipoli," 24. "Wellywood" is an informal conflation of the name of New Zealand's capital city, Wellington. Hollywood is a reference to the film production business established in the city by New Zealand film director Sir Peter Jackson and special effects companies Weta Digital and Weta Workshop. Sir Richard Taylor, creative director of the *Gallipoli: The Scale of Our War* exhibition development team, is the founder, creative director, and head of Weta Workshop. Both Jackson and Taylor—who are personally very interested in the First World War—are recognized for making the New Zealand film industry known internationally and have almost "mythic" status in the country, in which their efforts have contributed to New Zealand's sense of national identity.

20. Ross, "Conceiving and Calibrating Gallipoli," 24.

21. Williams, *Memorial Museums*, 25.

22. Ibid., 31.

23. Museum of New Zealand Te Papa Tongarewa, "World War I Teachers' Resource Pack," 3, accessed July 8, 2017, https://www.tepapa.govt.nz/sites/default/files/ww1_teacher_resource_pack_0.pdf.

24. Ross, "Conceiving and Calibrating Gallipoli," 28.

25. Ibid., 29.

26. Ibid., 28.

27. Ibid., 26.

28. Ibid.

29. Ibid., 27.

30. Ibid.

31. Ibid.

32. Ibid.

33. Ibid.

34. Museum of New Zealand Te Papa Tongarewa, "Messages," accessed November 28, 2016, and July 11, 2017, http://messages.gallipoli.tepapa.govt.nz.

35. Williams, *Memorial Museums*, 40.

36. Museum of New Zealand Te Papa Tongarewa, "Te Papa Marks a Record Year for *Gallipoli: The Scale of Our War*," modified April 25, 2016, accessed June 4, 2017, https://www.tepapa.govt.nz/about/press-and-media/press-releases/2016-news-and-media-releases/te-papa-marks-record-year-for.

37. Williams, *Memorial Museums*, 6.

38. Artificial poppies are worn as a remembrance symbol on Anzac Day, April 25.

39. Williams, *Memorial Museums*, 5.

40. Museum of New Zealand Te Papa Tongarewa, "Te Papa Marks a Record Year for *Gallipoli*."

41. Williams, *Memorial Museums*, 4.

42. Jay Winter, *Sites of Memory, Sites of Mourning: The Great War in European Cultural History* (Cambridge: Cambridge University Press, 1995), 85.

43. "The Great War Exhibition," accessed April 21, 2018, https://www.greatwarexhibition.nz.

44. "About the Great War Exhibition, accessed June 4, 2017, http://www.greatwarexhibition.nz/about-us/.

45. "Sir Peter Jackson Dishes on New Gallipoli Trench Exhibit," TV3 Newshub, accessed April 22, 2018, http://www.newshub.co.nz/home/new-zealand/2018/04/sir-peter-jackson-dishes-on-new-gallipoli-trench-exhibit.html.

46. "Sir Peter Jackson Dishes."

47. Ibid.

48. The part of the title of this section in quotation marks is from Ian McGibbon, "Chunuk Bair: A New Zealand Epic," in *Wartime* 47 (2009), accessed February 28, 2018, https://www.awm.gov.au/wartime/47.

49. Ian McGibbon, "Gallipoli," in *The Oxford Companion to New Zealand Military History*, ed. Ian McGibbon (Auckland: Oxford University Press, 2000), 198.

50. Christopher Pugsley, *Gallipoli: The New Zealand Story* (Sceptre: Auckland, 1984), 7.

51. Ken Inglis, *Sacred Places: War Memorials in the Australian Landscape*, 3rd ed. (Carlton, Victoria: Melbourne University Press, 2008), 433–44.

52. This critique is largely confined to Australia. Examples include James Brown, *Anzac's Long Shadow: The Cost of Our National Obsession* (Collingwood, Victoria: Redback, 2014); and Marilyn Lake and Henry Reynolds, *What's Wrong with ANZAC? The Militarisation of Australian History* (Sydney: University of New South Wales Press, 2010).

53. Chris Pugsley, "Malone, William George," *Dictionary of New Zealand Biography* 3, Te Ara—the Encyclopedia of New Zealand, 1996, accessed July 5, 2017, https://teara.govt.nz/en/biographies/3m40/malone-william-george.

54. Jay Winter, *Sites of Memory, Sites of Mourning: The Great War in European Cultural History* (Cambridge, UK: Cambridge University Press, 1995), 94.

55. For more discussion of this work and its Australian "pair," *Birth of a Nation*, see Kingsley Baird, "The Anzac Pair: An Allegory of National Identity," in *The Anzac Pair*, ed. Kingsley Baird (Waiouru, NZ: National Army Museum Te Mata Toa, Wellington, Massey University, 2017), 6–33.

56. Jay Winter, "Museums and the Representation of War," in *Museum & Society* 10 no. 3 (2012): 161, accessed February 28, 2018, https://journals.le.ac.uk/ojs1/index.php/mas/article/view/211/224.

57. Winter, *Remembering War*, 226.

58. Ross, "Conceiving and Calibrating Gallipoli," 27.

59. Ibid., 23.

60. Ibid., 26.
61. Young, "Memory and Counter-Memory," 5.
62. Ross, "Conceiving and Calibrating Gallipoli," 27.
63. Ibid., 30.
64. Williams, *Memorial Museums*, 8.
65. Ibid., 8.
66. Ibid.
67. Ibid., 25.
68. Winter, *Remembering War*, 283.
69. Ibid., 282–83.

CHAPTER 20

Dealing with a Dictatorial Past

Fascist Monuments and Conflicting Memory in Contemporary Italy

FLAMINIA BARTOLINI

THIS CHAPTER EXAMINES THE RECEPTION OF FASCIST MONUMENTS IN contemporary Italy as an expression of how the country has dealt with its troubled dictatorial past. The variety of cultural heritage left by the regime is a distinctive feature of any Italian city and is today both a symbolic and a physical witness of the invasiveness of the totalitarian regime. Taking the period from 2010, with increasing public debate about how to deal with divisive and conflicting remains, this chapter looks at two emblematic case studies that can aid our understanding of Fascist monument culture in contemporary Italy. The first considers a monument erected in 2012 as a memorial to the infamous murderer Rodolfo Graziani, the Fascist marshal known as "the butcher" for his efficacy in the conquest of Ethiopia. Built in Graziani's resting place of Affile, the monument, which in 2017 was suggested to be demolished by orders of the national courts, shows how part of society still views Fascism as positive. The second examines how the city of Bolzano has dealt with a Fascist frieze on the Palace of Financial Offices representing Mussolini on horseback and how the monument has been disempowered through the addition in 2017 of an installation by the artists Arnold Holzknecht and Michele Bernardi. These two monuments, conceived in different times and for different purposes, illustrate the variety of political reasons that can inform monument building. The differing responses to these monuments reflect similar attitudes seen transnationally, at a time when the legacies of difficult pasts are being renegotiated and new values are inscribed or previous values removed from them.

RODOLFO GRAZIANI MEMORIAL IN AFFILE:
FORGETTING ITALY'S COLONIAL PAST

Marshal Rodolfo Graziani is one of the most controversial figures of the Fascist dictatorship in Italy. Included in the list of those eligible for prosecution by the United Nations War Crimes Commission after World War II for his repressive measures among civilians in Ethiopia, he is, however, considered by some to be a war hero. In 2013, on the grounds of his extensive military achievements, a mausoleum was dedicated to him in Affile, his resting place, by the far-right regional coalition led by Renata Polverini, in response to a request from the mayor of Affile, Ercole Viri (figure 20.1).[1]

But who was Rodolfo Graziani, and what does this memorial stand for? Marshal Rodolfo Graziani, viceroy of Italian East Africa, was the most prominent figure in the consolidation and expansion of Italy's empire, first in Libya and then in Ethiopia. In the 1930s, Graziani was appointed commander of the Italian Forces in Libya and is remembered for suppressing the Senussi rebellion, during which he constructed both concentration and labor camps.[2] His actions against this and other rebellions have resulted in his being remembered in very different ways in Italy and in Libya: at home he was granted the role of "Pacifier of Libya," whereas among Arab Berbers, he was nicknamed "The Butcher of Fezzan".[3]

During the second Italian-Abyssinian War of 1935–1936, Graziani was the commander of the southern front, attacking from Italian Somaliland: the successful operation was initially commanded by Marshal Emilio De Bono, who entered from Eritrea, and later by Marshal Pietro Badoglio.[4] At the conclusion of the Italian-Abyssinian War, Graziani was appointed Viceroy of Italian East Africa and Governor-General of Addis Ababa. Having survived an assassination attempt while visiting the Ethiopian Orthodox Church of Dire Dawa, in

Figure 20.1. Graziani Memorial, Affile, Italy.
Photo: Alessia Mastropietro for Flaminia Bartolini ©

1937, after a second assassination attempt in Addis Ababa, Graziani authorized a brutal retribution on civilians, known as Ykatit 12 or the Addis Ababa massacre.[5] Up to 30,000 civilians were killed indiscriminately, a further 1,469 were summarily executed, and over 1,000 notable individuals were imprisoned or exiled from Ethiopia; for this specific act of mass murder, he became known as the *Butcher of Ethiopia.*

This followed an earlier massacre at the ancient monastery of Debre Libanos, following the first attempt on his life, to punish the Orthodox clergy.[6] Following the fall of Mussolini on July 25, 1943, Graziani was the only marshal of Italy to remain loyal to Mussolini, and he became minister of defense in the Italian Social Republic of Salo'. After the war ended in 1945, despite being accused of war crimes by the Ethiopians, he was never prosecuted for those, although he was taken to trial in 1948 for collaboration with the Nazis during the Italian Social Republic of Salo' and spent four months in prison.[7]

Thus, it came as a great surprise to the international media, more than the local press, when in 2012, a monument evoking Fascist architecture and with words to the *Fatherland* and *Honor* was dedicated to Rodolfo Graziani in Affile.[8] The decision to erect a mausoleum using 160,000 euros of public money was decided initially by the right-wing regional president, Renata Polverini, with the addition of private funds gathered by the right-wing mayor, Ercole Viri. As the news reached the media, halfway through its construction, funds were suspended by the newly elected left-wing regional president, Nicola Zingaretti, and the mayor of Affile was accused by the National Association of Italian Partisans (ANPI) of being an apologist for Fascism.[9] In November 2017, the mayor was sent for trial and sentenced to almost three years in prison, and a mandate was issued by the tribunal to destroy the monument.[10] But how is it possible that an internationally recognized war criminal can be seen by some as a hero to the extent of publicly remembering him with a mausoleum?

At the time of this research, Mayor Ercole Viri had been already arrested, but as part of my fieldwork, I interviewed members of the local population and followed the media and social media debate. Affile as a town does not offer much as a tourist attraction when compared with other Italian towns of a similar size, with the exception of the mausoleum where the leading historical figure is Rodolfo Graziani and a marble head of him sits triumphantly as a gift from the mayor to the town.[11] It then takes only a tour of the local gift shops offering calendars and souvenirs of Graziani to realize that the memorial to the marshal has been used as a dark tourist attraction. Aside from the commercial impact of the monument, arguably what this site is expressing is a revised and distorted perception of the historical events of Italian colonialism and one of the most brutal expressions of Fascist violence. Italy's postwar renegotiation of the Fascist past is divided between the conflicting memories of post-fascists and anti-fascists, and as in the rest of Italy, a conspicuous portion of the debate sees heritage sites at the center of these conflicting claims.

Analyzing the discourse from the press of Ercole Viri, it is clear that in his view Graziani was primarily a war hero, unfairly accused of crimes that "*everyone else would have committed in his place, he was just taking orders.*"[12] What emerges from my interviews is that the local population in Affile support their mayor's decision, and they also advocate for a general "*revision*" of history, claiming that "*the history of Fascism has been written by the winners.*" What the memorial to the marshal represents is a view of history produced by the far-right in Italy, which sees the constant rereading and editing of the Fascist past on a revisionist agenda.

As Ventresca[13] and Focardi[14] have explained, the Italian postwar narrative on Fascism has been based on the revisionist paradigm of *Italians (are) good people*, in which, with the support of media film and popular culture, the public perception of Fascist violence has been erased from Fascism itself, leading to the creation of a comforting narrative of the *Good Italian* in contrast to the *Evil German*. This sanitization of Fascism was reinforced after 1989 and at the beginning of the Berlusconi era in Italy, which saw Berlusconi entering in to a coalition with the far-right, so they not only entered Parliament, as the Movimento Sociale Italiano (MSI) did previously, but were also in government. This new political scenario in Italy fermented a second wave of Fascist revisionism, in the footsteps of the historical revisionism set out in the monumental work on Fascism by scholar Renzo De Felice.[15]

Italian colonialism is among those aspects of the Italian Fascist past that the country has actively tried to forget, as argued by Angelo Del Boca[16] in his work on Italian Oriental Africa: films such as *The Desert Lion* and *Fascist Legacies*, which document Graziani's atrocities, have not passed Italian political censorship and have not been screened on Italian national television despite having been acquired by the state.[17] The legacy of Italy's colonial past has been hidden from public display, as in the case of the former Colonial Museum, whose collection has now been incorporated into the Museum of North Africa.[18] Graziani's concentration camps in Libyan and Ethiopia have slowly disappeared from the collective memory after years of the postwar revisionist effort, backed also by the widespread lack of trials and punishment for Fascist crimes; it is notable that Graziani, regardless of his brutality, was taken to trial for only his Nazi cooperation and not for his colonial crimes, creating in effect, a national justification of his vicious crimes.[19]

What this memorial ultimately proves, however, is how successful a revisionist strategy can be in changing people's perception of historical events, to the point of the distortion of memory and a fulfillment of the narrative of the existence of a *good Fascism*. Fortunately, as we shall see in the following case study, elsewhere in Italy, monuments are telling a different story.

DISEMPOWERING ARCHITECTURAL PROPAGANDA: THE MUSSOLINI FRIEZE ON THE PALACE OF FINANCIAL OFFICES IN BOLZANO

In the past couple of years, the fate of Fascist monuments still standing in Italy has been at the center of a heated debate, which has expanded from scholars to involve the popular press and social media. From the columns of *The New Yorker*, Ruth Ben-Ghiat created a wave of discontent in Italy by questioning why, in a time of monument debate following Charlottesville and the removal of Confederate monuments, Fascist monumental architecture had been left unquestioned in Italy.[20] At the national level, the debate surrounding some of the most iconic monuments saw the left-wing president of the Lower Chamber of Parliament, Laura Boldrini, campaigning for the removal or covering of the words *Mussolini DUX* from the obelisk at the center of the Foro Italico complex in Rome.[21] In this case, as also in the Ben-Ghiat article, public debate was quite unanimous in criticizing any reworking or removal of such monuments.

Public perception of Fascist material legacies in contemporary Italy falls into what can be described as having been depoliticized; this emerged from my own ethnographic interviews, in which regardless of people's political views, Fascist monuments in contemporary Italy are seen as part of the rest of the country's vast cultural heritage legacy. Until recently, this conspicuous material legacy of the dictatorship had been left undisturbed in the landscape, very often reused for its original purpose or given a new use. Destruction was very limited and stemmed largely from the actions of the Allies' government of the country in the immediate postwar period or because of aerial bombing during World War II.[22]

The so-called defascistization process saw the removal of fasces and other Fascist symbols from public buildings but was very often limited to the removal of the word *Mussolini* and the axes from the fasces. Many Italian cities are still full of not only Fascist monuments but also infrastructures, such as train stations, gyms, and schools, which very often still present Fascist symbols that escaped the removal. Sculpture symbolizing Fascism has also been removed from public spaces, such as the so-called *Bigio* in Brescia—a colossal sculpture of the Fascist era—which since its postwar removal, has been waiting for relocation[23] or the reworking of the sculpture of the *Genius of Fascism*, which has been transformed into *Genius of the Sport* in the EUR (Esposizione Universale Roma) neighborhood of Rome.[24]

In Rome, Mussolini's obelisk was at the center of a fierce debate because of the words "*Mussolini DUX*," President Boldrini arguing that this visual image of Mussolini's name could be offensive to those who fought in the Resistance.[25]

The very idea of removing the obelisk earned the president accusations of acting like a "Taliban," a reference to their habit of blowing up monuments. Within this hotly contested debate stands the project for the monumental frieze of Hans Piffrader on the top of the Palace of Financial Offices in Bolzano, in which Mussolini is depicted next to the Fascist motto *Believe, Obey, Fight* (figure 20.2). This frieze, originally meant for the Fascist Party headquarters, is the largest Fascist symbol on a public building still standing in Italy and represents the history of Fascism in fifty-seven panels and is over thirty-six-meters in length. Following the national debate on what to do with the remaining Fascist symbols in the country and social tensions around this monument, the town hall opted for a public consultation; what emerged was a need for the message this building still conveyed to be "rewritten."

The issue of how to deal with Fascist monuments was not new to the town of Bolzano; in 2014, the city opened an exhibition space beneath the Victory Monument, a Fascist triumphal arch celebrating Italy's World War I victory in the Alto Adige.[26] Following public interest and the general success of the Victory Monument operation, the town hall decided to hold a public consultation on the best way to give a new meaning to the overimposing narrative on the Palace of Financial Offices; it was felt that a new contemporary dialogue was needed to make sure Fascist symbols, and consequently values, were not just left unquestioned. The consultation process resulted in an invitation for artis-

Figure 20.2. Arnold Holzknecht and Michele Bernardi's installation on the Palace of Financial Offices, Bolzano, Italy.
Photo: Laura Egger for Flaminia Bartolini ©

tic projects to express a contemporary reinterpretation of the specific monument and of Fascism more broadly; that of Arnold Holzknecht and Michele Bernardi was finally selected from 486 submissions.[27]

The concept was of an illuminated phrase hung onto the frieze, luminously covering Mussolini's face, showing a readaptation of a famous motto of the philosopher Hannah Arendt, who rephrasing Kant, said *"No one has the right to obey"* as an answer to Mussolini's notorious motto of *Believe, Obey, Fight.* The luminous installation covers the length of the entire frieze and is repeated in three languages: Ladin [the regional language], Italian, and German (because 70 percent of the population of the region is of non-Italian origin). What makes this installation unique, aside of course from its artistic value, is its attempt to give new meaning to the monument visually, recoding its semantic value. Using the words of Hannah Arendt as a symbol to oppose the dictatorship, as a battle between dialogue and imperative orders, has proved to be a noninvasive means of reinterpreting a contested monument. The new added meaning of an open rejection of Fascist values, which brought protests from the far-right party CasaPound, stands for a cry of "not in my name" from the city of Bolzano, something which is unique in Italy.

REMEMBERING AND FORGETTING A DICTATORIAL PAST: AN ONGOING PROCESS

As these two case studies have shown, dealing with a traumatic dictatorial past is a complex process for a nation. Postdictatorial societies are communities left with both traumatic memories of the regime and material traces that act as constant reminders. In Italy, following the fall of the dictator, first to be attacked was his iconography, followed by renegotiation of the symbols of the dictatorship, a process that in Italy was called defascistization. This process of visual cleansing expresses the need to challenge and publicly question past values, even when the monument itself is still standing. In this edited version, Fascist monuments remain in public places but are read differently by different parts of society. For anti-fascists, they will always represent traumatic memories of the past regime; for sympathizers of *Il Duce*, they will stand in memory of his past glories. For most Italians, these monuments do not represent a threat, and given the cultural landscape in Italy, the question of moving them into a museum is not an option because the removal of monuments is not legally possible. While the removal of symbols, as happened in the aftermath of World War II, would still be a viable option for many, current legislation on the protection of cultural heritage does not allow it. Finding new ways to add a contemporary layer of meaning to monuments that carry unacceptable values from the past is challenging because postdictatorial societies usually have multiple conflicting memorial narratives of this past. These same narratives can foster social division because they question ideas regarding identity, sense of place, and ownership of the past.[28]

As we saw with the first monument—Graziani's memorial in Affile—under the right political circumstances, conflicting memories can emerge and legitimize dark memories of even international massacres. Because heritage is always the result of a political decision and symbolic power that the past has on societies, it is crucial to understand the political meaning behind the erection of a monument and therefore its symbolic narrative.[29] In the case of Affile, the far-right coalition wanted to renegotiate the memory of Italy's colonial past, providing a reading that makes Graziani's massacres acceptable within the context of military actions. The complexity of Graziani's mausoleum is also expressed in the counter-memory narrative that protesters painted on the walls as an example of how heritage is a process of constant renegotiation and never just one fixed discourse.

The second case study, the installation on the Fascist frieze at Bolzano, stands at the opposite end of the spectrum in ways to deal with a dictatorial past. In this case, the town hall felt quite the opposite of Affile's case: they wanted to express disapproval of the values that this monument still represented and did so through the artistic medium of an installation. The luminous words are visibly and symbolically a new layer that builds on the monument, without taking anything away from it, preserving its materiality but working on the semiotic of the heritage discourse. The installation is removable, allowing for a different form of interpretation to be given should this new added meaning be superseded in the future, but gives a very powerful message that breaks Fascist rhetoric of order and obedience. In the light of the rise of far-right movements in Italy and beyond, considering the symbolic power these monuments exercise and how easily they could be instrumentalized, it is crucial to find ways to disempower memories of dark times.

ACKNOWLEDGMENTS

I would like to thank my supervisor and adviser at the University of Cambridge, Dr. Simon Stoddart and Prof. Robert Gordon, for their constant support, and the Cambridge Heritage Research Group for their assistance. A special thanks go to Arnold Holzknecht and Michele Bernardi for discussing their work with me, Catrina Appleby for reading this article, and Laura Egger and Alessia Mastropietro for the photographs. I would like to thank the following for their financial support: the Department of Archaeology (University of Cambridge) and St. John's College for their research grants, the Dorothy Garrod Trust, and the Anthony Wilkinson Fund.

NOTES

1. G. Pianigiani, "Village Tribute Reignites a Debate about Italy's Fascist Past," *New York Times*, August 28, 2012.

2. A. Del Boca, "Il colonialismo italiano tra miti, negazioni, rimozioni e inadempienze," *Italia Contemporanea* 212 (1998): 589–603; A. Del Boca, *Italiani, brava gente?* (Neri Pozza: Vicenza, 2014); M. Dominioni, *Lo sfascio dell 'impero. Gli italiani in Etiopia 1936-1941* (Rome and Bari: Laterza, 2008); G. Rochat, *Le guerre italiane 1935–1943* (Einaudi: Milano, 2008); G. Rochat, *Le guerre italiane in Libia e Etiopia, dal 1896 al 1939* (Gasparri Editore: Udine, 2009); L. Sáska, *Fascist Italian Brutality in Ethiopia, 1935-1937: An Eyewitness Account*, trans. Béla Menezer, ed. Balázs Szélinger (Trenton, NJ: Africa World Press, 2015); and D. Fargacs, "Italian Massacres in Occupied Ethiopia," *Modern Italy* 21, no. 3 (2016): 305–12, doi:10.1017/mit.2016.29.

3. Del Boca, "Il colonialismo italiano tra miti, negazioni, rimozioni e inadempienze"; Del Boca, *Italiani, brava gente?*; and Rochat, *Le guerre italiane 1935–1943*.

4. Rochat, *Le guerre italiane in Libia e Etiopia, dal 1896 al 1939*; Del Boca, *Italiani, brava gente?*; and Sáska, *Fascist Italian Brutality in Ethiopia, 1935–1937*.

5. A. Del Boca, "L'attentato a Graziani," in *Gli Italiani in Africa Orientale. III La caduta dell'Impero* (Mondadori: Milano, 1996); I. Campbell, *The Plot to Kill Graziani: The Attempted Assassination of Mussolini's Viceroy* (Addis Ababa: Addis Ababa University Press, 2010; reprinted Addis Ababa: Eclipse, 2015); I. Campbell, *The Massacre of Debre Libanos, Ethiopia 1937: The Story of One of Fascism's Most Shocking Atrocities* (Addis Ababa: Addis Ababa University Press, 2014); I. Campbell, *The Addis Ababa Massacre: Italy's National Shame* (London: Hurst, 2016); Sáska, *Fascist Italian Brutality in Ethiopia, 1935–1937*; and Fargacs, "Italian Massacres in Occupied Ethiopia."

6. Del Boca, "L'attentato a Graziani"; Campbell, *The Plot to Kill Graziani*; Campbell, *The Massacre of Debre Libanos, Ethiopia 1937*; Campbell, *The Addis Ababa Massacre*; Saska, *Fascist Italian Brutality in Ethiopia, 1935–1937*; and Fargacs, "Italian Massacres in Occupied Ethiopia."

7. Pankhurst, R. (1999) "Italian Fascist War Crimes in Ethiopia: A History of Their Discussion, from the League of Nations to the United Nations (1936-1949)." *Northeast African Studies*. 6:1–2; Fuller, M. (2006) *Moderns Abroad: Architecture, Cities, and Italian Imperialism*. London and New York: Routledge. Ben-Ghiat, R. and Fuller, M. (eds) (2005) *Italian Colonialism*. New York and Basingstoke: Palgrave Macmillan

8. Pianigiani, "Village Tribute Reignites a Debate about Italy's Fascist Past."

9. A. Mariozzi, "Sacrario a Rodolfo Graziani, l'ANPI denuncia il Sindaco di Affile," *Il Messaggero*, Ottobre 5, 2012.

10. J. Phelan, "Italian Mayor, Councillors Jailed over Monument to Fascist General," *The Local*, November 8, 2017.

11. Pianigiani, "Village Tribute Reignites a Debate about Italy's Fascist Past."

12. Mariozzi, "Sacrario a Rodolfo Graziani."

13. R. A. Ventresca, *From Fascism to Democracy: Culture and Policy in the Italian Election of 1948* (Toronto: University of Toronto Press, 2006).

14. F. Focardi, *Il cattivo tedesco e il bravo italiano* (Milano: Edizioni Laterza, 2014).
15. P. Santomassimo, "Il ruolo di Renzo De Felice," *Storia Contemporanea* 212 (1998): 555–63.
16. Del Boca, "Il colonialismo italiano tra miti, negazioni, rimozioni e inadempienze."
17. R. Caroll, "Italy's Bloody Secrets, BBC 1989 Documentary *Fascist Legacy*," *Guardian*, June 25, 2003; G. Lannes, "Ustica 1911, il lager della vergogna," *L'Unita'*, September 14, 2001.
18. M. Margozzi, *Dipinti, sculture e grafica delle collezioni del Museo Africano. Catalogo generale* (Roma: ISOAO, 2005).
19. Pankhurst, "Italian Fascist War Crimes in Ethiopia."
20. R. Ben-Ghiat, "Why Are Fascist Monuments Still Standing in Italy?" *The New Yorker*, October 5, 2017.
21. M. Valenza, "Laura Boldrini, cancellate al scritta *DUX*," *Il Giornale*, April 17, 2015.
22. J. Arthurs, *Excavating Modernity: The Roman Past in Fascist Italy* (Ithaca and London: Cornell University Press, 2014).
23. D. Bacca, "Piazza Vittoria cerca un'alternativa al Bigio," *Corriere della Sera*, 16 Giugno 2013.
24. A. Kallis, "From CAU to EUR: Italian Fascism, the 'Myth of Rome' and the Pursuit of International Primacy," *Patterns of Prejudice* 50, no. 4–5 (2016): 359–77.
25. Valenza, "Laura Boldrini."
26. S. Michielli and H. Obermair, eds., "BZ '18-'45: One Monument, One City, Two Dictatorships," Monument to Victory, Bolzano, Exhibition Text, 2014; H. Hökerberg, "The Monument to Victory in Bolzano: Desacralisation of a Fascist Relic," *International Journal of Heritage Studies* 23, no. 8 (2017): 1–16.
27. C. Invernizzi-Accetti, "A Small Italian Town Can Teach the World How to Defuse Controversial Monuments," *Guardian*, December 6, 2017.
28. S. Macdonald, *Difficult Heritage: Negotiating the Nazi Past in Nuremberg and Beyond* (London and New York: Routledge, 2009).
29. M. L. S. Sørensen and D. Viejo-Rose, eds., *War and Cultural Heritage: Biographies of Place* (Cambridge: Cambridge University Press, 2015).

BIBLIOGRAPHY

Ciriaci, Valerio, dir. *If Only I Were That Warrior*. New York: Awen Films in collaboration with Centro Primo Levi, 2015.

Pieri, G. "The destiny of the arts and artifacts." In *The Cult of the Duce: Mussolini and the Italians*. Edited by S. Gundle, C. Duggan, and G. Pieri, 220–40. Manchester and New York: Manchester University Press, 2013.

Rochat, G. "L'attentato a Graziani e la repressione italiana in Etiopia." *Italia Contemporanea* 118 (1975): 3–38.

Smith, L. *The Uses of Heritage*. London and New York: Routledge, 2006.

CHAPTER 21

Avoiding Iconoclasm

How the Counter-Monument Could Settle a Monumental Debate

Scott McDonald

IN THE PAST COUPLE OF DECADES, COMMUNITIES IN NORTHERN IRELAND HAVE made significant progress in shortening the social and political divides that have gripped the region for more than four hundred years. This progression is in part due to the progress that has been made by politicians in Northern Ireland who, since the Northern Ireland Conflict (1968–1998), have worked to provide its people with a stable and peaceful foundation from which they can rebuild. New generations are progressively moving away from a divided mentality, reliving the troubles of the nation's past through the memories of their parents and grandparents. Like many split nations, progress is being made by its citizens, who choose to set aside the dark memories of their past in favor of recognizing the similarities that unite them. Both sides continue to remember the unspeakable acts and the death toll in the recent conflict, but as the years go by, they are finding constructive and progressive ways to commemorate their loss. Northern Ireland has a rich history of using images in public space, many of which are often contested; opposed; and in some cases, vandalized.[1] However, in recent years there have been several public art projects that have attempted to tackle the problem of sectarian imagery in an effort to close the divide.

The progress made in Northern Ireland has the potential to settle similar debates around the world in communities that find themselves divided over the presence of a public monument, mural, or memorial. The Confederate monument debate in the United States, for example, in which two sides are deeply entrenched, have a chance to adopt some of the methods that have been put into practice in the divided communities in Northern Ireland.

A TROUBLED PAST

After the signing of the Good Friday Agreement in 1999, Northern Ireland and the surrounding regions found themselves in a period of transition. During this time, there were no plans to publicly commemorate those who had lost their lives during the conflict, due to the fragility of the political situation, but individual artists backed by their local communities began to find inventive ways to voice their anger, grief, and hopes for the future.[2] Cities and towns saw the emergence of large murals, illegal monuments, and temporary sculptures, public forms of expression that could be completed quickly with readily available materials at a relatively low cost. At a time when communities felt that their voices were unheard, murals rapidly became the most efficient way of communicating the feelings that still lay below the surface and continue with a similar function today.

Artists in Northern Ireland have been painting walls in this way since the beginning of the twentieth century. They began by depicting Protestant images of British imperial power, the Battle of the Somme, and the picture of King Billy, but it wasn't until the late 1980s that the murals became an emblem of factional territory. The artwork acted as a continuation of political talks happening behind closed doors, but the difference here was that the conversation was happening in an unrestricted public forum. The Northern Ireland murals have become a permanent and infamous feature of the nation's urban landscape, often painted on the side of residential buildings and homes within communities that still hold deep grievances from their recent past. However, their infamy is the result of portraying a message that represents the principles of only one community or even part of a community, in some cases a mural may be representative of an area that may have continued affiliation with an organization that participated in the Northern Irish Conflict. For those who seek to move on from *The Troubles* or those who harbor an opposing affiliation, these murals serve as a constant reminder of the differences that haunt the region.

The murals fell victim to vandalism, particularly in the late 1980s and throughout the 1990s, as feuds erupted and territories changed hands. Political, territorial, and destruction of cultural heritage also occurs in war zones across the globe; as one side begins to dominate the conflict, they instinctively erase the symbols of their adversary and mark the territory as their own. On a much larger scale, we may see the victor seek to orchestrate the complete destruction of all iconography from a former regime; the United States and Soviet occupation of Germany after the Second World War, for example, is a classic case of iconoclasm. However, in Northern Ireland it was a cease-fire and negotiation for peace that brought the conflict to an end; there was no single victor, which meant that the murals adopted a different role. Some professed that areas were still under the protection of specific groups or reminded their community that there was "no surrender," whereas others just wanted to commemorate the lives that had been lost (figure 21.1). They became part of a public conversation between communities, an exchange of images that acted as a reminder of collective identities and local history in a time of cease-fire and hopefully peace.

Figure 21.1.   James McCurrie and Robert Neill Memorial Garden (Lower Newtownards Road, Ballymacarrett) (c) copyright of Martin Melaugh.
Source CAIN (cain.ulster.ac.uk).

After so many deaths in the region, there was tension under the surface and a wide variety of emotions that had no official medium of public commemoration. The murals were quick and cost effective, but eventually, commemoration took a new form. In 2017, it was reported by the *Belfast Telegraph* that there are over one hundred illegal paramilitary memorials on Housing Executive land across Northern Ireland.[3] The memorials exist without the permission of local councils, and the majority of them commemorate those who lost their lives in the thirty-year conflict. They appear in a similar setting to the painted murals, often on the side of someone's home or in the open spaces of a community that are affiliated with specific groups. However, they are constructed more permanently, consisting of plaques, obelisks, crosses, and gravestones. Often, these sites are fenced in, surrounded by a stone or a concrete perimeter with a gate for access, and in some cases, there are even outdoor benches, plant life, and water features housed inside the construction.

There is strong opposition to the memorials constructed in this way, mostly from those who live outside of the communities in which they are situated and from those who are looking to move on from Northern Ireland's troubled past.[4] However, those who voice concerns over the memorial's presence do so not because they disagree with commemoration but because they do not affiliate themselves with the motivations of particular organizations that participated in the conflict. Many see these memorials as a way of commemorating individuals who were loyal to a terrorist organization or groups that were responsible for many deaths in the region, whereas others see them as a way of remembering the lives of their relatives and neighbors.

BUILDING PEACE THROUGH THE ARTS

In recent years, there has been a concerted effort to change the face of public commemoration in Northern Ireland; the task has been implemented by local community groups and several broader government initiatives to move away from a sectarian public image. The aim has been to neutralize the imagery and symbols that act to divide communities with new images of a collective ideology. Even though local community groups have had some success in removing or manipulating murals, it is the government initiatives that have been most successful. This success is the result of the methods that projects such as *Re-Imagining Communities* used between 2006 and 2008, as Hill and White explain:

> In each case plaques have been installed that make explicit the rationale for the transformation, and (where relevant) include images of the previous mural—suggesting that this process of commemoration played some part in convincing local residents that new murals could be produced without entirely losing the mural that had been there.[5]

In most cases, the sectarian imagery was replaced with murals depicting collective history or the local landscape, subjects that focus on local identity in a way that predates the recent dispute. This approach has the potential to work because it does not seek to erase our memory of past events completely. Instead, it aims to continue honoring the original murals' purpose while pushing to remove imagery that could further reinforce community division. The most important part of this process is how these projects open a dialogue with members of the community on both sides of the divide; often, they find common ground in the community's need for regeneration and the potential to attract new business in the area.

However, as Hill and White have observed, the *Re-Imaging Communities* project managed to complete only thirty-nine murals at the time out of a possible two thousand due to a lack of funding. Between 2013 and 2015, the Arts Council of Northern Ireland ran a new project that built on the progress already made by *Re-Imagining Communities* and the ongoing work of the local community organizations. *Building Peace through the Arts: Re-Imagining Communities* (BPTTA) began with a much more prominent aim in mind, eventually supporting fifty-three community arts projects and installing thirty-two site-specific public art pieces across Northern Ireland and its border counties. The project sought to close the community divide by encouraging cohesion, reconciliation, and community communication, with the aim to bring regeneration and more inclusive public works of art.

BPTTA invited both local and international artists to construct new and inclusive public works of art, the majority of which are site-specific counter-monumental sculptures and were conceived by working with members of the community on both sides of the divide. In this instance, the artists acted as objective mediators, independent from local councils, government, and community groups, with the aim to reach an outcome that is reflective of the entire community. The artwork did not reject memories of recent history as one might initially expect. The artists' aim was not to selectively edit how locals remember past events. In fact, many artists chose to include the element of community division but in a constructive way. During the initial trial phase, which manipulated murals, they developed an approach that is respectful of the Northern Ireland Conflict, seeking to paint a truthful portrait of the past.

Jason Mulligan's *Unity—The Caledon Cogs* is an example of a unifying approach (figure 21.2). Mulligan's sculpture, which is in Caledon, County Tyrone, focuses on the area's rich industrial history and can be found on the site of a restored waterwheel mill built in the early 1800s. The regenerated site already stands as a reminder to Caledon's once famous mill industry, the loca-

Figure 21.2. *Unity—Caledon Cogs*, Caledon, County Tyrone, Northern Ireland.
© Jason Mulligan 2018

tion of the only housed beam engine in Ireland; it is a site of national industrial pride. Locally, it reminds residents of Caledon's once-thriving woolen industry; it is part of their identity and collective history. The sculpture consists of two giant cogs made from Kilkenny Limestone sitting on a concrete foundation; the two cogs sit interlinked as if they were working together as part of a much larger mechanism. On the face of the lighter-colored cog, Mulligan has embedded a series of small bronze reliefs depicting images that relate to local history. The artist made these images by working directly with "postcards, book cuttings, maps and archived images." Mulligan translated these images into ten-by-ten-centimeter plaster tiles that were approved by a local regeneration group before eventually having them cast in bronze.

Caledon is a relatively small town with no more than five hundred residents. The size of the community and the remote location of the town exemplify the extent to which Northern Ireland is divided, deeply entrenched in the national psyche. Even Caledon has been a site for protest and social turmoil. In Mulligan's sculpture, the placement of the two cogs side by side is a depiction of this. The only difference between the two is in their tonality. Essentially, they are the same object in size, presence, and functionality. If this divide were depicted using different objects or shapes, then the two sides might appear to be opposing forces; however, the decision to use the image of the cogs provokes thoughts of unity in a way that is anchored to the history of the site. Similarly, the bronze reliefs are embedded on only one side of a single cog, meaning that the viewer does not see a divided history or see themselves relating to one side over the other.

Holger C. Lönze had three sculptures commissioned for the BPTTA project; the works are in County Tyrone, County Down, and County Antrim. *Conor's Corner* was completed in 2015 on the Shankill Road, Belfast (figure 21.3). Shankill Road is one of two roads in the city that became notorious for violent sectarian clashes during *The Troubles*. Along with the Falls Road, it is still home to a vast number of the city's communal murals and memorials. These two densely populated areas are an example of how deeply divided a community can become. They have been the sites of violence and protest and still evoke feelings of grief and anger today. Lönze's sculpture addresses the history of the place through a combination of traditional figurative sculpture and contemporary technology, which is reflective of the city itself. *Conor's Corner*, as Lönze puts it, was to be "an iconic urban landmark for the North Belfast area as a whole."[6] The sculpture depicts Belfast-born painter William Conor, a working-class artist whose work primarily focused on the vigor of the working-class population in Northern Ireland. Conor was a painterly genius, a trait that would not be possible without his industrial working-class background, something that was thought to be impossible in early twentieth-

Figure 21.3 *Conor's Corner*, Shankill Road, Belfast, Northern Ireland.
© Holger Lönze 2018

century Northern Ireland. Four Corten steel light boxes surround the figure of William Conor; each light box illuminates an image of the working class in several different environments through Conor's work.

The collective memory that *Conor's Corner* aims to emphasize is clear and objective; Northern Ireland has another history of which it can be proud, the struggle of the working class is a unifying identity that predates sectarian division. Since its completion, Lönze's sculpture has been the victim of vandalism and modification but not by individual members of the community. The commissioners of the project manipulated the sculpture almost entirely before it was unveiled to the public, a move that Lönze still adamantly condemns. The sculpture now has "William Conor: The Peoples Painter, 1881–1968" spray-painted on its central face, with the light boxes completely rearranged to promote it very clearly as a tribute to the painter, straying from the BPTTA's original message of reconciliation. The decision highlights just how fragile the use of public imagery is in the region and how working closely with the community is vital to this work. Despite this dispute, the sculpture has replaced a former Ulster Volunteer Force mural that many in the local community perceived to be contentious and dividing.

The BPTTA project demonstrates the role that counter-monuments can play in divided communities, mainly when monuments, murals, and memorials find themselves at the heart of the debate. Counter-monuments exist in places that find it difficult to confront their past, dark periods of history where the pride of a monument would be unfitting or distasteful. For example, Germany is home to the highest concentration of counter-monuments in the world. As a nation with a regrettable past, it seeks reconciliation by voicing regret and heeding a warning to future generations.[7] If in periods of conflict an inhuman act is committed, then we often see commemoration for the deceased or for individuals who resisted the cause by exercising their humanity. German public sculpture is one of the few examples in the world where military deserters can be celebrated alongside the commemorated victims of genocide.[8] Nations such as Rwanda and Bosnia have also begun to show signs of healing, and it is evident through the recent emergence of public counter-monuments. The historical, political, and social aspects of each of these conflict zones differ wildly, but their approach to dealing with past trauma is very similar. Each of these countries seeks to rebuild its sense of identity, something that can be obtained only by confronting the troubles of the past and constructing a new collective and inclusive memory.

THE ROLE OF THE COUNTER-MONUMENT IN NORTH AMERICA

The Confederate monument debate also highlights the usefulness of the counter-monument; in this instance, communities find themselves divided by the presence of a public monument. The result in many of these cases is often to have the monuments destroyed, an action that instantly removes the focal point of the debate but fails to unite the local community as it favors one side over the other. It does not address the root of the problem because the act of destroying an object is a manifestation of the animosity displayed by both sides. Here, we begin to see similarities between the community divides across the United States and those in Northern Ireland, where one side seeks to commemorate its ancestry and the other side disagrees with its affiliated cause. In a very similar way, these monuments are separatist, in the sense that their presence turns communities against one another.

The similarities between the two debates lead one to believe that the Confederate monument issue could be resolved by implementing an initiative like that in Northern Ireland, where a controversial mural, monument, or memorial is replaced with a neutral image of collective pride, with a plaque or a picture of the memorial that previously stood on the site. It is vital that we remind the public of what stood before for two reasons. First, by completely removing a memorial and offering no alternative, we invite new and inventive ways for communities to commemorate their heritage (just as we have seen from the illegal memorials in Northern Ireland). Second, they serve as both a warning to future generations of the mistakes our society has made in the past and a reminder that we are making progress in altering the symbols that aim to divide us.[9]

However, there is an alternative to manipulating existing memorials and monuments, an approach that has been utilized in Europe and Africa. Counter-monumentalism is a reactionary practice that actively seeks to oppose the traditional elements of the monument; it is the result of either ideological hatred toward a single memorial or a devotion to counter-memory. As a result, the counter-monument (or anti-monument as it is also known) is an anti-authoritarian endeavor; it challenges the meaning behind these permanent public objects and offers an alternative perspective on the way we recall past events. The *Memorial to Justice and Peace*, which has been constructed in Montgomery, Alabama, is the first US memorial to the victims of lynching, and it will stand in a region of significance to both Confederate and black history.[10] The *Memorial to Justice and Peace* mirrors the *Memorial to the Murdered Jews of Europe* in Berlin and the *Kigali Genocide Memorial* in Rwanda. The memorial is dedicated to the dead and counter-memory; its immersive quality and scale combat the selective Confederate memory of the Jim Crow South.

Each of these memorials acts as a signifier to a change in collective ideology and, particularly in the case of the United States, the progressive ways in which we can begin to challenge existing symbols of the past. The counter-monument questions the meaning of existing monuments by offering an alternative memory, undermining the original message of power and authority.[11] Counter-memory does not challenge the controversial monument physically; it does, however, inform and enlighten the people who interpret its meaning. Therefore, the strength of the counter-monument is its ability to change the definition of other monuments over time.

CONCLUSION

To close the gap that divides a community, we must first try to understand the reasons why the divisions persist. The answer lies in the way that we exercise our collective memory and sense of self; the way that we remember the past enables us to establish our place in the world. An understanding of our history allows us to form an identity concerning those around us. If another group challenges our memory of events, the way we record our history, or our sense of identity, then we instinctively build an "us and them" divide. In other words, in divided communities, both sides of the debate remember the events of the past differently, and the only way to move forward toward a unified identity is to establish a new collective memory.[12] This progressive way of thinking is taking place in Northern Ireland, Germany, Rwanda, and former

Soviet nations where progress has slowly been made to unify a national sense of identity with collective imagery.

The key is to acknowledge the identity, history, and principles of all the parties involved. More importantly, this includes the symbols, flags, and iconography of individual groups. If their methods of commemoration are suppressed, then they will naturally seek to uphold the divide. We cannot just remove a monument that commemorates the lives lost in a time of conflict with the hope that people will forget. We must, however, focus on symbols that encapsulate a broader collective memory of the past. Only a unified approach will allow individuals to exercise their sense of identity alongside those on the other side of the divide.

NOTES

1. B. Rolston, "Re-Imaging: Mural Painting and the State in Northern Ireland," *International Journal of Cultural Studies* 15, no. 5 (2012): 447–66.

2. P. Gough, "From Heroes' Groves to Parks of Peace: Landscapes of Remembrance, Protest and Peace," *Landscape Research* 25, no. 2 (2000): 213–28.

3. Adrian Rutherford, "Illegal Paramilitary Memorials on Housing Executive Land in Northern Ireland," *Belfast Telegraph*, accessed January 15, 2018, https://www.belfasttelegraph.co.uk/news/northern-ireland/illegal-paramilitary-memorials-on-housing-executive-land-in-northern-ireland-35640868.html.

4. P. Pinkerton, "Resisting Memory: The Politics of Memorialisation in Post-Conflict Northern Ireland," *British Journal of Politics & International Relations* 14, no. 1 (2012): 131–52.

5. Andrew Hill and Andrew White, "Painting Peace? Murals and the Northern Ireland Peace Process," *Irish Political Studies* 27, no. 1 (2012): 71–88.

6. "Holger C. Lönze—Sculptor," accessed January 15, 2018, http://www.holgerlonze.info/public-projects/#/belfast-2015/.

7. J. Young, "The Counter-Monument: Memory against Itself in Germany Today," *Critical Inquiry* 18, no. 2 (1992): 267–96.

8. S. Welch, "Commemorating 'Heroes of a Special Kind': Deserter Monuments in Germany," *Journal of Contemporary History* 47, no. 2 (2012): 370–401.

9. T. Stubblefield, "Do Disappearing Monuments Simply Disappear?: The Counter-Monument in Revision," *Future Anterior* 8, no. 2 (2011), xii–11.

10. K. Capps, "Hanged, Burned, Shot, Drowned, Beaten: Memorializing America's 4,384 Known Victims of Lynching" *The Atlantic* 320, no. 4 (2017): 30.

11. Q. Stevens, K. Franck, and R. Fazakerley, "Counter-Monuments: The Anti-Monumental and the Dialogic," *Journal of Architecture* 17, no. 6 (2012): 951–72.

12. M. Van Den Eeden, "Performing the Past: Memory, History, and Identity in Modern Europe," *European Review of History: Revue Europeenne D'histoire* 18, no. 4 (2011): 616–18.

CHAPTER 22

On Creating a Usable Future

An Introduction to Future Monuments

EVANDER PRICE

> If we need another past so badly, is it inconceivable that we might dis-
> cover one, that we might even invent one? Discover, invent a usable past
> we certainly can, and that is what a vital criticism always does.
>
> —Van Wyck Brooks[1]

HOW WE IMAGINE THE FUTURE AFFECTS HOW WE ACT IN THE PRESENT. WHEN
Van Wyck Brooks argued in *The Dial* (1918) for the need to create a past helpful to the present, he was referring to the narrower context of American historical and cultural criticism. His essay, "On Creating a Usable Past," is a staple in
the American studies canon. If the past, as currently imagined, is not of direct
use to Americans in the present, why not simply imagine a different one?[2] A
"usable past" might provide a more fruitful root for American culture to grow
from. This collective historical imagination contours our self-understanding
and self-fashioning as well as our ethical processes of decision making. What
precisely that past is or ought to be, well, that is still up for discussion. I would
like to propose that, in the intervening century since Van Wyck Brooks, that
we flip his manifesto on its head: What would it mean for Americans to create
a usable future?

Can imagining an optimistic future preclude the fatalism of imagining a
pessimistic one?[3] How have American folks imagined the future in the past?
Who is or isn't included in that future? When and where does that future end?
And how does that measurement shape individual and collective actions in
the present? Are there normative claims on futurity? What sort of principles
ought to frame an ethical imagination of the future? What sorts of practices or
inventions are possible to divert an unethical future ideation? Just how much
future was there? How much is there now?

These questions are too broad for the purposes of this brief essay, but I
would like to posit them here to open this discussion of monument culture to
a wholly new category of analysis: the future monument. Future monuments

are an excellent lens for asking these questions. Unlike conventional monuments, which commemorate the past, future monuments are built explicitly to manifest an imagination of the future. That is, they commemorate the future. They are often complex, temporally speaking, because they are subject to a medley of temporal metaphors jockeying for prominence. They show us how much future there is imagined to be. They inherently betray the aspirations and anxieties of the cultures that built them. They simultaneously highlight both the creativity and the myopia of their makers. And they tend to appear at critical points in history—when the future puts pressure on the present, artists, intellectuals, and entrepreneurs produce future monuments. And though they frequently invoke utopian visions of the future and attempt to bring them into existence, they only very rarely succeed.

In time, when the future does not come to pass as expected, future monuments become tombstones for alternate histories, for parallel worlds that were imagined but never realized. This irony is, perhaps, among the most "usable" qualities of future monuments: they shed light on this historical gap, this tension between ideological imaginations and material realities. It is this contradiction between potentials and outcomes, between foresight and myopia, between anticipations and realizations, that future monuments refuse to leave unreckoned.

Future monuments can be ephemeral or permanent, conceptual or concrete, and are probably best understood by example. Take the 1939 New York World's Fair in Flushing Meadows Corona Park, which was both concrete and fleeting. The fair attracted some forty-four million visitors to wander its acres of exhibitions over the course of two seasons. A six-hundred-foot needle, the Trylon, was readily visible from Manhattan. It was paired with a two-hundred-foot sphere, the Perisphere. Together, the two comprise the symbolic heart of the fair. The pair beckoned to visitors, inviting folks far and wide to visit the utopian *Democracity* exhibition housed inside the Perisphere.[4] Almost as popular was General Motors' utopian *Futurama* exhibition, GM's bid at a car-filled, streamlined utopian future. The World's Fair was built on what was originally a sprawling natural swamp, where five million New Yorkers had, for decades, daily dumped the fly ash from their coal burning furnaces by the ton. It was this landscape that inspired F. Scott Fitzgerald's description of an existential hell on earth, the so-called valley of ashes in *The Great Gatsby* (1925). And it was Fitzgerald's description that compelled Robert Moses, sometimes called the "master builder" or "Baron Haussmann" of New York, to lasso together funding to replace this dump with the World's Fair. Fitzgerald would have been surprised to see the very landscape he imagined was the hellish end of the Jazz Age rebranded under the theme "Your World of Tomorrow," a testament to pre–World War II technophilia and an orgastic faith in a future of streamlined highways and chromed cars. The *Official Guidebook* to the fair explained the theme:

> The eyes of the Fair are on the future . . . presenting a new and clearer view of today in preparation for tomorrow; a view of the forces and ideas that prevail as well as the machines.[5]

The Fair was a gargantuan festival to the future, a place where one would come to marvel at all the promise and wonder of what surely would be.

Moses's vision did not last: his colossal Modernist monuments to the future were soon thereafter dismantled for the war effort. Yet the dream of the World's Fair persists in Flushing, in Fitzgerald's fictional description of the valley of ashes, in the material remains of those millions of tons of fly ash, still simmering beneath ten inches of topsoil. The future monument of the World's Fair, however fleeting, fictional, ambitious, and hopeful, reveals how past visions of the future can still haunt contemporary spaces, often despite various efforts to erase or revise these many palimpsests. Indeed, one can still buy authentic souvenir pins handed out by the hundreds of thousands at the 1939 World's Fair, each stamped with the bold declaration: "*I HAVE SEEN THE FUTURE.*"[6]

A second example: The Long Now Foundation is a nonprofit organization currently working on its flagship future monument—a colossal clock designed by the writer Stewart Brand, the engineer Danny Hillis, and the musician Brian Eno and funded by the CEO of Amazon, Jeff Bezos.[7] The clock is hidden away in a desert cave, meant to measure time at the scale of ten thousand years. The clock ticks slowly. Tocks once a century. Cuckoos chime (designed by Eno) every millennium. It sounds like something out of a science fiction story, yet it is astoundingly real; construction is under way.[8]

The clock is meant to inspire ten-thousand-year thinking, a temporal ethics that insists on considering the ramifications of decisions over a time span roughly equal to human history. What decisions—individual, political, cultural—would you, or wouldn't you, make if you considered the ramifications of those choices ten thousand years into the future? The clock asks us to think like a glacier. It measures time in units fit for radioactive decay. It recalls the Doomsday clock.[9] It highlights the temporal problem at the heart of global warming—that is, the temporal limitation of human perception to perceive changes invisible on the scale of human time frames, yet astoundingly clear when seen on a planetary timescale.[10] It is an object in conversation with what geologists, ecologists, and environmentalists call the "Anthropocene," the period of time after which human beings began to have an influence over the planet comparable to and measurable on the scale of geology. Will the Anthropocene last for an epoch, an age, or an era? What exactly is the post-

Anthropocene? What does it mean if the clock stops? The clock is an ambitious attempt to grapple with all these questions at once.

Stewart Brand has his own answers to these questions. He and a team of eighteen professors, scientists, and technophiles have penned a manifesto urging a capitalist reimagination of the climate crisis—suggesting, in the spirit of the 1939 World's Fair, that technology can turn back the clock of global warming "to re-wild and re-green the Earth."[11] In another project, Brand proposes—in all seriousness—the resurrection of extinct species (woolly mammoths, passenger pigeons, and more) from tattered DNA remains archived in museums or frozen in glaciers.[12]

Is there a point at which technophilia becomes technomania? How are we to reconcile the idea that Jeff Bezos is funding this ten-thousand-year clock with its ten-thousand-year ethics, when his greatest gift to the planet so far has been Amazon two-day Prime? It is worth asking to what extent such Long Now thinking is a privilege and pastime of the wealthy. It is also worth considering to what degree this future monument merely memorializes its builders. But what if Brand's optimistic vision of human survival ten thousand years into the future—his colossal ticking clock—is precisely the sort of mindset necessary to stave off the environmental apocalypse?

The Long Now Foundation's clock is in part influenced by the idea of preserving at least a portion of humanity such that it could survive the global environmental catastrophe predicted by so many scientists. The foundation solves this problem by building its clock in a mountain, but it had looked to others before it who had considered similar predicaments. Carl Sagan, the cosmologist and popular scientist, had grappled with a similar question in the face of the Cold War threat of global nuclear holocaust.[13] He came to a different solution: a collective relic called the Golden Record.

Sagan's Golden Record is an LP made of gold strapped to NASA's Voyager 1 and 2 space probes, which launched in 1977 and promised to be the first human-made objects to leave the solar system. The Golden Record comprises images and music from Earth, greetings in hundreds of languages, and music—J. S. Bach, Chuck Berry, Javanese Gamelan, Navajo Night Chants, and even humpback whale songs.[14] NASA even included a record player aboard the Voyagers.[15] Sagan and his team had selected what he hoped would be a representative sampling of human culture; it was, in the words of one member of his team, "a mix tape of the gods."[16]

Because there is very little to damage the Golden Record in space and because it is free from the erosive forces of wind, water, and human beings, it promises to be the most lasting monument to humankind yet made. Some estimate that the Golden Record will be recognizable for billions of years. By temporal comparison, the pyramids of Egypt look like melting mounds of butter in the desert. Even if human beings obliterate all vestiges of life on earth, the Golden Record will preserve some slice of our memory into cosmic perpetuity.

Though this Cold War artifact might seem a conventional monument to the past, Sagan intended it as a gift for some alien civilization, which—in some far future—might retrieve it and, indeed, play it. In its immortality, the Golden Record takes on mythical proportions. The Golden Record is as eternal and inaccessible as the Golden Fleece or the Golden Bough, retrievable only by some chosen hero like Aeneas or Jason. NASA, through Sagan, has effectively repurposed and converted a mythological symbol into a material object—the hero's quest is no longer defined by gods who conjure golden goals for heroes to achieve but by some cosmic equivalent. What, then, would it mean to retrieve the Golden Record? What does it mean that human beings can make objects that exist on immortal-cosmological timescales? What does it mean to project a collective image of humankind into a near-infinite future? What sort of image should be collectively presented to the cosmos? Is it hopeful in imagining that someone or something might receive this golden gift? Or is it rather nihilistic, a kind of cosmic cenotaph acknowledging our galactic loneliness? What do we do with the humbling reality that the most lasting vestiges of the human species will ultimately be our space trash?

Despite its invisibility and inaccessibility, this far-flung future monument remains fast in the public imagination even forty years after its launch into space. A group that calls itself SETI-X remixed the record into a seventy-minute concept album that imagines what aliens "flirting with copyright violation on an interstellar scale" might send back to us.[17] Multiple books of poetry have been written imagining some of the many possible futures.[18] A recent Kickstarter campaign even went so far as to suggest the record should be reprinted in its entirety. Their goal was to raise $198,000; they raised nearly $1.4 million.[19] The finished product even won a Grammy.[20] For now, the Golden Record is just that: a creative writing prompt, a concept album, a literalized thought experiment asking its audience to reflect on its place in the universe, a vehicle for carrying future thinking to the limits of temporal possibility.

The 1939 World's Fair, the Clock of the Long Now, and the Golden Record are just three major examples of the category of future monument. But there are many more in American culture. When Elon Musk successfully launched his rocket, the *Falcon Heavy*, into space, for example, he attached to it a Tesla Roadster, driven by a dummy they named "Starman."[21] It too will likely survive an eternity in space. Starman has much in common with the three preceding future monuments. It is an echo of the 1939 World's Fair technophilic mentality that firmly believes science and technology can solve any problem. Starman reminds us that monument making is often the pastime of wealthy elites hoping to guarantee their legacy. And Starman is a reflection of the surficial hopefulness of future monuments that, in this case, stretches toward Mars to the tune of David Bowie's "Space Oddity." With Starman, Musk demonstrates that future monuments need not take themselves so seriously. They may also be cosmic kitsch, an interplanetary joke.

Future monuments can also be menacing. While Confederate monuments reflect the efforts of various white supremacist groups to create a usable past more fitting to their racist agenda, they simultaneously anticipate, reify, and endeavor to affect an alternative future—one in which the Civil War is simply one lost battle in a greater war extending across centuries and into a future where white power has regained racial dominance.[22] It is not just the past that they commemorate but also the future they anticipate that makes Confederate monuments so insidious and abominable. To remove them, then, is to foreclose the future they reify. Confederate monuments thus also demonstrate that not all futures are necessarily just. The risks inherent to creating a "usable past" also extend to usable futures.

Future monuments are temporally strange by definition. They show us what could be, and what might have been. They highlight the ways in which various and distinct historical forces competed to compel specific imaginations of futurity. They provide a vehicle through which it is possible to ask what it would mean to imagine an ethical—or, in the case of Confederate monuments, an unethical—future. Returning briefly to Brooks's essay, we might note that at each instance that he employs the word "past," we might just as well interchange the word "future" to impart the same wisdom:

> The past is an inexhaustible storehouse of apt attitudes and adaptable ideals; it opens of itself at the touch of desire; it yields up, now this treasure, now that, to anyone who comes to it armed with the capacity for personal choices.[23]

In other words, if we need another *future* so badly, is it inconceivable that we might discover one, that we might even invent one? There is an adage of uncertain origin that quips, "The future isn't what it used to be." Future monuments surely demonstrate as much. But they also suggest that the future probably shouldn't be what it used to be.

NOTES

1. Van Wyck Brooks, "Past, on Creating a Usable," *The Dial* 64 (January 3, 1918): 337.
2. Brooks is arguing for a more freethinking, creative play with history—a consideration for the literary–historical past that focuses less on the rigorous establishment of a plodding series of facts beholden to European academe. His essay is something of a culturally nationalist project, an effort to separate American academic criticism from its perpetual, self-negating subservience to the European scene.

3. Incidentally, and not unrelated to the concerns of this essay, this very question is the subject of a recent Disney film, *Tomorrowland*. Brad Bird, dir., *Tomorrowland* (Walt Disney Pictures, 2015).

4. The very *Futurama* that Matt Groening's cartoon is eponymously named after.

5. Roland Barker, ed., *Official Guide Book of the New York World's Fair, 1939* (New York: Exposition Publications, 1939), 46.

6. It is of note that the 1964 World's Fair was also hosted on the same site as the 1939 World's Fair, though by most measures it was far less popular. The Unisphere and some of the buildings from this second world's fair remain in Flushing Meadows Corona Park today.

   I'm particularly indebted to the research of Joseph Corn and Terry Smith and the collections at the Queens Museum in Flushing Meadows Corona Park: Joseph J. Corn, *Yesterday's Tomorrows: Past Visions of the American Future* (Baltimore: Johns Hopkins University Press, 1996); Joseph P. Cusker et al., *Dawn of a New Day: The New York World's Fair, 1939/40* (New York: Queens Museum; New York University Press, 1980); and Terry Smith, *Making the Modern: Industry, Art, and Design in America* (Chicago: University of Chicago Press, 1993).

7. For some primers on the Clock of the Long Now, see Stewart Brand, *The Clock of the Long Now: Time and Responsibility*, 1st ed. (New York: Basic Books, 1999); Danny Hillis and Alexander Rose, *The Clock of the Long Now: Mechanical Drawings of the First Prototype* (Lexington, KY: The Long Now Foundation, 2010); and "Introduction—10,000 Year Clock—The Long Now," The Long Now Foundation, accessed December 31, 2018, http://longnow.org/clock/.

8. "Bezos-Backed 10,000 Year Clock under Construction," *BBC News*, February 21, 2018, accessed February 27, 2018, http://www.bbc.com/news/technology-43143095.

9. The Doomsday Clock is monitored by the *Bulletin of the Atomic Scientists*: John Mecklin, ed., "2018 Doomsday Clock Statement," *Bulletin of the Atomic Scientists*, accessed February 27, 2018, https://thebulletin.org/2018-doomsday-clock-statement.

10. For this point, I have Timothy Morton's works in mind: Timothy Morton, *Hyperobjects: Philosophy and Ecology after the End of the World* (Minneapolis: University of Minnesota Press, 2013); Timothy Morton, *Dark Ecology: For a Logic of Future Coexistence*, Wellek Library Lecture Series at the University of California, Irvine (New York: Columbia University Press, 2016).

11. The full manifesto is available here: "A Manifesto to Use Humanity's Extraordinary Powers in Service of Creating a Good Anthropocene," An Ecomodernist Manifesto, accessed April 24, 2017, http://www.ecomodernism.org/.

12. "Help Us Turn the Tide on Species Loss," Revive & Restore, accessed April 29, 2017, http://reviverestore.org/.

13. Sagan published a book with Richard Turco about the "nuclear winter," a concept that Turco had published about in the early 1980s: Carl Sagan, *A Path Where No Man Thought: Nuclear Winter and the End of the Arms Race* (New York: Random House, 1990).

14. For technical specifications of the *Voyager* mission and the Golden Record, see Christopher Riley, Richard Corfield, and Philip Dolling, *NASA Voyager 1 & 2: Owners' Workshop Manual* (Newbury Park, CA: Haynes Publishing, 2015).

15. Sagan and his team concurrently published a book describing the scope of their project: Carl Sagan, *Murmurs of Earth: The Voyager Interstellar Record*, 1st ed. (New York: Random House, 1978).

16. Timothy Ferris, "The Mix Tape of the Gods," *New York Times*, September 5, 2007, accessed 28 February 2018, https://www.nytimes.com/2007/09/05/opinion/05ferris.html.

17. "Scrambles of Earth," earthscramble.com, accessed April 14, 2016, http://earthscramble.com/.

18. For example, Srikanth Reddy, *Voyager* (Oakland: University of California Press, 2011).

19. "The Voyager Golden Record: 40th Anniversary Edition," Kickstarter, accessed October 31, 2016, https://www.kickstarter.com/projects/ozmarecords/voyager-golden-record-40th-anniversary-edition.

20. For Best Boxed or Special Limited Edition Package, see "60th Annual GRAMMY Awards (2017)," GRAMMY.com, accessed February 28, 2018, https://www.grammy.com/grammys/awards/60th-annual-grammy-awards.

21. Leonard David, "Where Is Starman? Track Elon Musk's Roadster as It Zooms Through Space," Space.Com, published February 22, 2018, accessed February 28, 2018, https://www.space.com/39777-track-elon-musk-tesla-starman-website.html.

22. Jess Bidgood, "Confederate Monuments Are Coming Down across the United States. Here's a List," *New York Times*, modified August 16, 2017, accessed February 28, 2018, https://www.nytimes.com/interactive/2017/08/16/us/confederate-monuments-removed.html.

23. Brooks, "Past, on Creating a Usable," 339.

Index

and, 78–79; for history, 32, 214; humanitarianism for, 94n9; memory and, 209; in New Zealand, 219–28, *224*, *226*; of Ōpūkahaiʻa, 18–19; politics and, 17, 46n5, 101–2, 178–80; propaganda and, 4, 8–9, 38–39, 44–45, 66–67, 236; protests against, 174; psychology of, 102–3; of religion, 3, 16–17; in Spain, 10n6; violence by, 25–36, 66–68, 71–72, 76, 80n2, 88, 96n38, 99–106, *102*; voice as, 217n22

Azoulay, Ariella, 194

Baard, Frances, 90, *91*, 92
Badoglio, Pietro, 234
Baker, Bryant, 53–54
Bakgatla-Baga-Kgafela, 89
Barsotti, Carlo, 146–47
Bates, Ralph, 7–8
Becker, Wolfgang, 166
Ben-Ghiat, Ruth, 237
Benjamin, Walter, 153, 155
Berkhofer, Robert, 145
Berlin Wall, 166
Bernardi, Michele, 233, *238*, 238–39
Bezos, Jeff, 255–56
bigotry: by authority, 85–90, *91*, 92–94; communism and, 6; deracialization and, 87–88; hierarchy of, 49–58, *50*, *55*; history of, 8–9, 11n14; in media, 7; memory, 58; politics of, 19–20, 258; in US, 5
Black Lives Matter, 7
de Blasio, Bill, 143, 148
Bligh, William, 13–14
Blight, David, 143–44
Blythe, Ernest, 119n17
body language, 177–81, *182*, 183
Boldrini, Laura, 237
De Bono, Emilio, 234
Borgoño cartel, 100–106, *102*
Bowie, David, 257–58
Brand, Stewart, 256

British Empire. *See* Europe; United Kingdom
Brock, Thomas, 111, *112*
Brooks, Van Wyck, 253, 258, 258n2
Budd, Clint, *193*
butcher of Ethiopia. *See* Graziani
Byrd, Richard E., 29

California: culture of, 58; history of, 49, 52. *See also* San Francisco; United States
Cambodia, 35–45, *36*, 46n5
Canada, 194
Carson, Anne, 156–58
Carson, Kit, 52
de Las Casas, Bartolomé, 144–45
Castro, José, 52
Catholicism. *See* religion
censorship: of art, 170; of history, 61–69, 166–68, *167*; illegal monuments, 177–81, *182*, 183–86, *185*; of politics, 103–6
di Cesnola, Luigi Palma, 146–47
Charlottesville (VA), 1–9, 143–44
Chazin, Pinchos J., 5
Cheetham, Mark, 157–58
Chile, 99–106, *102*
China: economics of, 40; in globalization, 39; UK in, 110–11
Christianity. *See* religion
The Civil Contract of Photography (Azoulay), 194
civil religion, 226
Civil War: politics of, 2; in Spain, 5; in US, 51
Clark, Frank, 229n13
Clark, Helen, 229n13
climate change. *See* ecology
Col, Pilar, 77–78, *78*
Cold War, 35–36, 41–43, 199–200, 257
colonialism: authority for, 54–56, *55*; culture of, 19; France in, 39, 41; genocide and, 56–57; history of, 20, 37–38, 42–43, 51–52, 87; imperial

253–58; of protests, 6; psychology of, 215; of religion, 128n14; revisionism of, 236; of science, 25–26; of South Africa, 85–90, *91*, 92–94, 95n10; of South East Asia, 35–45, *36–37*; of Tahiti, 13; technology for, 206, 209, 213; Topography of Terror (documentation), 61–62, 213–14; of torture, 102–3; tourism and, 217n20, 221, 235–36; of Turkey, 127n8, 225–26; of US, 10n5, 177; of violence, 93–94, 106n2, 107n6, 143–44; of women, 53–54; World's Fair for, 259n6

Hite, Katherine, 74–75

Höcke, Björn, 181, *182*, 183

Hofmeyr, Steve, 86

Hoheisel, Horst, 197–98

the Holocaust, 61–69, 88; Austria in, 205–10, *207*, *211*, 212–15; education of, 196–97, 217n27; for Europe, 131–39, *134*, *138*; in history, 181, *182*, 183; memory and, 193

holograms, 183–84

Holzknecht, Arnold, 233, *238*, 238–39

Homage to Catalonia (Orwell), 6

Horn, Roni, 153, *154–55*, 155–62

Huanca, Clodoaldo, 76

Hughes, John, 115, *115*

Hughes, Langston, 6

humanitarianism: for authority, 94n9; ecology and, 159; human rights, 72, 76, 78, 79, 80n2, 101; *Human Rights in Camera* (Sliwinski), 194; in identity, 222–23; politics of, 64–65; war crimes and, 233–34

Hussein, Saddam, 180–81

Hyperobjects (Morton), 158–60

Iceland, 153, *154–55*, 155–62

iconoclasm: counter-monument ideology and, 243–52, *245*, *247*, *249*; as propaganda, 109–18, *112*, *115*

identity: art and, 230n19; history for, 252; humanitarianism in, 222–23; politics of, 126–27; psychology, 125

illegal monuments, 177–81, *182*, 183–86, *185*

Imagined Communities (Anderson), 194

immigrants, 147

imperial symbols, 109–18, *112*, *115*, 244

inclusivity, 56–58

An Inconvenient Truth (Gore), 153

Independence Monument, 25–45, *36*

India, 111

international politics, 180

The Invisible Camp--Audio Walk Gusen (Mayer), 205–10, *207*, *211*, 212–15

Iraq, 180–81

Ireland: colonialism for, 109–18, *112*, *115*; Northern Ireland and, 243–52, *245*, *247*, *249*

Irving, Washington, 144

Italy, 146, 207, 233–40, *234*, *238*

Jackson, Peter, 224–25, 230n19

Jackson, Stonewall, *174*, 174–75

James Lick Pioneer Monument (Happersberger), 49–53, *50*, 55, 58

Japan, 178–80

Jara, Victor, 99, 106n1

Judaism. *See* religion

Kadalie, Clements, 89

Kalafatis, Chrysostomos, 122–23

Kansas, 54–55, *55*. *See also* United States

Kazakhstan, 165

Kennedy, John F., 41

Kent, Flor, 134–35

Khatide, Lindokuhle, 96n35

Khmer. *See* Cambodia

Khodorkovsky, Michael, 174

Kikotis, Giorgos, *124*

Kindertransport (Samuels), 132

kindertransports, 131–39, *134*, *138*

murals, 246–47
Musk, Elon, 257–58
Muslims. *See* religion
Mussolini, Benito ("Il Duce"), 8, 233–40
Mutal, Lika, 73–75, *74*, 77–78, *78*

Nameless Library (Whiteread), 161
narratives, 143
Narváez, Rosario, 71
nationalists: in Antarctica, 25–32; in
    colonialism, 39; globalization for,
    31–32; history for, 36, 117–18; in
    Italy, 239; politics of, 3, 14, 191–200,
    192–93; in protests, 1, 4; psychology
    of, 122–23, 169; refugees for, 131–39,
    134, 138; in Spain, 1–2
National Security Agency (NSA), 183
Nazism, 61–69, 197–98. *See also*
    Germany; the Holocaust
Ndlozi, Mbuyiseni, 86
Neal, Eric, 117
Neill, Robert, *245*
Nelson (Lord), 110–11
neutrality, 43
New Orleans, 178
New Zealand, 219–28, *224, 226*, 229n5,
    229n6
Nishi, Tatzu, 141
Niven, Bill, *138*
Nokwe, Duma, 90
Non-Sites, 157–58, 163n11
North Carolina, 194
Northern Ireland, 243–52, *245, 247, 249*
North Korea, 178–80
Norway, 28–29
Nott, Henry, 14
NSA. *See* National Security Agency
Ntjie, Sipho, 96n35
Ntrama Genocide Memorial Center,
    62–69
nuclear power, 29
Nunneley, David, 57–58
Nuremberg Interventions (Evol), *185*
Nyembe, Dorothy, 90

O'Connell, Daniel, 111
Ojo que Llora (memorial), 71–80, *74, 78*
Oklahoma, 53–54, 56–57. *See also*
    United States
Olympic Games, 174
On Collective Memory (Halbwach),
    141–42
"On Creating a Usable Past" (Brooks),
    253
O'Neil, Megan, 110
The One I Was (Graham), 137
Ōpūkahaiʻa, 18–19
Ortiz, Gisela, 72, 76
Ortiz, Luis Enrique, 76
Orwell, George, 1, 6, 9

Paniagua, Valentín, 72–73
Papeiha, 18
Pardo Villalón, Luis Antonio, 26–27
Patiño, Margarita, 77–78, *78*
Patuxai, 35–45, *37*, 45n1
Peru, 71–80, *74, 78*
Phillips, Jock, 219–20
Phnom Penh, 35–45, *36*, 46n8
photography: *The Civil Contract of
    Photography* (Azoulay), 194; for
    culture, 165–71, *167, 172*, 173–75,
    174; *Human Rights in Camera*
    (Sliwinski), 194
Phoumma, Souvanna, 37
Piffrader, Hans, 238
Pinochet, Augusto, 99
pioneers. *See* colonialism
Pioneer Woman (Baker), 53–54, 56
Pokémon Go, 178
Poland, 199
politics: of Apartheid, 85–90, *91*, 92–94;
    of art, 141–48, 205–6; of ATS, 27,
    31–32; authority and, 17, 46n5, 101–
    2, 178–80; of Berlin Wall, 166; of
    bigotry, 19–20, 258; for Black Lives
    Matter, 7; of Borgoño cartel, 100–
    106, *102*; censorship of, 103–6; of
    Civil War, 2; of Cold War, 35–36; of

colonialism, 112–13; of Columbus, 149n17; of communism, 9, 198–99; of culture, 54–55, 87, 125–26, 168; of democracy, 192, 205; of ecology, 92–93, 153, *154–55*, 155–62; EFF in, 87; of fascism, 233–40, *234*, *238*; of FDR, 10n4; futurity in, 253–58; in Germany, 61–62, 181, 197–98; globalization of, 25–26; graffiti as, 168–69, 171; history and, 28, 30–31, 72–74, *74*; of humanitarianism, 64–65; of identity, 126–27; of illegal monuments, 177–81, *182*, 183–86, *185*; international politics, 180; of kindertransports, 131–39, *134*, *138*; of media, 161–62; of memory, 251–52; of miniature monuments, 184–86, *185*; minorities in, 96n37; of missionaries, 19; of nationalists, 3, 14, 191–200, *192–93*; of Olympic Games, 174; propaganda and, 30, 238; of protests, 94n9; psychology of, 114; of QVB, 116–17; of religion, 13–14, 44, 46n8, 121; in Russia, 165–71, *167*, *172*, 173–75, *174*; of science, 256; social darwinism in, 49–50; of socialism, 169–70; in Spain, 2–3; of terrorism, 245–46; of torture, 99, 107n13; of tourism, 30, 76; in US, 5–6, 243, 250–51; of vandalism, 173, 249; violence in, 73–74

"Politics and the English Language" (Orwell), 9

Polynesia, 13–22, *15–16*

Pōmare II (King), 14

popular culture, 210

de Portolá, José, 52

poverty, 92–93

prison: culture of, 103–4; *Prison Ship Martyrs 2.0* (memorial), 183–84; psychology of, 74; torture and, 100

Prison Ship Martyrs 2.0 (memorial), 183–84

propaganda: authority and, 4, 8–9, 38–39, 44–45, 66–67, 236; in Cold War, 257; history and, 15, 17–18, 21–22, 253–58; for missionaries, *15–16*; politics and, 30, 238

Prosthetic Memory (Landsberg), 142–43, 194

protests: activism and, 179; anarchists in, 8; against authority, 174; history of, 6; for inclusivity, 56–58; in media, 1–2, 4; nationalists in, 1, 4; politics of, 94n9; against religion, 16; in Spain, 5–6; symbolism, 178–80; in US, 85–86, 174; vandalism as, 71–72, 85, 113, 219, 237–38

psychology: of art, 217n18; of authority, 102–3; of cooperation, 212–13; of counter-monument ideology, 191–200, *192–93*; of culture, 126–27, 147–48; of democracy, 212–13; of futurity, 65, 67, 69; of Germany, 135–36, 138–39; of history, 215; identity, 125; of narratives, 143; of nationalists, 122–23, 169; *On Collective Memory* (Halbwach), 141–42; of politics, 114; of prison, 74; technology and, 256; of victims, 75–76, 79–80; of violence, 66–67; of voice, 208–10, 216n9. *See also* memory

Pugliese, Stanislao, 147

Pugsley, Christopher, 219–20

Queen Victoria Building (QVB), 116–17

Quinn, Teachta Dála Ruairi, 114

QVB. *See* Queen Victoria Building

racism. *See* bigotry

Radermacher Norbert, 198

Rambelli, Fabio, 109–10

Reconstruction, 2

refugees, 127n3; culture of, 137–38; heritage sites for, 121–27, *124*; for nationalists, 131–39, *134*, *138*

Reinders, Eric, 109–10

religion, 5; authority of, 3, 16–17; civil religion, 226; colonialism and,

20–21, 110–11; culture of, 14, 18, 128n15; in heritage sites, 123–25, *124*; history of, 128n14; politics of, 13–14, 44, 46n8, 121; protests against, 16; science and, 29–30; in South East Asia, 43; violence and, 20, 122–23, 131–32, 135–36
revisionism, of history, 236
Rhodes, John Cecil, 85–86, 94n9, 229n3
Rodriguez Cabrillo, Juan, 52
Roosevelt, Franklin D. (FDR), 2, 10n4
Roosevelt, Theodore, 85–86
Ross, Kirstie, 222
Russia: Cold War for, 43; genocide in, 170; politics in, 165–71, *167, 172*, 173–75, *174*
Russo, Gaetano, 146
Rwanda, 62–69, 250

Sagan, Carl, 256
Samuels, Diane, 132
San Francisco, 49–51
Sayasithsena, Tham, 35, 37, 40–41
Schreiner, Olive, 89
science, 163n24; in Argentina, 27–28; *Falcon Heavy* (rocket), 257–58; history of, 25–26; nuclear power, 29; politics of, 256; religion and, 29–30; technology and, 38
Sebald, W. G., 137
"A Sedimentation of the Mind: Earth Works" Smithson, 157–58
Sen, Hun, *36*, 44
Seo-kyung, Kim, 179
Serra, Junipero, 52, 58
Setthathirath (King), 41
Shackleton, Ernest, 26–27
Sihanouk, Norodom, 37–38, 44, 45n4, 46n5
Silwinski, Sharon, 194
Simon, Roger I., 64–67
Simons, Jake Wallis, 137
Sims, J. Marion, 85–86
The Sky of our Childhood (film), 170
Skyspace (Turrell), 156

Smithson, Robert, 157–58, 163n11
Snowden, Edward, 183–84
Soberón, Francisco, 76–77
social darwinism, 49–50, 52–53
socialism, 169–70. *See also* fascism
social media, 191–200, *192–93*
South Africa, 85–90, *91*, 92–94, 95n10, 229n3
South East Asia, 35–45, *36–37*
South Korea, 178–80, 183
Soviet Union. *See* Russia
"Space Oddity" (Bowie), 257–58
Spain: authority in, 10n6; Civil War in, 5; in colonialism, 52; communism in, 4; nationalists in, 1–2; politics in, 2–3; protests in, 5–6; terrorism in, 11n15
spectacle, 219–28, *224, 226*
Sutter, Johann, 52
Suyin, Han, 42–43
Sydney Opera House, *193*
symbolism, 178–80
Syria, 138
Szydlowska, Malgorzata, 199
Szydlowski, Bartosz, 199

Tahiti: culture of, 15–16, 21; history of, 13. *See also* Polynesia
Tappe, Oliver, 40–41
Taylor, Richard, 220, 230n19
technology: education and, 89–90; *Falcon Heavy* (rocket), 257–58; Golden Record (Sagan), 256–57; for history, 206, 209, 213; holograms, 183–84; MP3 players, 207, 210, 217n20; psychology and, 256; science and, 38; 3-D digital maps, 221–22; video games, 177–78
Telepbergenova, Dalmira, 171, *172*, 173
Te Papa Tongarewa (museum), 219–28, *224, 226*
terrorism: in France, 191–93, *192–93*; globalization of, 195–96; NSA, 183; politics of, 245–46; in Spain, 11n15; violence and, 90

About the Contributors

Johnny Alam is a Canadian artist, curator, and scholar, based in Montreal, and holds a PhD in visual culture, a master's in art history, a master's in fine arts, and a bachelor's in history. Alam's work examines relations between art, memory, technology, and representation. He is currently working on a number of artworks and publications that focus on transnational tokens of identity and conflict in contemporary art and photography.

Kingsley Baird, a visual artist and professor of fine arts at Massey University (Wellington, New Zealand), investigates memory, memorialization, and remembrance through the design of memorials, such as the *New Zealand Memorial* in Canberra, *The Tomb of the Unknown Warrior* in Wellington, and *The Cloak of Peace* in Nagasaki, as well as temporary installations in museum residencies, solo exhibitions, and published textual outputs reflecting on and contextualizing his practice.

Flaminia Bartolini is a classical archaeologist specializing in the heritage of the dictatorship. She holds an MPhil in heritage studies and is finalizing her PhD in fascist heritage at the University of Cambridge while currently teaching MPhil students on the topics of heritage of the sictatorship. She has several years of professional experience in the cultural heritage sector and was a fellow at ICCROM (International Centre for the Study of the Preservation and Restoration of Cultural Property) in Rome in 2017.

Derek Boetcher is a PhD candidate at the University of Florida working on a dissertation project about the erection and "lives" of monumental art in Ireland and the Dominions from the late eighteenth century to the early twenty-first century. His interdisciplinary research interests include concepts of British imperial, national, and colonial identities, in both imperial and post-imperial manifestations, particularly as they are expressed through various cultural, literary, and artistic objects.

Nausikaä El-Mecky (PhD, Cambridge University, 2013) is an art historian specializing in attacks on art from antiquity until today. She is currently a postdoctoral fellow at Heidelberg University.

Basil Farraj is a PhD candidate in anthropology and sociology at the Graduate Institute, Geneva. His work focuses on political prisoners and the violence directed against them and ways in which they resist the incarcerating regimes.

Chiara Grilli is an Italian independent researcher. Her doctoral dissertation investigates Italian American myths of migration in literature and culture.

Dan Haumschild, PhD, is the Holocaust Education Fellow at Cardinal Stritch University and the Nathan and Esther Pelz Holocaust Education Resource Center in Milwaukee, Wisconsin. Trained in philosophy and critical theory, his research focuses on collective memory by addressing the relationship between public history and reconciliation in communities that have experienced mass violence.

Ingo Heidbrink is professor of maritime history at Old Dominion University in Norfolk, Virginia. His research focuses on international maritime economic conflicts as well as the history of Antarctica and contemporary social science questions related to Antarctica. He is a member of the International Polar Heritage Committee as an international scientific committee within the framework of ICOMOS.

Ñusta Carranza Ko is an assistant professor of political science in the Department of History, Political Science, and Geography at Ohio Northern University. Her research interests include cross-regional research on transitional justice processes in Latin America and East Asia, including policies of memorialization in Peru and South Korea and questions of indigenous people's rights in Peru.

Elliot Krasnopoler is a PhD student at Bryn Mawr College, writing his dissertation on different aspects of landscape in contemporary art. His work focuses on how notions of absence or emptiness in a place are able to signify history and conjure memory.

Runette Kruger is head of the Department of Fine and Applied Arts at the Tshwane University of Technology, South Africa. Her research interests include Afrofuturism, utopia, agency, dissent, cities, globalization, time, and space.

Scott McDonald is a PhD researcher in the Liverpool School of Art and Design at Liverpool John Moores University, United Kingdom, specializing in the history of modern and contemporary sculpture. Scott is also a guest lecturer and practicing sculptor in the city of Liverpool. Scott's primary focus is to address the role of temporary public sculpture, counter-monumental sculpture, and anti-monumental sculpture in public space.

Zeliha Nilüfer Nahya is a social and cultural anthropologist at Erciyes University, Turkey. She did research on Turkish converted Protestants in Ankara (MA) and image and othering in the context of the European Union in a group of Ankara University and Middle East Technical University students (PhD). She also studies religion, ethnicity, and religious minorities in Turkey and food culture.

Roger Nelson is an art historian, independent curator, and postdoctoral fellow at Nanyang Technological University, Singapore. He is a cofounding co-editor of the scholarly journal, *Southeast of Now: Directions in Contemporary and Modern Art in Asia*.

Saim Örnek is a research assistant at Erciyes University, Turkey. He studied the modern Greek language and literature at Ankara University and obtained his MA at Hacettepe University, with his dissertation on rites of passages in a Karamanli village in Greece. He is currently a PhD student at Gazi University. His research interests are migration, food culture, and Greek folklore studies.

Cynthia Culver Prescott is associate professor of history at the University of North Dakota. She is the author of *Gender and Generation on the Far Western Frontier* (2007) and *Pioneer Mother Monuments: Constructing Cultural Memory* (2019).

Evander Price is a PhD candidate in American studies at Harvard University. He is broadly interested in time and the many ways people conceive of it. His dissertation on future monumentality is forthcoming.

Tanja Schult is an associate professor at Stockholm University, where she teaches art history and visual studies. She is the author of *A Hero's Many Faces: Raoul Wallenberg in Contemporary Monuments* (2009/2012) and the editor (together with Diana Popescu) of *Revisiting Holocaust Representation in the Post-Witness Era* (2015). Her current research project, *Making the Past Present: Public Perceptions of Performative Holocaust Commemoration since the Year 2000* (in cooperation with Popescu), is financed by the Swedish Research Council.

Carmen S. Tomfohdre, a native of the United States, holds a PhD from the University of Hong Kong. Her current research investigates impacts of Christian missionaries on culture in Polynesia, 1797–1830.

Alex Vernon is a professor of English at Hendrix College outside Little Rock, Arkansas. His books include two military memoirs (*Most Succinctly Bred* and *The Eyes of Orion: Five Tank Lieutenants in the Persian Gulf War*); three works of scholarship (*Hemingway's Second War: Bearing Witness to the Spanish Civil War*; *On Tarzan*; and *Soldiers Once and Still: Ernest Hemingway, James Salter, and Tim O'Brien*); and four edited collections (*Teaching Hemingway and War*; *Critical Insights: War*; *Approaches to Teaching the Works of Tim O'Brien*; and *Arms & the Self: War, the Military, and Autobiographical Writing*).

Masha Vlasova is an interdisciplinary artist and filmmaker. She's a recipient of the Fulbright Fellowship in filmmaking, Alice Kimball Traveling Fellowship, and JUNCTURE Art and Human Rights Initiative Fellowship at Yale Law School. Her films and objects have been exhibited at La MaMa and La Galleria, Smack Mellon, Anthology Archives, and Abrons Arts Center in New York; Leeds College of Art, United Kingdom; Temple University and Vox Populi in Philadelphia; ArtSpace in New Haven; and Carpenter Center for the Visual Arts at Harvard University, Cambridge.

Amy Williams is a PhD researcher in history at Nottingham Trent University, financed by the Midlands3Cities AHRC Doctoral Training Partnership. She is working on a study of the *Memory of the Kindertransport in National and International Perspective*, exploring the way the Kindertransport has been represented in novels, museums, memorials, testimony, and autobiography.

About the Editor

Laura A. Macaluso researches and writes about murals, monuments, material culture, and museums. In 2018, her published work includes *The Public Artscape of New Haven: Themes in the Creation of a City Image* and "Public Art Inside and Outside the Museum," in *The State of Museums: Voices from the Field*. She previously published *Art of the Amistad and the Portrait of Cinqué* for the American Association for State and Local History Series for Rowman & Littlefield (2016). She has a PhD from the Humanities/Cultural & Historic Preservation departments at Salve Regina University in Newport, Rhode Island.

Made in the USA
Middletown, DE
09 January 2023

21727386R00179